Hard White

Hard White

*The Mainstreaming of Racism
in American Politics*

RICHARD C. FORDING
AND SANFORD F. SCHRAM

OXFORD
UNIVERSITY PRESS

OXFORD
UNIVERSITY PRESS

Oxford University Press is a department of the University of Oxford. It furthers
the University's objective of excellence in research, scholarship, and education
by publishing worldwide. Oxford is a registered trade mark of Oxford University
Press in the UK and certain other countries.

Published in the United States of America by Oxford University Press
198 Madison Avenue, New York, NY 10016, United States of America.

Library of Congress Cataloging-in-Publication Data
Names: Fording, Richard C., 1964– author. | Schram, Sanford, author.
Title: Hard white : the mainstreaming of racism in
American politics / Richard C. Fording, Sanford F. Schram.
Description: New York : Oxford University Press, 2020. |
Includes bibliographical references and index.
Identifiers: LCCN 2020007497 (print) | LCCN 2020007498 (ebook) |
ISBN 9780197500484 (hardback) | ISBN 9780197500491 (paperback) |
ISBN 9780197500521 (online) | ISBN 9780197500507 (updf) |
ISBN 9780197500514 (epub)
Subjects: LCSH: Racism—Political aspects—United States. |
United States—Race relations—Political aspects. | Whites—United States—Politics
and government. | Whites—Race identity—United States. |
Identity politics—United States. | Trump, Donald, 1946—Influence.
Classification: LCC E185.615 .F569 2020 (print) |
LCC E185.615 (ebook) | DDC 305.800973—dc23
LC record available at https://lccn.loc.gov/2020007497
LC ebook record available at https://lccn.loc.gov/2020007498

1 3 5 7 9 8 6 4 2

Paperback printed by LSC Communications, United States of America
Hardback printed by Bridgeport National Bindery, Inc., United States of America

Contents

Preface

We had been researching the enduring legacy of racism in American politics for years when we decided in 2016 to conduct a study on who was supporting Donald Trump for president. Like many political scientists, we were especially struck by the fact that Trump's popularity continued to rise throughout the 2016 campaign despite a series of scandals (e.g., the *Access Hollywood* tape) as well as his consistent use of explicitly racist rhetoric in his campaign speeches. Everything we thought we knew about contemporary politics suggested that either of these things—the scandals or the racist rhetoric—should have sunk his campaign. As we know, Trump not only survived both but went on to win the presidency. How could this possibly have happened?

Our first attempt to answer this question focused on some important differences between supporters of Trump and his opponent Hillary Clinton that we discovered from survey data collected during the 2016 primary season. Among Trump voters, it turned out, there was a bloc that were significantly more likely to display what psychologists call a low need for cognition, which simply means that they were more likely to avoid (or at least dislike) cognitively complex tasks. This trait was politically meaningful for two reasons. First, it meant that a non-trivial number of Trump supporters were less likely to consult alternative sources of political information and therefore more likely to take Trump's claims, especially about demonized outgroups, at face value. Second, according to prior research on the need for cognition, it suggested that Trump supporters might emphasize emotional responses over cognitive processing and therefore would be more susceptible to racial stereotypes and prejudice. Indeed, our initial research confirmed that much of the effect of the need for cognition on candidate support was mediated by indicators of racial hostility. These initial findings, which we first reported in the *Washington Post*'s *Monkey Cage* blog on election day in 2016, sparked many more questions. While it seemed clear enough that Trump's racist appeals probably helped him more than they hurt him, how was this possible? How exactly did Trump's racism help him win? And more generally, how has racism changed American politics in the Trump era? These questions quickly led to a research agenda that culminated in this book.

This project represents a shift in focus for us, but in some ways it felt like coming home. Years before we, like most graduate students in political science, had learned a lot about studying elections. After years of not focusing on electoral behavior, we were forced to return to that topic with a real sense of urgency in 2016. Our prior research had confirmed that race was central to American politics and public policy, social welfare policy in particular. Yet like most political scientists, we were surprised by how far Trump was willing to go in exploiting simmering racial resentments that had been building in recent years. We also noticed that he was exploiting more than just white resentment toward African Americans. In a post-9/11 age of globalization and immigration, white "outgroup hostility" better captured the resentment that included anger toward the Latinx and Muslim populations as well as African Americans. We also recognized the need to broaden our focus beyond electoral behavior to include how white outgroup hostility stormed into the mainstream of American politics via social movement organizing. Trump rode to the White House by exploiting an organized movement that fanned the white resentment toward outgroups. These developments have led to what we term a "mainstreaming of racism" in American politics—something that goes beyond electoral politics and is likely to outlast Trump's presidency. The research we review in this book confirms this conclusion in great detail; consistent with that assessment, we end this book by suggesting what can be done about this troubling development that lends irony to the term "post–civil rights era."

We consulted a wide variety of colleagues as we sought to bring together research on social movements and electoral behavior. We want to thank Cathy Schneider and Kim Williams for their deep knowledge of social movement theory. As he has so often before, Mark Peffley provided sage advice on the study of racism and helped push us in the direction of studying the effects of racial attitudes on political action. Frances Fox Piven helped improve our arguments by reminding us about the dangers posed by resurgent racism in the era of Trump. Christopher Parker provided great suggestions on a full draft, as did Heath Brown. David Abraham also read the full manuscript and provided extremely helpful commentary and corrections. Brianne Wolfe provided initial copyediting as she has done so competently in the past for us. Ryan Schram gave us the title for the book and offered sound criticism on terminology, including among other considerations about how to characterize the sources of white outgroup hostility and the ethnocentric dangers of calling polarized politics "tribalistic." Jack Schram provided an informed and detailed perspective on the new white extremist groups. Joan Schram commented effectively on our prose. Horace Bartilow, Alan Draper, Fred Exoo, George Hawley, Ruth Milkman, Dana Patton, Charles Tien, John Wallach, Lina Newton, Michael Lee, and Leah Nelson also contributed much-appreciated, thoughtful comments about the arguments in the book as we were writing. Daisy Crispin supplied effective research assistance, especially regarding Chapter 6. Finally, we are grateful to Brenda Hanson and Matthew Thomas for providing valuable research assistance as well as Heidi Beirich and her staff at the Southern Poverty Law Center for providing the data on white nationalist groups that we use throughout the book.

Our editor, Angela Chnapko, was excellent in shepherding the book from inception to completion. She made critical suggestions regarding the focus and the production of the book. The staff more generally at Oxford University Press professionally produced the book, and we are most appreciative of their competence as well as their kindness. Haripriya Ravichandran effectively managed the production of the book. The anonymous reviewers who read the manuscript did so very carefully and recommended improvements that greatly strengthened the final manuscript.

We have been researching and writing together for years. Once again our collaboration was its own source of joy, this time just the two of us without our other longtime collaborator Joe Soss, whose insights and efforts we missed. There were the usual tensions regarding deadlines, but the intellectual frisson from learning from each other was beyond anything either of us could rightly expect. We hope the final result will give readers a sense of not just how fraught our racial politics is today, but how if we work together to study it and think through what to do about it, we can make a meaningful difference.

1

The Mainstreaming of Racism
in American Politics

Race casts a long shadow over the history of U.S. politics.[1] In recent decades white Americans have been prone to convince themselves that the civil rights movement (CRM) of the 1960s put racism in the past. A post–civil rights society, it was said, was color-blind. It was almost Christian; the Reverend Martin Luther King Jr. died for our sins, and now we were saved. By the time Barack Obama became the first nonwhite president, many people, white and nonwhite, could tell themselves that maybe we were becoming a post-racial society.

Yet today our politics makes that idea more than contestable. To be clear, racism has never ceased to be a factor in American politics. It is true that national opinion polls in recent decades have indicated that there has been a long-term decline in "old-fashioned" or "Jim Crow" racism that espouses an explicit racial hierarchy with whites on the top.[2] Nevertheless, surveys indicate that a significant minority of whites exhibit some form of racial prejudice, whether it takes the form of traditional racism or a "symbolic racism" that sees African Americans not necessarily as inferior but instead as threatening to whites.[3] And today, with issues of globalization, immigration, and demographic diversification achieving greater public salience, racism is more likely to manifest itself in the form of a generalized ethnocentrism that expresses "outgroup hostility" toward a diverse set of groups.[4] The United States has historically been a country where white people are identified as the "ingroup" and various nonwhite groups are constructed as threatening "outgroups."[5] In today's politics Donald Trump's rise as a political force was based in good part on stoking white outgroup hostility, especially toward the Latinx and Muslim populations, as well as African Americans.

The increasing politicization of white outgroup hostility is reflective of the cyclical nature of politics, in which movements are countered by other movements.[6] In the post–civil rights era, in recent years progressive

Hard White, Richard C. Fording and Sanford F. Schram. Oxford University Press (2020). © Oxford University Press.
DOI: 10.1093/oso/9780197500484.001.0001

white attitudes on race have been increasingly challenged by the mobilization of outgroup hostility, reflective of a reactionary movement that has
enabled white racism to move from the political fringe to the mainstream.
In this book we explain why this has happened, how it happened, how it has
changed the landscape of American politics, and ultimately, what can be
done to reverse it.

In many ways our book is closely related to the growing body of scholarship that attempts to explain the rise of Donald Trump. Like the authors of
those works, we advance an argument that accounts for the rise of Trump,
and like much of the most recently published work, we emphasize the role of
racial hostility as the key to Trump's success.[7] Yet our book differs from this
work in several important respects. First, prior studies are generally "Trump-
centric" in that they identify the rise of white nationalism in American politics as primarily due to Donald Trump's candidacy. We agree that Trump
did a lot to attract white nationalists to his campaign—more so than any
other major party candidate since George Wallace in 1972—but while
Trump's presence may have been a necessary condition, it was hardly a sufficient condition for the mainstreaming of racism in American politics. As we
argue, Trump's racially conservative base was already in place by the time he
launched his candidacy in 2015, having been awoken and mobilized by the
resistance to Barack Obama's presidency. Second, and following from this
misconception regarding the primacy of Trump, is the misperception that
Trump succeeded because Americans became more racist. Actually, Trump
succeeded despite the fact that Americans actually became *less* racist, at least
during the critical period between 2012 and 2016 when Trump was planning
his run for the White House. Trump was able to secure the presidency, we
argue, through the mechanism of mobilization. While he may not have initi-
ated this mobilization, he certainly capitalized on it and in the process lured
white racial extremists and conservatives from the fringe to the mainstream
of American politics.

Two Levels of Mainstreaming

The political mainstreaming of racism has occurred at both the elite level
and the mass level, each of which has served to reinforce the other. We argue
that elite use of what we call "racialized political narratives" served as "collective action frames" to help stoke white outgroup hostility in the mass public.[8]

The elite-mass interaction points to the relationship of structure and agency, in which changes in the political structure are exploited by political actors who use their agency to further the mainstreaming of racism.[9] The racialized political narratives pushed by elite hatemongers like Trump accelerate the mainstreaming of white racial extremists into electoral politics while authorizing more mainstream racial conservatives to act on their outgroup hostility. In the chapters that follow we examine the mainstreaming of racism at both the elite and mass levels to show how changes in the political structure opened possibilities for people to use their agency (their capacity as free agents to act on their own).

At the elite level, the political mainstreaming of racism has been most evident in the rhetoric and behavior of Donald Trump, first as presidential candidate and then as president. Trump is not the first Republican candidate in the modern era to rely on race-baiting as a campaign strategy. Ever since the Democrats aligned themselves with the CRM during Lyndon Johnson's presidency, Republican candidates have successfully built on Richard Nixon's southern strategy, which used race to flip southern states to the Republican column. They have pushed narratives that demonize nonwhites, African Americans in particular.[10] In fact, the Republicans' success in flipping the South also led some Democrats to succumb to electoral pressures to follow suit, as Bill Clinton did with "New Democrat" promises to get tough on crime and "end welfare as we know it."[11] Some presidential hopefuls, most dramatically Pat Buchanan, relied on even more explicitly racist themes during unsuccessful bids for the Republican nomination in the 1990s. Yet prior to Trump, racial appeals were most often stated implicitly, with "dog whistles" that preserved deniability to others.[12] The dog whistling reflected the fact that espousals of white supremacy had become verboten in the post–civil rights era.

This changed in the age of Trump. He was the perfect politician to mainstream the most extreme and explicit racist ideas. While long known as a fringe media character with eclectic interests in public affairs, Trump has a consistent history of racism stretching back decades.[13] As a landlord, he settled with the federal government a suit regarding refusal to rent to nonwhites. Trump gained notoriety when he took out an ad in the *New York Times* insisting that five nonwhite teenagers who became known as the Central Park Five should be given the death penalty for the beating of a white female jogger who survived the attack in the spring of 1989. The Central Park Five were eventually exonerated after being wrongly convicted and serving extended prison sentences. As is his wont, Trump never backed down on their guilt even years later as president.

Trump's racism as a candidate and then as president is no doubt reflective of his own personal racist past, but it is also an outgrowth of the resurgence of racism in American politics in the post–civil rights era. Candidate Trump was not alone in his race-baiting. He and other political elites in recent years were especially drawing on the growing white resentment that boiled over during Obama's tenure as the first nonwhite president. Trump shared that resentment and capitalized on it for a base of support to finally make a major-party run to succeed Obama as president. Trump consciously went out of his way to attach himself to white nationalist extremists, many of whom were associated with the so-called alt-right.[14]

The alt-right predated Trump's 2016 presidential campaign but was a relatively new effort to mainstream white nationalist extremism into conventional politics. Its political mobilization increased dramatically in reaction to Obama's presidency. Trump opportunistically chose to align himself with that movement. By 2011 Trump had succeeded in becoming one of the leaders of the burgeoning birther movement, which propagated the wild conspiracy theory that Obama was not really an American citizen but instead was a foreigner born in Kenya as a Muslim. Trump took his leadership of that campaign and folded this racist narrative into an effort to replace Obama as president.

Trump was also aligning himself with a resurgent nativism that had been percolating for some time in the Western world more generally in reaction to increased globalization, immigration, and demographic diversification.[15] In this way, Trump was further aligning himself with the alt-right. He brought political agitators Steve Bannon and Stephen Miller into his campaign, both of whom had strong ties to the alt-right community and its leaders, including Richard Spencer. Bannon and Miller were undoubtedly instrumental in the formulation and implementation of Trump's strategy to emphasize racial hostility. Trump's candidacy shared with the alt-right an affinity for Vladimir Putin, who as president of Russia has actively worked to stoke white nationalist fervor throughout the Western world. Like the nativism of right-wing populists in Europe, the resurgence of white racial resentment in the United States had evolved. In the United States, racism was no longer just about African Americans. With increased globalization, immigration, and demographic diversification, it broadened to include Muslim and Latinx populations as two other outgroups threatening to whites. Trump's campaign did not just give voice to this new racism; it sought to inflame it.

Donald Trump and the Mainstreaming of Racism in the 2016 Campaign

Over the course of his 2016 campaign for the presidency, Trump consistently worked to rally his white nationalist base of supporters with barely disguised barbs directed at African Americans, Muslims, and the Latinx population. That strategy was evident from the moment he formally announced he was joining the race for the Republican nomination in 2015, when he declared, "When Mexico sends its people, they're not sending their best. They're sending people that have lots of problems. . . . They're bringing drugs. They're bringing crime. They're rapists. And some, I assume, are good people."[16] Trump's campaign closely followed Richard Nixon's southern strategy by routinely stoking white fears of black crime, often repeating false crime statistics for cities such as Chicago, Oakland, and Philadelphia and portraying predominantly African American urban neighborhoods as urban hellscapes.[17] And in one of his most important campaign promises, Trump supported a ban on all Muslim immigration, claiming that "a lot of them[,] I mean a lot of them [hate the United States]."[18]

In addition to his racist rhetoric disparaging targeted outgroups, throughout the campaign Trump consistently acted in a way that can only be explained as an attempt to overtly court the support of white racists, including even the most extreme among them. For example, Trump often retweeted messages from white supremacists, such as the following tweet from a Twitter user displaying the well-known white supremacist phrase "white genocide" in his Twitter handle: "@WhiteGenocideTM: @realDonaldTrump Poor Jeb. I could've sworn I saw him outside Trump Tower the other day!"

When asked about David Duke's endorsement of his candidacy during the Republican primary campaign, Trump claimed, "I don't know anything about David Duke. Okay?" Although Trump eventually acknowledged Duke's endorsement, he seemed to dismiss its significance when he responded to CNN's Jake Tapper: "Okay, all right. I disavow, okay?" And in what was explained away as simply a mistake by an intern, the Trump campaign circulated a campaign poster in which Nazi SS soldiers appeared next to a picture of Trump's face.[19]

Mainstreaming Racism in the White House

Trump's presidency has remained true to its racist and nativistic roots. In the first three years it was marked by significant instances in which Trump continued to stoke the fire of white racism in the country. Immediately after being elected, Trump followed through on his promise to ban travel to the United States from certain Muslim-majority countries, a ban that ultimately survived in revised form. His repeated attempts to build a wall on the southern border also reflect his racist inclinations, given how he has framed the issue as a need to build barriers to stop an "infestation" of immigrants from Latin America.

In his first year in office Trump was still largely dog whistling in public statements his allegiance to white nationalism. At that time, so it seems, he was not yet prepared to openly espouse white supremacy as a legitimate ideology in the way that, for instance, southern members of Congress routinely did in the decades prior to the CRM.[20] At an October 2018 rally on behalf of Senator Ted Cruz's re-election campaign, Trump called himself a "nationalist," even going out of his way to note the term had acquired negative connotations and thereby admitting that he was implicitly embracing the supposedly forbidden *white* nationalism as his political identity. His "nationalism" was coded white, just as his presidential campaign slogan "Make America Great Again" implicitly suggested to many "Make America White Again."

Early in his second year in the White House, Trump backed out of a major bipartisan deal on immigration, asking in an Oval Office meeting with congressional negotiators, "Why are we having all these people from shithole countries come here?," in reference to immigration from South America, the Caribbean, and Africa.[21] Later that same week he said he wanted instead more immigration from countries like Norway. And Trump continued to fumble his response to the outbursts of racist violence that were increasing with his ascension to the White House.

In spite of the Republicans' losing forty congressional seats in the midterm elections in 2018, Trump, already eyeing his re-election, doubled down on stoking outgroup hostility when he chose on July 14, 2019, to attack "The Squad," four newly elected Democratic congresswomen: Alexandra Ocasio-Cortez (D-NY), Ilhan Omar (D-MN), Ayanna Pressley (D-MA), and Rashida Tlaib (D-MI).[22] As leaders of the new crop of members of Congress elected in 2018 in opposition to Trump's racist presidency, they drew his ire.

Trump dropped almost all pretense when he called for these elected representatives to "go back" to their countries of origin, as if they were not U.S. citizens, let alone duly elected members of Congress. Trump painted them as
nonwhite interlopers, glossing over the fact that three of them were born in
the United States and the fourth was a naturalized citizen who immigrated to
the country at the age of twelve. They were not to be seen as real Americans
and could be cast out for their failure to honor Trump's presidency. The
House of Representatives, which gained a new Democratic majority in the
2018 midterm elections due to the negative reaction to Trump's presidency
and now under the leadership of Nancy Pelosi as Speaker, moved quickly to
pass a resolution condemning Trump, the first such instance of House condemnation of a president in more than one hundred years.

It was no accident that Trump focused on The Squad, who perfectly personified the key groups targeted by the new ethnocentrism's outgroup hostility. These female members of Congress were all nonwhites, members of
the African American, Muslim, and Latinx populations. They personified
the targets Trump had campaigned against and constantly sought to vilify
in his quest to agitate his base of anxious white supporters. His rallies featured a new chant. Whereas in his 2016 campaign supporters had chanted
"lock her up" (in reference to Trump's opponent, Hillary Clinton), now they
chanted, "send her back" (in reference to Ilhan Omar). Trump's fearmon-
gering exposed him now most clearly as the race-baiter he is. He became explicit about pushing the new ethnocentrism's outgroup hostility, and he was
doing it as president of the United States. As president he, more than anyone
else, was accelerating the normalizing of white racism in its new form and
expressed via a virulent white outgroup hostility.

Yet the race-baiting of The Squad was most explicitly depicted not by
Trump but when the Illinois Republican County Chairmen's Association
posted an image of them on Facebook on July 19, 2019 (see Figure 1.1). This
was at the height of Trump's attacks on The Squad via social media, at rallies,
and even in what had become his frequent sessions with journalists on the
front lawn of the White House. The image was titled "Jihad Squad" and
depicted the four congresswomen as ominous and threatening, holding guns
and standing in defiant poses. The source of the image was a Republican-
aligned political action committee, and its president quickly apologized.
The post was taken down two days later. Yet the image had already gone
viral, serving to remind a wide audience that at least in the minds of some
of Trump's allies, The Squad was deserving of vilification. The image even

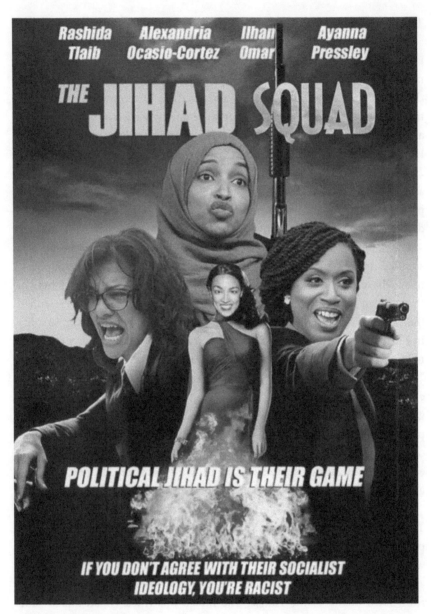

Figure 1.1 Jihad Squad

tries to anticipate being called out for racism by boomeranging that criticism at the bottom: "Political Jihad Is Their Game: if you don't agree with their socialist ideology, you're racist." The image was in fact a stark reminder that under Trump's leadership the Republican Party was primed to stoke outgroup hostility via what we call racialized political narratives. These narratives painted whites as the real victims, with every right to feel threatened by these outgroups.

The Jihad Squad depiction pointed to the process of racialization in these narratives but did so by offering a new twist. Up until then, racialized political narratives of outgroups were more often than not about racializing Muslims as threatening nonwhites who could be lumped in with African Americans and Latinos. Yet the Jihad Squad depiction reverses that process. It Muslimizes African Americans and Latinos so that they all can be seen as terrorists. Either way, the racialized political narratives about The Squad, whether visually depicted or not, were using their ethnicities to demonize them as archetypes of the key outgroups threatening to whites. The Squad served as a paradigmatic example of how racialized political narratives were being used by political elites to stoke outgroup hostility.

By the time of the attack on The Squad, it was clear that Trump had opened a Pandora's box of hate. He knowingly exploited simmering white resentments, with the intention of inflaming white anxieties about outgroups for his own political advantage. Trump had by then totally cast his fate with a loyal base of anxious whites whom he knew he must never betray. There were a variety of voters that comprised Trump's base, to be sure, and as we will show, the majority could not be classified as racists. Yet, while some were not happy about Trump's inflammatory rhetoric, they nonetheless tolerated and thereby became complicit in his efforts to appeal to even the most extreme of white nationalists.

Trump's base stayed with him in late July 2019 when he mounted an explicitly racist attack on Rep. Elijah Cummings (D-MD). Trump said Cummings was responsible for problems in the city of Baltimore, where part of Cummings's congressional district was located. Apparently mad at Cummings for chairing investigations of Trump's policy of separating immigrant children from their parents at the border, Trump blamed Cummings for Baltimore's shortcomings, calling the city "a disgusting, rat and rodent infested mess" and saying "no human being would want to live there."[23] Trump would never use such dehumanizing rhetoric about poor white rural communities, but he invoked the rats and infestation terms he often likes to spew when it comes to communities of color.

Many people condemned Trump as a white supremacist and racist agitator, but he denied all the accusations, and his standing with his base remained unchanged. Trump had by then re-mainstreamed explicit racism by normalizing and legitimizing as president the hateful rhetoric that in recent decades had been banished to the margins. Trump's mainstreaming had unleashed a diabolical dynamic in which extremist rhetoric was normalized and ordinary people were now authorized to express support for that extremism.[24]

No president since Woodrow Wilson was ever so explicitly associated with white extremism, and Trump arguably outdid even Wilson in his embrace of white nationalism. It was nothing less than shocking.

Mainstreaming Racism at the Mass Level

The mainstreaming of racism among the mass public reflects profound changes in what has been called the political opportunity structure.[25] It was greatly accelerated by the election of Barack Obama as the nation's first black president. Obama's election affected the political behavior of white racists in a number of important ways. As we show in the next chapter, it was associated with an increase in hostility toward minorities, especially African Americans, the Latinx population, and Muslims. Racial prejudice became more politicized than at any other time in the post–civil rights era. It became a more powerful predictor of whites' political attitudes. Yet perhaps most important, the election of Obama was associated with an increase in anger toward a government led by a black man. This contributed to a significant increase in the mobilization of white racial extremists, reflected in a surge of activity within the white nationalist movement (WNM), which had long been languishing on the fringe of American politics. It was at this point that the political mainstreaming began in earnest. Discouraged by the lack of progress made by traditional white supremacist groups, white nationalists began to shift the focus of their efforts to achieving greater acceptance for their agenda in the mainstream of conventional politics. Some white nationalist groups, such as the American Freedom Party, began to run candidates under their own party labels. Yet much of this new energy was funneled into the Republican Party through the Tea Party movement (TPM), which first formed in 2009 as an antitax movement. By 2010 the movement had spread across the country and, as we show in Chapter 4, had co-opted a significant faction of the WNM. In 2010 the *New York Times* identified 138 Tea Party candidates for Congress. They ran on a platform that reflected not just antitax and antigovernment sentiment, but overtly racist, anti-immigration appeals as well. White extremists responded with great enthusiasm, contributing to the election of 50 percent of the Tea Party candidates to the U.S. Senate and approximately one-third of those to the U.S. House.

Soon after 2010, the TPM began to wane. Although a congressional Tea Party caucus was formed in the aftermath of the election, it still lacked a charismatic national leader who could appeal to a broad coalition of voters. For white nationalists, the TPM also proved to be a disappointment because its national leaders were largely ineffective in implementing the TPM's antiminority agenda. Although Donald Trump did not explicitly identify himself as a Tea Party candidate, he regularly praised the TPM, its goals, and its supporters. Indeed, the first major endorsement he received from a national political figure came from Sarah Palin, one of the TPM's favorites. Most important, though, is that Trump adopted much of the Tea Party agenda, especially its most racist elements. As a result, Trump became the new hope for white racists who had been lured to electoral politics by the promise of the TPM but had become disillusioned by its lack of progress.

White nationalist support for Trump was both frequent and visible throughout the 2016 campaign. As early as the Iowa caucus, a group that called itself the American National Super PAC received national attention due to its robocall campaign urging Iowans to vote for Trump. Based on the name of the PAC, one would never know that this was simply a front for white nationalist activists or that the person speaking in the call was none other than Jared Taylor, publisher of the white nationalist *American Renaissance* magazine and one of the most prominent alt-right figures in the country. The most important white nationalist political party, the American Freedom Party, decided not to run a presidential candidate because they felt they already had one in Trump. On the eve of the election, they engaged in a robocall campaign that contacted nearly 200,000 landlines in Utah to convince voters that they should not vote for Evan McMullin, the third-party alternative who threatened to steal Utah from Trump. The reason given was that McMullin was gay.[26] And as the most well-known white supremacist, David Duke, declared on his radio show, voting for anyone other than Trump would represent "treason to your heritage."[27] The white nationalist base followed suit and became a regular presence at Trump rallies, often broadcasting live to their followers[28] and in some cases, inciting violence.[29]

After Trump's victory, activists in what had crystallized as the now re-surgent WNM were more empowered than they had been in decades. The most prominent event occurred during Trump's first year in office, when hundreds of white nationalists from all over the country converged on Charlottesville, Virginia, in April 2017 for a gathering billed as the "Unite the Right" rally.[30] According to the organizers of the event, Charlottesville was chosen as the site because of the removal of a statue of Robert E. Lee by local authorities. The statue had been removed in response to the 2015 Charleston, South Carolina, massacre, in which the young white nation-alist Dylan Roof murdered nine African American members of the Emanuel African Methodist Episcopal Church. Roof's murderous rampage was a reminder that white racism remained a threat to peace and stability in the United States many years after the CRM of the 1960s had accorded African Americans basic protections against discrimination. The Charlottesville rally further served to underscore that white racism was not just a problem of isolated, alienated youth. Instead, it was a coming out party for the newly energized WNM, which was moving into the mainstream of U.S. politics and focused on undoing the legacy of the CRM. During the two-day period of the Charlottesville rally, disturbing images of white nationalist protestors wearing Klan robes and carrying Nazi flags were broadcast around the world. Yet perhaps equally disturbing in another way was that the original protesters on the first night of the rally wore khakis, as if to signal their desire to be seen as mainstream, even as they stomped around with torches reminiscent of a Nazi rally. As the number of counterprotestors grew, the event eventually devolved into a massive street brawl, leading to the death of counterprotester Heather Heyer and the subsequent deployment of the Virginia State Police to impose order after the fact.

The Charlottesville riots, as they have since been called, served as an ugly wakeup call that white racism was far more prevalent in the post–civil rights era than Americans had perhaps led themselves to believe. Prior to Charlottesville, most Americans were aware that the WNM and its offspring, the alt-right and other hate groups, existed on the fringes of the political system. This type of white extremism was not new. Yet after the victories of the CRM of the mid-1960s and the subsequent widespread (although some-times reluctant) acceptance of African Americans into mainstream society by the white establishment, this resistance had dissipated, and white liberal Americans could tell themselves that white racists would never again play a significant role in American politics. Charlottesville made it extremely clear that things might not have changed as much as people wanted to believe. Not only had there been an underestimation of the scale of the WNM as a countermovement to the CRM, but when President Donald Trump stated in the wake of the riots that there was violence "on many sides," his despicable pandering to white nationalists brought home the reality to many Americans that white nationalists once again had political clout in the White House.

Trump's pattern of subtle appeals to white nationalists in his responses to racist-inspired violence has continued throughout his first term. In late October 2018, over a seventy-two-hour period at the height of the midterm elections, white nationalist rage once again broke into the headlines. First, a white nationalist killed two African Americans after failing to get into a black church in Louisville, Kentucky.[31] Next, the "Maga Bomber" (as he was to be called) sent pipe bombs to several of Trump's critics. When reporters asked the president if he would tone down his rhetoric, Trump demurred, saying he thought he should "tone it up."[32] The next day, in response to the mass killing of Jewish congregants at the Tree of Life Synagogue in Pittsburgh, Pennsylvania, Trump refused to take any responsibility for his rhetoric about "globalists." This was another dog whistle, one that he had used in his 2016 presidential campaign and that singled out Jews who opposed his nationalism.[33] The Pittsburgh assassin had actually claimed he was not a Trump supporter, saying that Trump was too much of a globalist and affiliated with Jews who condoned immigration and diversification.[34] Nonetheless, Trump stuck to his race-baiting. It remained a key campaign strategy during the 2018 midterm elections, which he intentionally made into a referendum on his racially divisive policies.

The violence soon got even worse when another white male inspired by nationalist rhetoric took an assault weapon to a Walmart in El Paso, Texas, on August 3, 2019. He killed twenty-two people and wounded eight others in just a heartbeat. He surrendered and immediately told the police he had come to kill Mexicans. Shortly before the killing spree, he had posted an online statement explicitly indicating he had become enraged that the United States was suffering from an "invasion" of immigrants. He noted that his ideas predated Trump but did not disavow Trump's relationship to them. In fact, subsequent reports indicated that Trump had used words like "invasion," "killers," "animals," and other pejorative terms more than five hundred times when talking about immigrants at his rallies from 2017 until just before the shooting.[35] While for many Americans the connection between Trump's rhetoric and racist violence was obvious and repellent, to a significant share of Trump's racist base these connections were precisely why they had voted for him; their unwavering support provides little incentive for him to change his behavior.

Overview

In the chapters that follow we describe exactly how the outgroup hostility that Trump and other race-baiters have inflamed has enabled racism to move back into the mainstream of American politics. We explain why this has happened and why it is likely to persist. Our explanation begins by clarifying what racism is today. To date, the literature on the resurgence of racism in American politics has focused almost exclusively on white racial prejudice or, in some cases, white racial identity. We emphasize that while it is important to understand the formation of racial attitudes and their relation to political attitudes, the mainstreaming of racism in American politics cannot be attributed simply to extremists becoming more vocal or aggressive in their individual behavior. We must also consider how and why racial extremists were able to pursue their racist goals through participation in various forms of collective action, including mainstream electoral politics. Accordingly, we look to the social science literature on social movements, and especially the importance of the political environment in movement mobilization, to better understand how white racial extremists have increasingly organized to participate effectively in conventional politics.[36]

We highlight two important features of the political environment that we argue have led white racists to place greater emphasis on conventional politics. First, we highlight the importance of race-baiting elites in promoting a mass white racial consciousness among the mainstream as well as the fringe. We stress that race-baiting elites may have had their own economic interests uppermost in their minds but they were keen to promote an economic populism that was filtered through white racial resentments. Effective here were collective action frames designed to encourage a white racial consciousness among the voting populace.[37] These collective action frames relied on racialized political narratives that operated to racialize selected groups of people as threatening "outgroups" in opposition to whites as the "ingroup." Second, we show how the political opportunity structure for white racial extremists became more open, leading to an increase in opportunities for them to participate in conventional politics. We argue that both factors had already converged prior to 2016 to lay the foundation for Trump's success. The mainstreaming of racism, however, would not be nearly as complete had it not been for Trump's unique abilities as the supreme race-baiter on the contemporary political scene. He fostered white racial consciousness among more mainstream whites while providing disaffected white racial extremists with the confidence that their goals were justified and their time had finally come to participate in conventional electoral politics.

We take an empirical approach throughout the book, wherein each chapter provides a focused analysis to add to the story of mainstreaming. We rely on a variety of data to tell this story of resurgent racism, including survey data on public opinion, textual data from political elites and movement organizations, and detailed data on WNM organizing dating back to 2000. Throughout the book we focus on a concept that we term "outgroup hostility" as a relatively new ideology of racism. Chapter 2 begins by surveying the literature on white racial prejudice and voting behavior. We show that over the last four elections, white hostility toward African Americans, Latinx immigrants, and Muslims has become increasingly intertwined and forms the basis for what we define as a contemporary form of ethnocentrism expressed in white outgroup hostility. We confirm the results of other studies that have shown that while the effect of outgroup hostility on vote choice greatly increased in 2016, the level of outgroup hostility actually declined between 2012 and 2016. Therefore, to properly understand the political mainstreaming of racism over the 2010s, we argue that we must not only consider the evolution of whites' racial attitudes but also examine the processes by which outgroup hostility is translated into political participation. To accomplish this task, we introduce a theoretical framework that combines insights from social identity theory to understand changes in whites' racial attitudes with theories of political participation originating from the social movement literature. The framework thus emphasizes the highly contingent nature of the relationship between white racial consciousness, outgroup hostility, and political mobilization. Specifically, we outline a model of the process by which racialized political narratives help activate a politicized white consciousness that allows for outgroup hostility and serves as the basis for political mobilization.

One of the most important insights offered by social movement theory,[38] we argue, concerns the effects of the political environment on both the level and type of political participation of white racial extremists over the last three decades. In Chapter 3 we trace the history of the modern WNM. We

describe the ideology of white nationalists and the variety of racialized political narratives utilized by movement leaders to foster white racial consciousness. These narratives became increasingly resonant among white extremists
due to observable increases in racial diversity, which was portrayed as a
threat to white supremacy. Nonetheless, due to the relatively closed nature
of the political opportunity structure, white racists had few vehicles open to
them to express their frustration. From the 1980s until the election of Obama
in 2008, white extremists became increasingly disillusioned with contemporary politics. Most white racists sat out of politics altogether as an increasingly angry minority of extremists fueled a rapid growth in white nationalist
groups that were relegated to the political fringe.

One of the most important changes along these lines is represented by the
emergence of the TPM as an electoral protest movement in response to the
election of Barack Obama. In Chapter 4 we document the rise of the TPM
and how it evolved into an attractive vehicle for the expression of outgroup
hostility and the pursuit of racist policy priorities. We show that the TPM
not only mobilized a significant number of previously inactive white racial
conservatives but also co-opted a significant portion of the WNM, especially
the traditional white supremacist groups such as the Ku Klux Klan. In many
ways, the TPM thus set the stage for Trump by bringing more white racial
extremists and racial conservatives into electoral politics. Yet this newly
energized constituency lacked a national leader. Trump's emergence as a
presidential candidate thus represents the second critical change in the political opportunity structure. White racists and racial conservatives now had a
national leader who spoke directly to their outgroup hostility and their anger.

In Chapter 5 we provide evidence from Trump's speeches to show that he
was indeed the leading race-baiter who exploited the changed political environment in ways that not only garnered him a loyal base of white supporters
but also greatly facilitated in legitimating the mainstreaming of racism. As
we show in our analysis, Trump mainstreamed established white nationalist
thinking by echoing the major themes of the new racial outgroup hostility
through his repeated targeting of African Americans, Latinx immigrants,
and Muslims in his campaign rhetoric.

In Chapter 6 we focus on the role of a changing media landscape in disseminating misinformation to a disproportionately underinformed audience
who support Trump. We show how the Trump campaign and its allies, including the contract firm Cambridge Analytica as well as Russian operatives,
exploited the changing media landscape to spread misinformation to sow

racial division and stoke white outgroup hostility. We focus on the nexus between Fox News, fake news, and Trump to provide evidence of that specific connection that demonstrates the key role of the mass media, social media included, to help disseminate misinformation about outgroups and sustain high levels of outgroup hostility among whites.

Chapter 7 examines the success of the Trump campaign and its allies in garnering the support of "low-information voters," who were more vulnerable than informed voters to relying on emotions for making their vote choice. We show that "low-information" whites who had a low "need for cognition" were most likely to have high levels of outgroup hostility and were therefore most likely to be responsive to Trump's race-baiting.

Chapter 8 offers a thorough analysis of survey data from the American National Election Study (ANES), the Cooperative Congressional Election Study (CCES), and the Democracy Fund's Voter Study Group (DFVSG) to show that white outgroup hostility had a uniquely strong effect on vote choice in 2016. We also show that it was as important in predicting vote choice as party identification. Although many people have argued that a major factor in Trump's victory was increasing economic anxiety within the white working class,[39] we find the direct effects of economic anxiety in 2016 were relatively small compared to the effects of outgroup hostility and they were not really different than effects of economic anxiety on the presidential vote in prior years. To the extent that economic anxiety mattered in 2016, it largely operated indirectly by accentuating outgroup hostility. The influence of outgroup hostility is even more compelling once we consider its indirect effect on vote choice through its effects on party identification and ideology. Finally, this chapter specifies the causal pathways that are suggestive of a process by which (1) white identity becomes politicized and leads to the formation of white racial consciousness, (2) white racial consciousness is the result of the dissemination of racialized political narratives as propagated by race-baiting elites, (3) this dissemination of racialized political narratives agitates attitudes of outgroup hostility, and (4) that outgroup hostility was a critical factor in producing a winning coalition for Trump that furthered the mainstreaming of racism right into the White House.

In Chapter 9 we show that the Trump campaign's explicitly stated focus on mobilizing nonvoters in swing states paid off. We provide statistical evidence that Trump benefited more from mobilizing 2012 nonvoters than from getting 2012 Obama voters to switch parties and support him.[40] We show that Trump was in fact effective in mobilizing nonvoters in swing states, and he was able to do that on the basis of appealing to nonvoters' high levels of out-group hostility. The increased turnout of nonvoters in swing states was most likely a result of the campaign's avowed focus on mobilizing them through emotional internet ads tailored specifically to them. Our analyses provide a strong evidentiary basis for suggesting that the Trump digital campaign was a resounding success. Trump's rhetorical emphasis on outgroup hostility also resonated among the most hardcore racists within the WNM, including the emerging alt-right, leading to an unprecedented level of interest and involvement of white nationalist activists in Trump's campaign. By providing a more attractive venue for white nationalists to channel their activism, Trump has essentially facilitated the co-optation of a significant segment of the WNM into the Republican Party.

In Chapter 10 we review our findings and draw conclusions about what is to be done to respond to the mainstreaming of racism in the current era. Our findings regarding the important role of white outgroup hostility in our politics today are in many ways consistent with those of other studies.[41] The 2016 election has been characterized in these prior studies as representing a racialized backlash among voters who were concerned about the status of whites in a changing society. Yet our analysis leads us to slightly different conclusions about this backlash and the nature of white anxiety. Analysts accept that the level of white outgroup hostility did not increase in 2016, even among Republicans. The white racial backlash that helped propel Trump to victory had already peaked in 2012. We show that the more significant attitudinal backlash that occurred in 2016 was the anti-Trump backlash among racial moderates and progressives. Thus, what was most significant about racial attitudes in 2016, we argue, is that white outgroup hostility had become so polarized. Further, this polarization is most centrally over how whites feel about outgroups, not their affinity for whiteness as a source of their identity. Both these points have important implications not only for our understanding of what happened in 2016 but also for the future of American politics in the Trump era.

We emphasize that Trump's victory has helped solidify the mainstreaming of racism by leading to a massive reshuffling of the two major political parties. The parties are now more racialized, with the Republican Party overwhelmingly white and the Democratic Party much more racially diverse. The parties are highly polarized in their attitudes toward outgroups. We show that the polarization of the parties over outgroup hostility makes them more ideologically coherent but also more likely to practice a tribalistic politics of always resisting compromising with the other side, especially on race-related policy issues. As a result, racial antagonism is likely to persist as a central feature of electoral politics.

We argue that in a highly polarized and tribalistic political environment, it is unlikely that talking and listening, building bridges, and compromising are likely to defuse the situation. Listening and compromising are important, but are not effective with implacable racists. Beyond trying to get people to step down from responding to racist appeals, it is more important to mobilize the broader constituency of nonracists, white and nonwhite, who have low levels of outgroup hostility. In this sense, it might be best to emulate Trump, not in race-baiting but in his emphasis on mobilizing his base. Mobilizing racial liberals is likely to prove to be more effective in countering the white hostility toward outgroups.

There is an urgency in reducing polarization for, as some have noted, if people continue to be so polarized that they cannot talk to each other,[42] the hopes for an inclusive democracy can be derailed for dictatorship.[43] Whites increasingly are willing to express declining support for democracy given that it means to them a stronger government that supports outgroups.[44] From this perspective, trying to understand the resentful white people left behind in hollowed out, rural America or other places is the wrong focus.[45] A winning politics should help those people economically, but given the high levels of racialized outgroup hostility, it is futile to try to convert them or achieve common ground.[46] Mobilization of an opposition to white racism is more likely to prove effective than trying to persuade whites to switch sides. We provide evidence that the Blue Wave of the 2018 midterm elections was in fact energized by resistance to the racism that swept Trump into office. We conclude by suggesting that just as Trump was able to accelerate the mainstreaming of racism when he stoked outgroup hostility and mobilized disaffected whites, an effective countermovement must continue to mobilize a multi-racial coalition of racial liberals to begin the process of pushing resurgent racism back to the fringes of U.S. politics.

2

The Changing Face of Racism

Outgroup Hostility and Racialization in an Age of Globalization

Racism today has changed, and so too has our understanding of its role in elections. Prior to 2016 most studies focused on the effects of white attitudes toward a single group, usually African Americans. Many studies have found that white hostility toward African Americans has had a significant effect on a variety of electoral outcomes, including the partisan realignment that occurred in the South in the aftermath of the civil rights movement (CRM),[1] support for black candidates in biracial contests,[2] and most recently, support for Barack Obama.[3]

More recently scholars have discovered that hostility toward Latinx immigrants can also have important effects on political behavior. Americans have become increasingly divided over immigration, leading to what Abrajano and Hajnal refer to as a "white backlash" fueled by narratives that characterize Latinx immigrants as a cultural, economic, and security threat to white Americans.[4] This has had profound political repercussions. Research by Hajnal and colleagues finds that Democrats have become increasingly identified as the "immigration party," leading to a significant rightward partisan shift among white voters, much like the racial realignment in the South which occurred in the aftermath of the CRM.[5] Attitudes toward Latinx immigrants have also had an impact on vote choice, leading to greater levels of support for John McCain in 2008 and for Republican congressional candidates in 2010.

Studies of vote choice in 2016 generally reflect the trend in the literature of moving toward a broader conceptualization of racial attitudes that includes prejudice toward Latinx immigrants in addition to racial resentment toward African Americans. Indeed, in mid-2019 we identified twenty-four peer-reviewed, published studies of vote choice in the 2016 election. All but four of these studies included some measure of hostility toward African Americans in their analysis, and the majority (thirteen) also estimated the effect of

Hard White, Richard C. Fording and Sanford F. Schram. Oxford University Press (2020). © Oxford University Press.
DOI: 10.1093/oso/9780197500484.001.0001

hostility toward the Latinx population or Latinx immigrants on vote choice. Although fewer in number, a handful of studies have also considered the importance of attitudes toward another outgroup, Muslims.[6] Collectively the results from this literature convincingly demonstrate that hostility toward racial outgroups, broadly defined, mattered in 2016. Support for Trump was significantly more likely to be found among whites who displayed negative attitudes toward blacks, Latinx immigrants, and Muslims.

Although the elections literature remains dominated by studies that focus on white hostility toward racial outgroups, a number of studies have begun to recognize the importance of ingroup attitudes in understanding political behavior. These studies do not deny the importance of outgroup hostility. Instead, they argue that the exclusive focus on outgroups has come at the expense of attention to white racial identity, which they maintain played a critical role in explaining support for Trump in 2016. The most comprehensive study to advance the white identity thesis was published by Ashley Jardina. Similar to other studies in this camp, Jardina's makes two important claims regarding the importance of white identity. First, she argues that "in-group attitudes and strong in-group identities do not strongly correlate with out-group bias or negativity."[7] Second, she argues that white identity has a direct effect on political attitudes and behavior that operates directly and independently of outgroup hostility. Jardina finds consistent support for this hypothesis based on evidence from a variety of surveys and dependent variables, including partisan identification, policy attitudes, and vote choice (including support for Trump in 2016). Jardina's findings are supported by a handful of other analyses of elections in the post-Obama period,[8] including the comprehensive analysis of the 2016 election published by John Sides, Michael Tesler, and Lynn Varveck.[9]

Collectively the 2016 election studies have convincingly established the primacy of racial attitudes, broadly defined. Yet several important questions remain unresolved. In this chapter we begin to answer them. First, which racial attitudes are most relevant to understanding American politics in the Trump era? Although the 2016 election studies have been more likely to consider the effects of attitudes toward a broader set of racial outgroups, there are still relatively few studies that have examined the effects of the full range of ingroup and outgroup attitudes simultaneously. To the extent that different types of racial attitudes are correlated with one another, the findings from this literature must therefore be considered somewhat tentative. This is especially a concern for the estimation of the relative effects of ingroup and outgroup attitudes, which have often been found to be at least moderately correlated.[10]

Second, how do racial attitudes work to affect political behavior? Although several studies incorporate a broad range of ingroup and outgroup attitudes in their statistical analyses of voting behavior, this literature fails to provide much theoretical guidance concerning if and how these different racial attitudes might be related to one another. Rather, most studies implicitly assume that all racial attitudes operate independently of one another and that any correlation among them is theoretically meaningless.

Third, and perhaps most important, how and why did racial hostility become so important in 2016? To what extent was this was facilitated by Trump? And how did this contribute to Trump's historic victory in 2016? To answer these questions we must look beyond vote choice, which has been the primary focus of most of the elections literature. In an era of extreme polarization, in which voters are much less persuadable than they have been in the past, we must also turn our attention to how racial hostility is translated into political action, broadly speaking. To provide a better understanding of this process, we offer a general theoretical framework that integrates several bodies of social science research. We borrow from theories of social identity and ethnocentrism to motivate our approach to conceptualizing and measuring outgroup hostility. To understand the role of outgroup hostility in the generation of political action, we look to the social psychology literature on the formation of group consciousness and specifically how racialized collective action frames generate anger, which in turn serves as an important motivation to act. Finally, we draw from social movement theory to explain how the political energy generated by outgroup hostility is channeled by the political environment into different forms of political behavior.

Conceptualizing Racial Attitudes in the Trump Era: The Importance of Outgroup Hostility

Although we recognize the importance of both ingroup and outgroup attitudes, we argue that the construct that has the most powerful and proximate effect on vote choice and voter participation and therefore is most critical to understanding the mainstreaming of racism in American politics is what we call "outgroup hostility." Given its importance throughout the book, we begin our theoretical presentation with a detailed discussion of how we define and measure outgroup hostility, how the level of outgroup hostility has varied over time, and how it varies across a variety of politically relevant subgroups today.

Our conceptualization of outgroup hostility emerges out of a body of literature firmly established in the study of mass attitudes and voting behavior. Our framework is most closely related to the concept of ethnocentrism, which has been the subject of renewed interest in political science.[11] In this literature ethnocentrism is often conceptualized as a combination of two related constructs: ingroup favoritism and outgroup hostility. In studies of voting behavior, to measure ethnocentrism political scientists have generally followed Kinder and Kam,[12] who constructed a scale of ethnocentrism for whites by computing the average difference between the evaluation of whites as a racial/ethnic group and three outgroups, which in their labeling are "Blacks," "Hispanics," and "Asians." In addition to the work of Kinder and colleagues, this indicator of ethnocentrism has been utilized in several other studies of whites' racial attitudes.[13]

We agree with Kinder and colleagues that the most fruitful approach to understanding the role of racial prejudice in American politics today is to employ a broader conceptualization of racial animosity that goes beyond a focus on a single group to recognize that white voters have become increasingly motivated by a more generalized antipathy toward several racial or ethnic "outgroups" in their evaluation of candidates. Our approach to conceptualizing and measuring ethnocentrism, however, differs in two important ways. First, an established body of empirical research has found that ingroup favoritism and outgroup negativity are distinct constructs and only modestly correlated.[14] Therefore, rather than combining attitudes toward the ingroup and outgroup in a single concept, we treat white identity and outgroup hostility as separate, distinct concepts in our theoretical framework and utilize separate indicators of ingroup and outgroup evaluation for our multivariate analyses of the effects of ethnocentrism on political behavior.[15]

Second, in the current political environment, in which political behavior is strongly motivated by anger and fear, we argue that contemporary white outgroup hostility is better captured by attitudes toward a slightly different set of outgroups. We define outgroups as those who are seen as threatening to the white majority, especially given that its privileged majority status is increasingly perceived as fragile.[16] The white outgroup hostility that Trump was able to tap into grew out of anxieties directed not just toward the long-demonized "other" of white racist politics, that is, African

Americans. Instead, in an age of growing concern about globalization, immigration, and multiculturalism, outgroup hostility came to include other racialized groups, especially Latinx immigrants and Muslims. In the end, Trump's railing against these groups inflamed pre-existing anxieties about them, resulting in concerns about these groups cohering in the form of a new ethnocentrism, or outgroup hostility.

Measuring Outgroup Hostility Using Survey Data

We rely heavily on three sets of surveys to better understand the role of outgroup hostility in American politics. Our data options are somewhat limited because we must be able to measure attitudes toward all three racial outgroups: African Americans, Latinx immigrants, and Muslims. Fortunately we have three excellent options that provide the basis for most of the survey analysis in this book: the American National Election Study (ANES), the Views of the Electorate Research Survey (VOTER Survey), and the Cooperative Congressional Election Survey (CCES). Most of our analyses rely on the ANES and VOTER Survey because these studies utilize our preferred measures of outgroup hostility and allow us to track changes in outgroup hostility over time. The outgroup hostility items are available only for 2016 in the CCES, but the extremely large sample size is valuable for making regional and state-to-state comparisons.

To measure antiblack hostility, we rely on the racial resentment scale developed by Donald Kinder and Lynn Sanders.[17] Since the racial resentment scale more directly primes attitudes toward African Americans in a political context, it is not surprising that it has consistently been found to be related to political behavior across a variety of contexts.[18] And consistent with our theoretical arguments, the effect of racial resentment on candidate evaluation appears to be mediated by partisan-directed anger.[19] As for Latinos, research has found that negative attitudes toward the Latinx population are most likely to exist when they are associated with images of immigrants,[20] legal or illegal, as the two are often conflated in the minds of many whites.[21] Rather than relying on the feeling thermometers in surveys for "Hispanics," we follow Abrajano and Hajnal[22] and construct a multi-item scale measuring opposition to immigrants. The scale consists of the three items that tap attitudes toward immigrants and were included (in identical form) in the ANES from 2004 to 2016, specifically:

- The feeling thermometer score for "illegal immigrants," reverse-scaled as a measure of hostility.
- A five-point scale of responses to the question, "Do you think the number of immigrants from foreign countries who are permitted to come to the United States to live should be . . ." (increased a lot–decreased a lot).
- A four-point scale measuring responses to the question, "How likely is it that recent immigration levels will take jobs away from people already here . . ." (very unlikely–very likely).

Although the "immigrants" referenced in these questions do not represent a specific racial or ethnic identity, the vast majority of whites associate illegal immigrants with Latinx immigrants or immigrants of some other nonwhite origin, thus justifying the inclusion of this scale as an indicator of racial out-group affect.[23]

Finally, we include attitudes toward one additional outgroup, Muslims. Although "Muslim" is a religious categorization, scholars have increasingly recognized the "racialization" of Muslims in the United States, especially those of Arab and South Asian descent.[24] As a result, Muslims now occupy a subordinate position as an "ethnoracial" minority group in America's racial order.[25] Research has shown that these negative attitudes toward Muslims, especially when primed by the mass media, can have important effects on public approval of policies related to the War on Terror[26] and policies that are likely to impose harm on Muslims in the United States or abroad.[27] Attitudes toward Muslims worsened in the wake of the 9/11 terrorist attacks, and hostility toward Muslims became politically reactivated beginning in 2008 with the rise of the anti-Muslim movement and the proliferation of a number of national and grassroots organizations seeking to prevent Muslims from gaining influence in the United States. Working hand in hand with the Tea Party movement (TPM), the anti-Muslim movement has been successful in pushing many conspiracy theories, including the accusation that Barack Obama was a Muslim immigrant.[28] The political relevance of attitudes toward Muslims continued to increase throughout the 2016 campaign, as Donald Trump promised that if elected he would ban all Muslims from immigrating to the United States. To measure hostility toward Muslims, we utilize the standard feeling thermometer item, which we have reverse-scaled to create a measure of "coldness" toward Muslims. We use thermometer scores for Muslims but not African Americans and Latinos because the egalitarian norms that serve to bias scores for these groups do not apply to

Muslims.[29] This proposition is supported by the fact that among the major racial and ethnic groups in the United States (African Americans, Latinos, Jews, and Asians), Muslims receive the "coldest" rating by whites on the standard feeling thermometer scale, even lower than "illegal immigrants."

Validating Our Measure of Outgroup Hostility

Table 2.1 presents the results of several analyses that compare our measure of outgroup hostility to Kinder and Kam's measure of ethnocentrism. The results generally support the validity of our measure of outgroup hostility as well as the more general argument that the targets of outgroup hostility have changed over the last two decades. The top panel of Table 2.1 reports the results of an exploratory factor analysis that combined Kinder and Kam's three indicators of ethnocentrism (constructed as feeling thermometer difference scores: white-Asian, white-black, white-Hispanic) and our three indicators of outgroup hostility (racial resentment, anti-immigration index, Muslim feeling thermometer). The analysis relies on ANES data, pooled over the four election samples (2004–2016). The purpose of a factor analysis is to determine the degree to which several different indicators are measuring the same concept or if the indicators are measuring different concepts. The analysis returns two important results. First, it determines if the indicators are measuring a single concept (a single "factor") or multiple concepts (two or more factors). Second, it returns a measure of how strongly each indicator is related to each factor identified by the analysis. Our results provide clear evidence of the distinctiveness of Kinder and Kam's ethnocentrism scale and our outgroup hostility scale. The factor analysis returned two distinct factors, suggesting that the six indicators are measuring two different concepts. Our three preferred indicators of outgroup hostility consistently loaded on one factor, while the other three indicators of ethnocentrism consistently loaded on a second, distinct factor.

The second panel of Table 2.1 reports the results of confirmatory factor analysis (CFA) conducted for each set of scale items for the presidential election years, 2004–2016. Specifically, the table reports the coefficient of determination, which is a measure of how well each set of scale items collectively maps onto the underlying concept that the items are measuring. Although the three feeling thermometer–based ethnocentrism items consistently display a stronger fit, this is to be expected given the fact that the

Table 2.1 Factor Analysis and Validity Results for Racial Hostility Scales

Affect Items	Outgroup Hostility	Kinder and Kam's Ethnocentrism
	Factor Loadings (Pooled 2004–2016)	
Racial resentment	.83	−.06
Opposition to immigrants scale	.80	.04
Hostility toward Muslims (FT)	.73	.06
Asians (FT difference)	−.06	.89
Blacks (FT difference)	.04	.87
Hispanics (FT difference)	.04	.88
Sample size (2004–2016)	8,035	
Election Year	**Confirmatory Factor Analysis Results** *Coefficient of Determination*	
2004 (N = 687)	.64	.83
2008 (N = 1,165)	.61	.80
2012 (N = 3,144)	.67	.84
2016 (N = 2,526)	.83	.90
	Correlation with Right-Wing Authoritarianism Scale	
2004 (N = 678)	.31	.20
2008 (N = 1,154)	.34	.20
2012 (N = 3,116)	.39	.22
2016 (N = 2,524)	.53	.33
	Correlation with Social Dominance Orientation Scale	
2008 (N = 1,165)	.33	.11
2012 (N = 3,832)	.37	.08
2016 (N = 2,513)	.51	.26

Note: The sample for this analysis includes white (non-Hispanic) voters and is taken from the American National Election Time Series Study. Columns 1 and 2 of panel 1 report factor loadings for the first two factors that returned an Eigen-value >1.0. The factor analysis was conducted using principal-components factors and oblique rotation to allow for correlated factors. Panel 2 presents model fit results from confirmatory factor analyses of each set of racial affect items, for each election year.

feeling thermometer items share an identical question format. What is most interesting about these results is the trend in the strength of the fit of the models across the four elections. While the fit has increased since 2008 for both sets of items, the increase has been far more significant for the outgroup hostility items. The most significant increase in model fit occurred between 2012 and 2016, increasing from .67 to .83. This suggests that in 2016 attitudes toward African Americans, Latinx immigrants, and Muslims were significantly more connected than they have been in recent history. As we show in the chapters that follow, Trump was unique among recent presidential candidates in the way that he emphasized these three racial outgroups in his campaign platform and rhetoric. Therefore, this finding would seem to provide some preliminary evidence that the public followed along, previewing our findings in the chapters to come.

We created our outgroup hostility index by combining our measures of attitudes toward blacks (racial resentment scale), Latinx immigrants (opposition to immigration scale), and Muslims (feeling thermometer). Using the ANES, we are able to measure outgroup hostility in this way for the four presidential elections from 2004 to 2016. We also created an ethnocentrism scale of attitudes toward blacks, Hispanics, and Asians following Kinder and Kam.[30] That is, we summed the ingroup-outgroup thermometer difference scores across the three outgroups (Banks 2014, 2016; Hajnal and Abrajano 2015; Hajnal and Rivera 2014; Kam and Kinder 2012).[31] In the bottom two panels of Table 2.1 we present the results of two final analyses that provide additional information regarding the relative validity of the two scales.

In the third panel of Table 2.1 we present the yearly correlation between each scale and a version of the right-wing authoritarianism (RWA) scale, which has been found to be positively associated with ethnocentrism in many studies over the years.[32] The results indicate that the correlations are consistently stronger for the measure of outgroup hostility compared with the ethnocentrism scale. The bottom panel of Table 2.1 presents a similar analysis utilizing a version of the social dominance orientation (anti-egalitarianism) scale (SDO).[33]

As with the RWA scale, many studies have found the SDO scale measuring support for group inequality to be an important determinant of racial prejudice.[34] The pattern of correlations between SDO, outgroup hostility, and Kinder and Kam's ethnocentrism scale follow the same general pattern. Outgroup hostility is significantly related to SDO, and the strength of the association increased in 2016. The ethnocentrism scale consistently displays a far weaker correlation. These validity analyses provide strong evidence that our measure of outgroup hostility is not only a valid indicator but has become far more salient and cohesive as a racial belief system among the mass public in recent years.[35]

Outgroup Hostility in the Electorate

For ease of interpretation, we transformed our outgroup hostility scale to range from 0 to 1. Because the component items are measured so that the midpoint of the scale always represents a neutral opinion, the outgroup hostility scale has a natural midpoint of .5. In other words, a value of .5 on the index means that on average, the respondent is neutral toward blacks, Latinx immigrants, and Muslims. Values less than .5 indicate respondents who are generally more favorable toward the three outgroups, and values above .5 reflect those who are at least somewhat hostile toward the three groups, on average.

Table 2.2 reports the mean level of outgroup hostility for white respondents across several different politically relevant subgroups in 2016. The table shows descriptive statistics based on two different survey samples, the 2016 ANES and the 2016 VOTER Survey. As can be seen by comparing the numbers within each row, the two surveys provide very similar results.

The mean outgroup hostility score for all whites is .55 in the ANES survey and .54 in the VOTER Survey. This suggests that in 2016, on average, as a group whites overall tended to feel slightly unfavorable toward the three outgroups.

The results suggest that variation in outgroup hostility largely conforms to what we know about variation in racial prejudice more generally. Those who display relatively higher levels of outgroup hostility tend to be male, older, less educated, more religious, and less well off financially. In some cases, the differences are quite significant. Among the demographic categories, those with no more than a high school degree scored approximately .16 higher on the index than whites with a graduate degree. The differences among the other demographic subgroups were more modest, but all are statistically significant (at the .01 level).

The most pronounced differences in outgroup hostility, however, are seen across the subgroups representing different levels of economic optimism. The table reports the mean level of outgroup hostility across the values of two

Table 2.2 Mean Level of Outgroup Hostility in 2016, by Voter Subgroups

Voter Subgroups	ANES	VOTER
All whites	.55	.54
Economic evaluation (national)		
Much better	.40	.40
About the same	.55	.56
Much worse	.71	.66
Economic evaluation (personal)		
Much better	.47	.39
About the same	.55	.52
Much worse	.67	.64
Family income		
Below median	.58	.56
Above median	.53	.52
Education level		
High school or less	.60	.59
College degree	.51	.51
Graduate degree	.45	.43
Church attendance		
Never	.52	.48
1–2 times per month	.59	.56
Every week	.60	.59
Age		
18–30	.50	.41
31–50	.54	.48
51 and over	.58	.55
Gender		
Female	.54	.51
Male	.57	.57

Note: Cell entries are subgroup means for outgroup hostility scale, which ranges from 0 to 1.

different types of economic evaluation items: a question measuring retrospective evaluations of the national economy and a similar question based on the respondent's personal finances. In both cases, the outgroup hostility score for the most pessimistic whites exceeds that of the most optimistic by .20 to .31, depending on the item and the survey, suggesting the possibility that the political effects of economic and racial attitudes in the current period are by no means entirely distinct.

The Prevalence of White Racial Conservatives and Extremists

Although we sometimes discuss recent trends in the political behavior of racial liberals and racial moderates, the primary focus of our book is the bloc of voters who display higher than average levels of outgroup hostility. We think of these voters as falling into one of two general categories: racial conservatives and racial extremists. Perhaps the most visible racial extremists are white nationalists, who advocate for white separatism, often justified by an implicit or explicit ideology of white supremacism. It is unlikely, however, that most racial extremists personally identify as white nationalists or white supremacists. Nonetheless, while they are a small fraction of the whites who express the new form of outgroup hostility, we argue that racial extremists represent an important force behind the mass-level mainstreaming of white racism.

We define racial conservatives as voters with relatively high levels of outgroup hostility, yet their racial ideology falls short of racial extremism. Some voters in this category rely on conservative principles to oppose racial assimilation, integration, and public policies designed to reduce discrimination and overcome disadvantage based on race. Yet many racial conservatives have come to express high levels of outgroup hostility simply out of concern that the three targeted outgroups represent a threat to the status quo. Their outgroup hostility is grounded in their anxiety about these groups, independent of an embrace of supremacist ideology, nationalist sentiment, or conservative policy orientation. Although racial conservatives are less extreme in their outgroup hostility, they have become an important voting bloc in recent elections and along with racial extremists now comprise an important faction within the Republican Party.

Since there is no agreed upon methodology for classifying voters in this way, we must devise our own strategy. We fully acknowledge that this is a somewhat arbitrary and subjective task. Therefore we make no claim that ours is the only reasonable approach that one might take. Yet since we (like other social scientists) often refer to this ambiguous population of voters throughout the book, we believe it is useful to empirically identify them. With this caveat in mind, we define white racial extremists based on two guiding principles. We believe that if we take the term *extremist* literally, the population of extremists must be relatively rare and must display an unusually strong degree of hostility toward at least one racial outgroup.[36] Specifically, we identify a racial extremist as someone who (1) displays the maximum level of hostility for at least one of the three outgroups and (2) displays a higher than average level of hostility toward the remaining outgroups. We define racial conservatives as those who do not satisfy condition 1, but satisfy condition 2 for all three racial outgroups.

Table 2.3 displays the percentage of white racial conservatives and extremists by several politically relevant subgroups. Approximately 11 percent of whites were classified as racial extremists in 2016, and a nearly equal number (9.9 percent) were classified as racial conservatives. As we would expect, racially hostile whites are more likely to be male and less likely to have a college degree. Yet, the characteristic that best distinguishes white racial conservatives and extremists from the rest of the electorate can be seen by examining which presidential candidate they supported in 2016. Nearly 38 percent of voters who supported Trump were classified as either racially conservative or extremist, compared to merely 5.2 percent of Hillary Clinton's supporters. And approximately one in five (21.9 percent) of Trump's supporters were classified as racial extremist, compared to only 1 percent of Clinton's supporters.

Table 2.3 Percentage of White Racial Conservatives and Extremists in 2016, by Voter Subgroups

Sample	Percent Racial Conservatives	Percent Racial Extremists	Total Percentage
All whites	9.7	13.0	22.7
Trump voters	15.8	21.9	37.7
Clinton voters	4.1	1.1	5.2
White men	10.6	15.3	25.9
White women	8.9	10.5	19.4
Whites with less than a college education	10.6	16.3	24.0
Whites with a BA or graduate degree	7.8	6.6	14.4

Source: ANES 2016 Time Series Study.

In Search of a White Backlash

A common narrative in the mass media is that Trump's victory represents a "white backlash," or as CNN's Van Jones quipped, a "whitelash" against the perceived threat posed by growing racial diversity.[37] The implicit understanding in this narrative is that white racial hostility increased as a result of Trump's campaign and that this was responsible for Trump's success. As is often the case, however, the data reveal a far more complicated story. The top panel of Figure 2.1 presents the yearly means for the outgroup hostility scale for white respondents, along with the yearly means for the three component items from which the scale is constructed. The trends in all of these indicators tell the same story. Although outgroup hostility among whites generally increased somewhat between 2004 and 2012, outgroup hostility actually decreased in 2016. This decline in outgroup hostility in 2016 was not an artifact of changes in affect toward a single group. Indeed, for each of the three groups that comprise the outgroup hostility scale, white hostility for the period 2004–2016 reached its lowest level in 2016. This finding is also reported by Sides, Tesler, and Varveck for the same outgroup items, which they too acknowledge is hardly consistent with the dominant narrative of the 2016 election as a "white backlash" fueled by Trump's candidacy.[38]

The bottom panel of the figure presents the percentage of white respondents who were classified as racial extremists and racial conservatives over the four presidential elections based on ANES data (2004–2016). Similar to the trends in outgroup hostility, the data clearly show that there was a surge in the percentage of whites classified as racial extremists and conservatives in the immediate aftermath of Barack Obama's election. The most significant growth occurred for racial extremists. Indeed, in 2004 the percentage of racial conservatives (8.3) was approximately as large as the percentage of extremists (9.3), but by 2012 the percentage of extremists had doubled, reaching approximately 17 percent compared with about 12 percent for racial conservatives. Yet what is perhaps most interesting for our purposes is that the percentage of white racial extremists and conservatives actually declined between 2012 and 2016—in contrast to the conventional backlash narrative.

Finally, Figure 2.1 also presents the percentage of whites who displayed relatively high levels of white racial identity ("white identifiers"), based on the indicator that is most widely used in the literature ("How important is being white to your identity?"). Unfortunately, this indicator is only

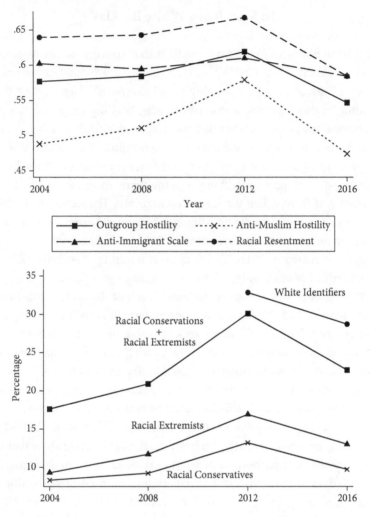

Figure 2.1 The surge and decline of outgroup hostility, 2004–2016

Note: The data for this analysis are taken from the ANES and include white respondents only.

available in the ANES for 2012 and 2016 (we discuss the measurement of white racial identity more fully in Chapter 8). But what is important here is that like the percentage of racial extremists and conservatives, there is no evidence that white racial identity increased prior to 2016. Not only did whites become somewhat less likely to express hostility toward racial outgroups; they also were less likely to view their race as an important dimension of their identity.

Yet our position is that it would be premature to dismiss entirely the "whitelash" narrative. The bottom panel of Figure 2.1 shows that even after the decline of outgroup hostility in 2016, the percentage of whites classified as racial extremists was still significantly larger than it was in 2004. Thus, there has been a long-term increase in racial extremism. But most important, the data merely tell us that Trump's whitelash did not come in the form of an overall increase in white racism. Rather, as we show later, the whitelash came in the form of an electoral mobilization of white racial extremists and conservatives that started well before Trump came onto the scene but was also intensified by his targeted race-baiting. To tell this story, we need a theoretical framework that combines the insights of theories of social identity and ethnocentrism to explain the attitudinal changes that preceded Trump with theories of social movements and collective action to explain the mobilization, and ultimately the mainstreaming, of white racism.

Understanding Racially Motivated Political Behavior: A Theoretical Framework

How and why has outgroup hostility come to have such a significant effect on political behavior? How did it help Trump? And how has this resulted in what we term the "mainstreaming of white racism"? To help answer these questions, we present a graphical summary of our main theoretical arguments in Figure 2.2. We begin with the upper half of the diagram, which describes the processes by which outgroup hostility is generated and politicized through the formation of white racial consciousness. This stage of the model also highlights our position concerning the causal roles of white identity and outgroup hostility. Given the importance of this debate in the current literature, we begin by discussing the relationship between ingroup and outgroup attitudes and their relative role in affecting political behavior.

White Identity versus Outgroup Hostility

The relative contributions of pro-ingroup attitudes (e.g., ingroup loyalty, superiority, preference) versus anti-outgroup attitudes (hostility, contempt)[39] have long been a subject of debate in the literature. As it was originally formulated in 1906, Sumner's conceptualization of ethnocentrism assumed that

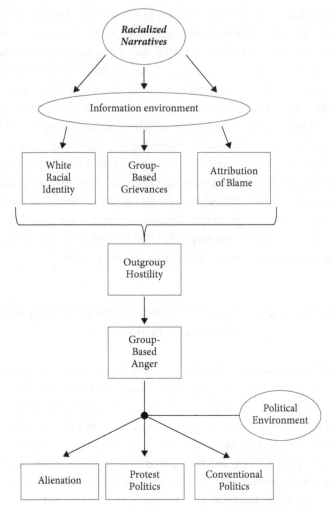

Figure 2.2 Understanding Racially Motivated Political Behavior: A Theoretical Framework

these two concepts comprised one dimension.[40] For decades afterward this view dominated the measurement of ethnocentrism in the literature.[41] Yet a large body of empirical research has found that ingroup favoritism and outgroup negativity are independent constructs, although often correlated.[42] Therefore, it seems appropriate to separate attitudes toward one's ingroup from outgroup evaluations in theoretical models and empirical analyses of the effects of ethnocentrism.[43] We follow the lead of scholars who have taken this approach to study the effects of white identity and outgroup hostility in recent elections.[44]

Scholars have varied in how they specifically define white racial identity (WRI). We follow the tradition in the social identity literature and conceptualize white identity as a form of group identity in which one comes to feel a strong sense of belonging to a racial or ethnic group.[45] In addition to a sense of attachment to a racial or ethnic group, "identity" is also thought to include a set of attitudes and emotions that are tied to group membership. Combining these two dimensions, Tajfel defines racial identity as consistent with "that part of an individual's self-concept which derives from his knowledge of his membership in a social group (or groups) together with the value and emotional significance attached to that group membership."[46]

One of our main points of disagreement with scholars advancing the WRI thesis concerns the causal proximity of white identity relative to outgroup hostility in our model of political behavior. As can be seen in Figure 2.1, in contrast to WRI scholars who argue that white identity has an important direct effect on political behavior, we argue that white identity primarily (if not exclusively) operates indirectly, through its effect on outgroup hostility. The argument that the causal flow runs from ingroup loyalty to outgroup hostility is consistent with important research on the subject. In his seminal study of prejudice, Allport argued that ingroup attitudes were "psychologically primary"[47] and that "familiarity, attachment and loyalty to one's ingroups comes prior to development of attitudes toward specific outgroups."[48] One interpretation of this formulation is that the political effects of white racial identity are therefore mediated through white outgroup hostility. In Chapter 8 we present a series of analyses that support this position.

The Formation of White Racial Consciousness

A critical way that white identity contributes to outgroup hostility is through its contribution to the formation of white racial consciousness (WRC), known more generally as an instance of group consciousness in the literature.[49] Although the literature reflects significant variation in its precise conceptualization, most theorists treat group consciousness as multidimensional, recognizing the importance of three general attitudinal components. First, group consciousness requires a high level of group identification. Second, research suggests that group consciousness also requires a subjective sense of group deprivation among group members. We refer to this sense of deprivation as "group-based grievances" in Figure 2.2. The third dimension of group consciousness (blame attribution) has been conceptualized in various ways and includes the related concepts of "system blame,"[50] "power discontent,"[51] "political trust" and "political efficacy."[52] These concepts share the common feature of referring to the attribution of blame for group-based grievances to the political system. Several studies have shown that the combination of group identity, group-based grievances, and a sense of political discontent (variously defined) has proven to be strongly related to participation in collective political action.[53]

We argue that WRC today represents a form of group consciousness that is defined by all three attitudinal dimensions. First, WRC requires a high level of white racial identity. In addition, for WRC to be fully realized whites must also experience a subjective sense of group-based deprivation or injustice. Today, group-based injustices felt by whites take a variety of forms rooted in perceived threats to white economic, political, and cultural supremacy. Finally, WRC also requires that whites attribute responsibility for their grievances to the political system, especially political elites who they view as responsible for advancing the status of racial minorities at the expense of whites. As we have already established, the minority groups that are most likely to be perceived as threatening by whites are African Americans, Latinx immigrants, and Muslims.

Numerous examples of the connection between group-based grievances felt by whites and government support of these three racial outgroups come to mind. Racially conscious whites in the United States have for several decades attributed responsibility for economic grievances to minorities who benefit from affirmative action. Many whites also blame political elites for the long-term increase in illegal immigrants, who they perceive as "stealing" jobs from whites due to their willingness to accept lower wages. They also believe immigrants pose cultural threats because many of them do not speak English, and because many practice a non-Christian religion (i.e., Muslims). Political threats to white political supremacy are naturally attributed to the growing representation of minorities in political office, especially African Americans and Latinos. For racially conscious whites, all of these threats are made even more urgent by the trajectory of current demographic trends, which project that white Anglos will cease to comprise a majority by the year 2045.[54]

Although WRC has likely existed among some segments of the white population since the CRM, there is considerable evidence to suggest that the growth in WRC has accelerated in recent years.[55] This growth has been facilitated by objective changes in the social, economic, and political environments that have come to be interpreted as threats to whites' status. Yet how do whites come to the conclusion that these changes represent threats? While many whites are undoubtedly capable of reaching these conclusions on their own, we argue that one of the keys to understanding the increase in WRC has been the development and diffusion of what social movement scholars refer to as collective action frames.[56]

Collective action frames are employed by movement entrepreneurs to promote the development of group consciousness by promoting a shared understanding of a group's deprived condition, assigning responsibility for that condition to the system, and by prescribing a course of political action that will effectively resolve the grievance. One of the primary ways in which these objectives have been accomplished with respect to WRC is through what we call "racialized political narratives." Narratives plot the relationship between actors. Racialized political narratives identify a victim (whites), a villain (minorities and/or elite sympathizers), and a plot that connects the two. In the process, these narratives reinforce a sense of group-based grievance; attribute responsibility for the grievance; and in many cases identify a "hero," a person, organization, or policy that will eradicate the grievance.

Racialized political narratives have long been used by political elites to mobilize whites. In Chapter 3 we show how these narratives have played an important role in the framing strategies of white nationalist groups, such as the Ku Klux Klan and the myriad neo-Nazi groups that continue to operate on the political fringe. Yet since the victories of the CRM, mainstream political leaders have generally relied on less explicit, "dog-whistle" rhetorical strategies to convey their message.[57] What sets Trump apart from other mainstream political leaders is that not only has he relied heavily on racialized narratives in his political speeches, he also has been far more willing to rely on explicit rhetoric in conveying these narratives.

Indeed, Trump is the paradigmatic example of how invoking these racialized political narratives could effectively activate whites' anxiety about their status as a threatened identity. Trump's campaign speeches are a treasure trove of empirical evidence on this score. As we show in Chapter 5, Trump, in contrast not just to Democrats like Clinton and Bernie Sanders, but also to his Republican primary opponents, hammered away on how

African American, Latinx, and Muslim populations posed threats that could undermine whites' status in American society, not just through demographic diversification and cultural change but also as a threat to whites' economic standing. These racialized political narratives helped make his campaign slogan to "Make America Great Again" easily be decoded to mean we need to "Make America White Again."

Trump did not stop with generalities; he pushed specific policies consistent with his goal to stoke white anxiety about these three outgroups. His ban to prevent immigration from selected Muslim countries was actually upheld by the U.S. Supreme Court (if in a more limited form than its original incarnation). Trump was not afraid to code "Muslim" as "terrorist" in his campaign speeches. He was equally tendentious in his campaign speech narratives about Latinx immigration. His push for a wall on the southern border to prevent Latinx immigration, including by legal asylum seekers, was never fully funded but remained a constant policy concern throughout his presidency. Trump equated immigration from the south with an "infestation." He told stories that made it seem as though all immigrants, mothers with children included, were not escaping unlivable conditions in their countries of origin but were gang-bangers in the notorious MS13 gang, which was prominent in some Latinx communities on both the East and West Coasts. Trump constantly equated southern border immigration with the illicit drug trade. His attempts to reach out to the African American community continued to run aground when he periodically would refer to African nations as "shit-hole countries." Trump's recurring insistence that the Central Park Five were rapists and deserved the death penalty continued even as president, in spite of the fact that the City of New York paid millions of dollars to the five men, who were falsely accused and spent years in jail. Trump's inauguration speech emphasized the "inner city" (code for black) as producing an "American carnage" that would now stop as he would "Make America Great Again." And then there was his attack on The Squad, elected members of Congress whom he told to "go back" to the countries they came from (see Chapter 1). All these racially driven narratives provide ample evidence that Trump continued from his campaign to his presidency to tell lies about African American, Latinx, and Muslim populations, and that these tendentious narratives reinscribed the African American, Latinx, and Muslim populations as inherently threatening to the established white order.

Through it all, Trump's racially inflected narratives were focused on piquing white anxiety about outgroup threats and underscoring that his policies were an alternative to that of liberal Democrats, who in the Obama era were allegedly making these threats to whites worse. Not all of these narratives originated from Trump. Indeed, as we show in Chapter 6, many of these narratives originated within a new information environment dominated by social media and highly partisan media sources that are more concerned with ideological advocacy than fact-based journalism. And as we show in Chapters 6 and 7, the types of voters attracted to Trump are precisely those ones who are most likely to consume these media. They are also least likely to venture outside their information bubbles to discover alternative narratives based on facts. In combination with the increased willingness of Trump and his media surrogates to push these narratives of demonization, a significant segment of the white population came to be attracted to Trump's candidacy on that basis, ultimately giving Trump the presidency. While other Republican presidents in the post–civil rights era won the presidency by playing the race card via tendentious narratives about threats to whites (Richard Nixon, Ronald Reagan, and George Herbert Walker Bush in particular), none did it with such a concerted effect as Trump.

The Activation of Outgroup Hostility and the Role of Emotion

We maintain that one important consequence of WRC is the generation of outgroup hostility. This proposition is supported by several theoretical traditions. In social psychology, social identity theorists have suggested that strong ingroup identity can have an important effect on outgroup affect. The way people experience ingroup-based grievances can facilitate an escalation of outgroup hostility.[58] As Brewer characterizes the role of ingroup preference, it can serve as a "platform for outgroup hate," especially when outgroups have been identified as a source of threat.[59] Although these authors do not work within the framework of group consciousness, the logic would seem to be directly applicable to WRC because it assumes the presence of a strong sense of white identity combined with a sense of threat from racial minorities. Writing from a sociological perspective, group position theorists have articulated a similar logic. According to Blumer,[60] racial prejudice among dominant group members (i.e., whites) is a direct result of the perceived threat posed by subordinate racial groups (i.e., blacks). Although the role of WRI was more implicit in Blumer's theory, it nevertheless supports the proposition that WRC—due to the experience of minority group threat—should be accompanied by negative affect (prejudice, outgroup hostility) toward the offending minority groups.

The generation of outgroup hostility, in turn, has important implications for political behavior. The experience of outgroup hostility is naturally accompanied by a range of negative emotions toward the offending outgroups. Indeed, Blumer recognized this fact in his original formulation of group position theory when he wrote that in response to threats posed by the subordinate group, the dominant group "thus develops fears, apprehensions, resentments, angers and bitterness which become fused into a general feeling of prejudice against the subordinate racial people or peoples."[61] Although political behavior has been found to be affected by several different emotions, the research suggests that one of the most politically potent emotions is anger.[62] Anger has been variously defined in the literature, but most definitions identify the sources of anger as threats or obstacles to achievement of personal well-being.[63] Anger is especially likely to be experienced when the threat or obstacle has been identified as being caused by an external source.[64] As a result, the experience of anger leads to a greater likelihood of a targeted, aggressive effort directed against the source of the grievance.[65] These conditions are naturally satisfied by the experience of WRC.

To the extent that individuals identify with a specific social group, group-based injustices and grievances may also trigger what collective behavior scholars term "group-based anger," which can serve as an important motivational force to seek retribution through collective (political) action.[66] For several reasons, we argue that WRC should often result in the experience of group-based anger. Indeed, the two constructs may even be mutually reinforcing. The identification of external outgroup targets as responsible for group-level grievances can contribute to the escalation of anger resulting from such grievances. In addition, anger leads to a greater reliance on motivated reasoning, a susceptibility to political misperceptions,[67] and a greater reliance on stereotypes in political decision-making.[68] This naturally leads to conditions favorable for the attribution of responsibility for ingroup grievances to one or more outgroups, as portrayed in racial narratives of white grievance. As a result, we expect outgroup hostility, as the targeted expression of group-based anger, to have a strong direct effect on political behavior as a means of addressing the perceived source of ingroup grievances.

The Political Opportunity Structure and
the Channeling of Outgroup Hostility

Outgroup hostility that is stoked by racialized political narratives provides what we might think of as a source of political energy, a strong motivation to act via the production of group-based anger. The social movement literature, however, has long recognized that the translation of discontent into mobilization is highly contingent upon the political opportunity structure: the features of the political environment that "alter the costs and likely outcomes of collective action."[69] Some of the most influential features of the political opportunity structure are the "openness" of the political system,[70] the probability of government receptiveness to the group's goals,[71] and the presence of allies within government.[72] These factors structure mobilization through their effects on the prospect for movement success, which is an important consideration in the cost-benefit calculation of potential movement participants.

In other words, the success of collective action frames, like the racialized political narratives Trump and other race-baiters employed in instigating political mobilization, are often contingent upon changes in the political opportunity structure. The political opportunity structure changed in two important ways for white racial extremists in the first two decades of the twenty-first century, and these changes have had a profound effect on their level of mobilization as well as the form their mobilization has taken. Following the successes of the CRM, the political system gradually closed for the most ardent racial conservatives. By the 1980s running on a platform of racial segregation had become unacceptable within the major political parties, despite the fact that a nontrivial percentage of white Americans continued to display nontrivial levels of traditional racial prejudice.[73] This had the effect of closing off formal institutional channels of influence, leaving white racists with just one option to participate in collective action to further their goals: organized "hate groups" such as the Ku Klux Klan, various neo-Nazi organizations, and a range of other organizations that prioritize an antiminority agenda. As we show in the next chapter, participation in these organizations grew at a fast pace throughout the 1990s and 2000s, reaching a peak during the first term of the Obama administration.

Yet compared with other forms of political participation, membership in these groups remained relatively small and was limited to whites with the most extreme views. One important reason for this is the high cost of participation in hate groups due to the stigma associated with being identified as a member of such a group. Participation in extremist groups is also limited by the fact that these groups are generally not viewed as being effective in promoting racist goals because by the 1980s they had become isolated from formal political institutions.

The first important change in the political opportunity structure came with the mobilization of the TPM. Although the TPM was originally founded in 2009 as an antitax, proliberty movement that emphasized fiscal issues, it soon grew to accommodate a broader set of priorities, including a strong opposition to immigration, opposition to less explicitly racialized policies such as welfare spending, and a general resistance to Barack Obama's presidency. Due to the highly racialized nature of the Tea Party agenda, coupled with the fact that the TPM was showing some success in recruiting and winning elections, the TPM became an attractive political alternative to white racists as a vehicle to advance their cause. As we show in Chapter 3, this had the dual effect of co-opting the most extreme elements of the white nationalist movement and mobilizing many white racial extremists who until this point had been politically disengaged because of the high costs of participation in white nationalist organizations and their sense of exclusion from the major political parties.

By mobilizing white racial extremists into conventional politics, the TPM thus facilitated the first major wave of the political mainstreaming of white racism. Despite the TPM's success in electing a number of candidates who identified as Tea Party "members" in 2010, the movement nonetheless soon began to lose steam. The most racist elements of the Tea Party agenda were never fully implemented for a variety of reasons, including the moderation of the agenda as it became co-opted by the Republican Party, as well as the fact that a Democrat occupied the White House and could effectively block the most radical policy proposals from being implemented. While this may have led to a demobilization of the TPM, at the same time it set the stage for the second phase of the political mainstreaming of white racism: the emergence of Donald Trump as a presidential candidate.

Trump's campaign further mobilized white racists into conventional politics at a level we have not seen in recent history. Although the TPM moved many white racists and racial conservatives from the sidelines into the mainstream of American politics, as the first major political party nominee to run on an explicitly racist agenda, Trump not only attracted whites from the

TPM, he also attracted a significant number of racially resentful whites who had bypassed the TPM but became engaged by the salience of the presidential race and the stark contrast between the two candidates in their positions on racial outgroups.

Outgroup Hostility and the Mainstreaming of Racism

Donald Trump shocked the world when he won the 2016 presidential election. Questions continue to arise as to how a presidential candidate could win while running on such an explicit platform of outgroup animosity. And while many observers predicted that Trump might moderate his rhetoric as president, it seems that the opposite has occurred. As president, Trump has remained committed to this strategy. In the process, he has helped facilitate the mainstreaming of white racism in American politics.

This chapter lays out the core argument that serves as the basis for the remaining chapters. Our central claim is that the key to understanding the mainstreaming of white racism is the growth and politicization of hostility toward the racial outgroups Trump has isolated as targets for white resentment: African Americans, Latinx immigrants, and Muslims. While white attitudes toward these groups have been found in prior research to be significant predictors of political behavior, we argue that these attitudes do not operate independently. Rather, we show that these attitudes operate powerfully in concert as a contemporary form of outgroup hostility.

While white outgroup hostility, more than white ingroup solidarity, is the critical factor affecting political behavior today, we argue that they are interrelated in important ways. In the chapters that follow we provide detailed evidence that the use of racialized political narratives has led to an increase in WRC, which in turn has contributed to an increase in outgroup hostility. We argue that this has been the most important and causally proximate factor in the mainstreaming of white racism.

Yet as the social movement literature reminds us,[74] the mainstreaming of racism is not simply the result of changes in white racial attitudes and behavior, but also of changes in the political opportunity structure that constrains and enables political possibility. What is needed to understand this interrelationship regarding mainstreaming of racism today is a theoretical framework that emphasizes the highly contingent nature of the relationship between WRC, outgroup hostility, and political mobilization. The remaining chapters work within that framework to provide evidence of changes in the external political environment that not only allowed the mainstreaming of racist attitudes but also helped enable disaffected white racial extremists to become active in mainstream electoral politics.

3

The Rise of the Modern White Nationalist Movement

The mainstreaming of racism in the current era involves more than changes in attitudes among whites already active in mainstream electoral politics. It also involves the activation of disaffected white racial extremists. In this chapter (and the next) we provide important empirical evidence on how a changing political environment enabled disaffected white extremists to become active in electoral politics and in particular to go on to join with other more mainstream whites to become a critical part of Donald Trump's constituency. This context proved critical to Trump's 2016 presidential campaign since changes in the political environment made the influx of new voters possible, and that helped compensate for the many votes Trump lost among racial moderates due to his use of explicit racial appeals. More so than any other candidate in recent years, Trump was able to mobilize white racial extremists, the majority of whom had been politically inactive prior to 2016 or had eschewed conventional electoral politics for fringe, protest politics. This chapter provides empirical evidence for how a changing political environment enabled racial extremists to become mainstreamed to the point that they became active in electoral politics, going on to become a critical part of Trump's constituency, especially within his activist base.

Although Trump mobilized racial extremists like no other candidate in recent history, their movement from the fringe to conventional politics had been underway for several previous elections.[1] Indeed, we argue that Trump would not have been able to attract so many racial extremists to his campaign if the white nationalist movement (WNM), in its many forms, had not already been partly absorbed into conventional politics through the Tea Party movement (TPM). Further, Trump's success in mobilizing white extremists to vote for him was also aided by their own efforts to insert themselves into mainstream politics via the burgeoning alt-right movement (ARM) and the more general turn toward electoral politics within the WNM. In fact, the mainstreaming of white extremists was a well-established two-way

Hard White, Richard C. Fording and Sanford F. Schram. Oxford University Press (2020). © Oxford University Press.
DOI: 10.1093/oso/9780197500484.001.0001

street. The extremists were for some time actively seeking inclusion in the mainstream even as they were being recruited. This fact is critical because it suggests that the co-optation of the WNM is not solely dependent upon Trump's candidacy. As long as there are like-minded political entrepreneurs within the Republican Party who, like Trump, are willing to promote a white nationalist agenda, the mainstreaming of white nationalism could persist long after Trump's exit from politics.

We begin here by tracing the recent history of the WNM from the 1970s through the election of Barack Obama. We examine the ideology of the movement through a detailed analysis of WNM issue statements and show how white racial consciousness (WRC) grew over time as a reaction to the perceived political threat posed by the rapid increase in minority political power. Our analysis emphasizes that throughout this period the political opportunity structure[2] provided few avenues for participation of white racial extremists in conventional politics. As a result, the WNM was largely relegated to the extremist fringe of American politics. This marginalization contributed to a steady increase in white nationalist group formation throughout the 1990s and 2000s, which peaked after the election of Barack Obama in 2008. By 2010, however, the stage was set for the movement of white racial extremists into the mainstream.

The Origins of the Modern White Nationalist Movement

Scholars have long recognized that social movements do not exist in isolation from other movements. One important effect that social movements often have, especially if a movement's goal is to challenge the existing status hierarchy, is to create conditions favorable for the emergence of a countermovement as "a conscious, collective, organized attempt to resist or to reverse social change."[3] The modern WNM emerged during the 1950s as an attempt to resist the demand for equal rights sought by African Americans and eventually, the policy victories of the civil rights movement (CRM). Although it did not achieve all of its goals, the success of the CRM ultimately changed the political opportunity structure in two important ways that would influence the trajectory of the WNM for the next four decades.

First, policies promoting racial equality provided valuable material for WNM organizers in their efforts to craft racialized political narratives to promote WRC. These narratives often portray whites as victims of government policies and programs that unfairly redistribute benefits from whites to nonwhites or extend rights to minorities that were previously granted only to whites. This has helped to fuel WRC in two ways: (1) by reinforcing a broad range of group-based grievances among whites and (2) by connecting the source of white grievances to racial outgroups as well as government officials, who are depicted as pursuing an antiwhite (i.e., antiracist) agenda. One of the most important changes in the political environment during the 1990s and 2000s that contributed to this sense of group-based deprivation was the redistribution of political power that resulted from the implementation of the Voting Rights Act. Between 1979 and 2002 the number of black elected officials more than doubled, from 4,584 to 9,430.[4] Similarly, the number of Latinx elected officials increased by 70 percent between 1983 and 2000, from 3,063 to 5,205.[5] This growth in minority political power far exceeded the growth rate of the minority population and was concentrated in states and communities where white nationalist sentiment was the strongest.

A second important change in the political opportunity structure resulted from the cultural effect that the CRM had on American society and ultimately, American politics. Prior to the CRM, surveys indicated that whites generally supported legalized forms of racial segregation and held many derogatory stereotypes of blacks. Over time, as legal forms of discrimination were struck down by Congress and the federal courts, the majority of white Americans came to reject the overt expression of racial prejudice.[6] As a result, it became unacceptable for mainstream political candidates to campaign on an openly racist platform.[7]

This transformation did not happen overnight, and it did not happen without resistance. Indeed, when George Wallace made his most successful run for president in 1968, he openly campaigned against recently enacted civil rights policies and the federal government's efforts to desegregate the South. Although he claimed he was not racist, he clearly positioned himself as the candidate of the white nationalist countermovement. During the campaign he once declared, "I am not against non-discrimination, but I am against the government of the United States in the name of civil rights trying to control the property rights of people. . . . and I feel the so-called Civil Rights Act is not in the interest of any citizen of this country, regardless of their race."[8] His campaign had direct ties to a broad range of white nationalist organizations prominent at the time, including the White Citizens Councils, the John Birch Society, and Liberty Lobby. A well-known figure in the WNM for many years, Liberty Lobby founder Willis Carto, authored a pamphlet for

Wallace titled "Stand Up for America: The George Wallace Story," in which he proclaimed that Wallace was the only candidate capable of beating back "blacky."[9]

Wallace ran one of the most successful third-party campaigns in modern election history, winning five southern states and forty-six electoral votes under the American Independent Party label. In 1972 he ran again, this time as a Democrat. In the four years since the 1968 election, even George Wallace had adapted to the new political environment, claiming that he no longer supported segregation and that he had always been a racial moderate.[10] Wallace got off to a good start in the Democratic primary. By mid-May he had won five states, more than 1968 nominee Hubert Humphrey or eventual 1972 nominee George McGovern. His campaign was cut short by an assassination attempt, which left him paralyzed for the rest of his life. After his recovery and return to politics, sensing that even in his home state of Alabama the political tide had turned, Wallace eventually apologized for his support for segregation and asked for forgiveness from black people.

Although there has been much speculation regarding whether Wallace was sincere or if his change of heart was a calculated political strategy, this marked the end of an era. No longer could a national political candidate run on an openly racist platform and expect to be successful. For white racial extremists, this meant that conventional electoral politics was no longer a viable option. By the 1980s simply being associated with a known white nationalist could potentially be enough to sink a mainstream campaign. This had a profound effect on the WNM. Many racial extremists withdrew from mainstream politics, some even choosing not to participate in any form of politics. Nonetheless, some white extremists were willing to absorb the costs of the stigma associated with the public support of a racist agenda. However, their only option was to organize outside of the major political parties through participation in one of a broad range of white nationalist organizations.

The Modern White Nationalist Movement: A Definition

Throughout this book we use WNM to refer to a broad set of groups who are set apart from other extremist groups on the far right by the fact that their agenda is largely dictated by their concern with protecting what they believe to be a threatened white racial identity. The most extreme adherents are what we legitimately term "white supremacists." These groups place a great deal of emphasis on the fact that their organization exists to promote the interests of the white race, which they believe is set apart from other races for a variety of reasons. The most common justification emphasizes whites' shared ancestry and culture. Many groups refer to whites as members of an "Aryan" race and tend to identify whites in the United States as members of a larger white nation that extends to the Anglo Saxon countries of Western Europe. Some white supremacist groups claim to want nothing more than separation from other races and the establishment of an all-white ethnostate, or at the very least homogenous white institutions, including schools, government, and all-white residential communities. Yet most white supremacists argue either implicitly or explicitly that the white race deserves to sit atop a racial hierarchy in the United States in which nonwhites assume a subordinate position. This ideology is often justified by some argument related to genetic or cultural superiority or in some cases the assertion that the United States was founded by whites as a white nation. An example of the cultural argument for white supremacy is offered by one of the most prominent neo-Nazi groups, the National Alliance:

> Our world is hierarchical. Each of us is a member of the Aryan (or European) race, which, like the other races, developed its special characteristics over many thousands of years during which natural selection not only adapted it to its environment but also advanced it along its evolutionary path. Those races which evolved in the more demanding environment of the North, where surviving a winter required planning and self-discipline, advanced more rapidly in the development of the higher mental faculties— including the abilities to conceptualize, to solve problems, to plan for the future, and to postpone gratification—than those which remained in the relatively unvarying climate of the tropics. Consequently, the races vary today in their capabilities to build and to sustain a civilized society and, more generally, in their abilities to lend a conscious hand to Nature in the task of evolution.[11]

Members of these groups oppose anything that they believe will dilute the purity of their unique white culture, including immigration, interracial marriage, globalization, and any form of multiculturalism. None of the groups that we label "white supremacist" would ever refer to themselves as white supremacists. Many white supremacist groups prefer to call themselves "white nationalists" or "white separatists."[12] However, the implication of the ideology is the same: members of these groups rigidly separate those who "belong" and those who do not based on race.

We refer to the remaining white nationalist groups simply as "(other) white nationalists." This category consists of groups that generally fall short in some way of the extreme ideology of white supremacist groups and includes many groups who in recent years have become labeled as the alt-right. Although we refer to these groups simply as "white nationalist," it is important to recognize that the line between what we call "white supremacist" and "other white nationalist" groups is often blurry, and many of the latter groups could be justifiably classified as white supremacist.

Trends in the White Nationalist Movement

To better understand recent changes in the WNM, we collected county- and state-level data for all white supremacist and other white nationalist groups in the United States that fit our definition, using data provided by the Southern Poverty Law Center (SPLC). The SPLC has been collecting data on what they call "hate groups" since the late 1980s, and its data provide the most extensive collection of hate group activity available. The SPLC collects data on many different categories of hate groups, some of which do not meet our definition of white supremacist or white nationalist groups. The most obvious example of such a category is "black separatist groups," but there are several others as well. Groups that are part of the "religious" right, such as the Christian Coalition, are not included. Neither are more narrowly focused antiabortion groups, anti-LGBT groups, radical Catholic groups, and groups classified as "Holocaust denial," despite their extremist views and tactics. Finally, we also exclude organizations that can be characterized as part of the militia and patriot movements. While it is true that "New World Order" conspiratorial thinking about a global cabal (often identified as led by Jews) is quite prevalent among militia and patriot groups, racism and anti-Semitism are not core aspects of their ideology.[13] Finally, the SPLC classifies some hate groups as "anti-immigrant" or "anti-Muslim." We do not consider these groups to be white supremacist or white nationalist in our analyses reported in this book because these groups are not explicitly founded on principles of white racial identity. We do, however, discuss and report trends in the growth of these groups in Chapter 4 because they represent an important manifestation of the increase in the new outgroup hostility discussed in Chapter 2. It is important to note that the SPLC only lists hate groups that were "known to be active" each year, where "activity" includes marches, rallies, speeches, meetings, leafleting, publishing literature, and criminal acts. Thus, this should exclude groups regardless of ideology that exist solely as a post office box or in cyberspace.

White Supremacist Groups

We define white supremacist groups as those that fall into one of four different SPLC group categories: Ku Klux Klan (KKK), neo-Nazi, Christian identity, and (racist) skinhead. The Klan is without doubt the oldest and most widely known of today's white supremacist groups. Its history can be traced back to white resistance to Reconstruction in the South after the Civil War. Originally it operated via local secret societies, becoming over time the most notorious of American hate groups and one of the largest. The KKK has had three distinct periods of ascendancy. During Reconstruction it terrorized freed blacks, burning churches and schools and lynching teachers and others who represented black freedom. After Reconstruction ended and white control of the South was reasserted, the Klan declined, but it rose again starting around 1915, in part spurred by the release of the film *The Birth of a Nation*.[14] Its membership increased dramatically in the 1920s, when it campaigned more openly as the defender of white culture and values. Today's "third-era" Klan originated in the 1950s in response to school desegregation and the successes of the CRM.

Throughout its existence the Klan has had a very violent history and has been responsible for many killings and acts of violence, even as recently as during the civil rights era of the 1960s. Compared to previous phases of mobilization, however, there is today far greater variation in the approaches taken by the many Klan organizations across the country. Some Klans, such as the Knights of the Ku Klux Klan (KKKK), now claim to be nonviolent "white civil rights organizations." This strategy reflects the tactical preference of their founder, David Duke, who at various times in his career has tried to be a player in mainstream politics. However, other Klan organizations, such as the Imperial Klans of America, continue to be associated with violent acts.

Neo-Nazi groups are distinct from the Klan because they are associated directly with the ideology and symbolism of Hitler's Third Reich. The origins of this faction among white supremacists can be traced back to the founding of the American Nazi Party by George Lincoln Rockwell in 1960. Rockwell was assassinated in 1967, and since then the movement has splintered into many different organizations. Some neo-Nazi groups are involved in electoral politics, such as the Traditionalist Worker Party, which has run candidates under its label and endorsed other candidates running under different party labels. Yet many neo-Nazi groups reject electoral politics and have often been associated with political violence. One of the most prominent neo-Nazi groups has been the aforementioned National Alliance, founded by Dr. William Pierce. Pierce, a former physics professor, was also the author of *The Turner Diaries*, a widely influential book in the WNM more generally that describes a "white revolution" and lays out a plot strikingly similar to the events surrounding the Oklahoma City bombing. Another prominent neo-Nazi-style organization linked to violence is the World Church of the Creator. It was once the largest neo-Nazi group, with eighty-eight chapters in 2002, but the organization quickly disintegrated upon the imprisonment of its leader— Matt Hale—who was convicted of conspiracy to murder a federal judge. One of the newest organizations and also one of the most popular today, with chapters in twenty-seven states, is Atomwaffen Division. As its name suggests (*Atomwaffen* is German for "atomic bomb"), Atomwaffen Division is linked to several violent acts, and at least eight members have faced federal charges ranging from possession of explosives to first-degree murder.

The third subgroup of white supremacist groups is "Christian Identity." The Christian Identity movement has long been one of the smallest hate group categories in the SPLC database, but this subgroup is important because of its radical white supremacist ideology, connection to survivalism, and occasional violent tendencies. Unlike most white supremacist groups, Christian Identity is a religion that has integrated its racist beliefs with Christian doctrine. Identity followers justify racial separation using two basic tenets. First, the Identity ideology holds that white Christians are the literal descendants of the lost tribes of ancient Israel and are thus God's chosen race on earth. Second, Identity believers argue strongly that modern-day Jews are not of what they call "Israelite heritage." Theories about the racial origins of Jews differ, but the most radical version (called the "seed-line doctrine") holds that the Jews are the direct descendants of Satan through the seduction of Eve by the devil in the Garden of Eden. This belief system, which literally demonizes Jews, has at times been relied upon to justify violence. For instance, the most notorious organized domestic terrorist group in the 1980s, the Silent Brotherhood (aka The Order), was made up largely of men connected to the virulently anti-Semitic seed-line version of Identity teaching. Most recently, a man inspired by Christian Identity doctrine murdered eleven congregants at the Tree of Life synagogue in Pittsburgh.[15] In most periods, Identity followers retreat to rural areas to exit modern society, which they regard as morally corrupt and antiwhite. Some prominent Identity groups are America's Promise Ministries, Church of Israel, Mission to Israel, and Scriptures for America Ministries.[16]

Neo-Nazi skinheads are the fourth subgroup of the American racist right included in our analysis. These gangs, whose origins trace back to 1960s Britain, are very similar in terms of ideology to the other neo-Nazis described in this chapter. However, skinheads tend to be younger, to be more violent (though mostly involved in hate crime vandalism and assault, not necessarily organized domestic terrorism), and to participate in their own youth subculture, with certain styles of dress and music. The music of the skinheads, known as "white power rock and roll," is one of the defining features of the subculture. It serves as entertainment, a recruitment tool, and ideological propaganda and has been known to incite violence. For many years the largest and most notorious group in this category has been Hammerskin Nation, which is associated with the annual racist music festival Hammerfest. Some of the other important, if smaller, groups in this category are Blood and Honour, Crew 38, and Firm 22.

Other White Nationalist Groups

Groups that do not fit easily into the preceding subgroups are included under a residual category that we refer to as "other white nationalist" groups. This is a diverse set of organizations that often reflect aspects of white supremacist ideology to one degree or another but do not identify or (typically) affiliate with the traditional white supremacist groups. The vast majority of these groups are now coded by the SPLC as "white nationalist" or "general hate"—separate categories that the SPLC started using in 2006. Some of the larger groups in this category include many that have existed for several years, including the Council of Conservative Citizens (CCC); David Duke's other main organization, the European-American Unity and Rights Organization (EURO); and the American Freedom Party, which began running candidates under its label (formerly American Third Position) in the early 2000s. We also include in this category groups categorized by the SPLC as "neo-Confederate," which promote a unique form of southern nationalism but otherwise espouse many of the themes of white racial identity thinking reflected in the broader WNM (especially the Klan).

In recent years a number of other miscellaneous white nationalist groups have emerged, many coded in the SPLC database under the label "alternative right." Richard Spencer, the controversial leader of National Policy Institute, is credited with first introducing this term in 2008 and quickly became recognized as the leader of the ARM. The ARM is commonly associated with younger people and has made much use of internet platforms such as 4chan and 8chan to recruit and exchange information. It is widely acknowledged that the term alt-right refers to a broader effort of certain factions within the WNM to rebrand themselves as a more moderate, intellectual, legitimate presence within the conservative movement. However, the ARM clearly rejects traditional conservativism, viewing its agenda as inadequate to achieve and secure rights for white people. These groups often refer to themselves as identitarians, a term that was first introduced by elements of the extreme right in France. Identitarians are less likely to explicitly advocate against the rights of racial minorities, preferring to frame their goals as motivated by a desire to preserve white heritage. Yet the implications are often the same, and many of the leaders under the ARM umbrella have roots squarely within the white supremacist movement. Spencer's National Policy Institute, Greg Johnson's Counter Currents Publishing, and Jared Taylor's American Renaissance are three of the more visible efforts to promote the intellectual roots of white nationalism. Although the ARM has been characterized as largely an online movement, a significant number of activist groups have sprouted up in the last few years under the alt-right brand, including Identity Evropa (renamed in 2019 as the American Identity Movement); The Patriot Front; and a number of local chapters of The Right Stuff, inspired by the popular alt-right blog with the same name.

Recent Trends in White Nationalist Movement Activity

Because of the WNM's association with opposition to the CRM, most Americans tend to think of it as more of a regional phenomenon that is more or less limited to the South. This is not entirely accurate, as white nationalist groups have spread to every state in one form or another. The most recent data on the geographic variation in white nationalist activity is summarized

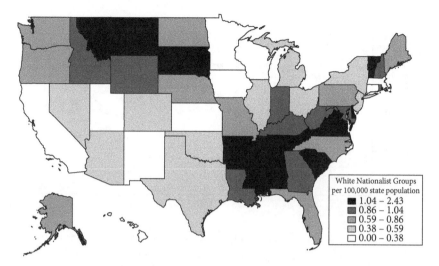

Figure 3.1 Geographic variation in white nationalist activity, 2015–2017

Source: Southern Poverty Law Center (Coding details available in our Online Appendix: https://rcfording.com/research/HardWhite).

in Figure 3.1, which displays the average number of active hate groups in the states for the years 2015–2017, controlling for the size of the white population (the number of white nationalist groups per 100,000 state white [non-Hispanic] population). Where are white nationalist groups most active? As can be seen on the map, white nationalist activity tends to be high in the South, as expected. Indeed, the two states with the highest density of white nationalist chapters are Mississippi (2.4) and Alabama (1.8). However, the northwestern and northeastern states also display higher than average levels of activity, with states such as Montana (1.8), New Hampshire (1.0), South Dakota (1.1), and Vermont (1.1) displaying activity levels in the top quartile. The southwestern and midwestern states, for the most part, display lower levels of white nationalist activity. This is particularly surprising for the southwestern states given the salience of the immigration debate in recent years and the large presence of Latinx immigrants in these states.

Perhaps the most counterintuitive development within the WNM concerns recent trends in the level of movement activity. We present these trends in Figure 3.2. The upper panel of Figure 3.2 shows the annual number of white supremacist chapters within each of the four subgroups during the period for which we have reliable data, 2000–2018. As can be seen, Christian Identity groups have always been the least numerous, having reached a maximum of

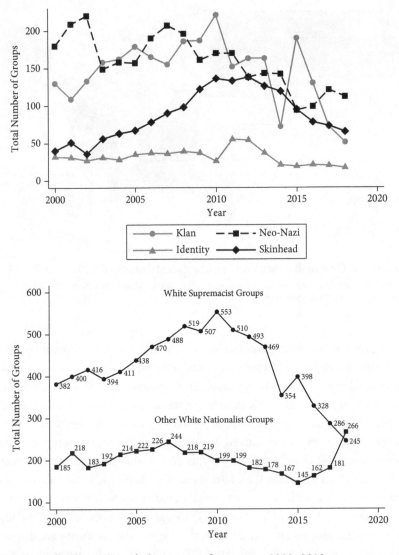

Figure 3.2 Total number of white nationalist groups, 2000–2018
Source: Southern Poverty Law Center.

just fifty-five in 2011. Racist skinhead groups are the only ones that experienced an increase during the 2000–2018 period, increasing from forty in 2000 to sixty-five in 2018. Ku Klux Klan and neo-Nazi groups have historically represented the two largest categories of white supremacist groups, reaching approximately two hundred active chapters on several occasions.

The most notable feature of these trends, however, is that during the latter half of the 2000–2018 period the number of white supremacist groups has steadily declined across all four subgroups. This decline in activity is more evident in the bottom panel of Figure 3.2, which displays the aggregated total of white supremacist groups along with the annual count of chapters that we categorize as "other white nationalist" groups. The total number of white supremacist groups increased steadily from 2000 to 2010, peaking at 553 active groups in 2010. Since then the number of white supremacist groups has consistently declined, and by 2018 they totaled just 245 active chapters. This represents a decrease of over 50 percent since 2010. The number of other white nationalist groups has followed a somewhat similar pattern, increasing in number from 2000 to 2007 and then experiencing a steady decline through 2015. Unlike the white supremacist groups, however, the number of other white nationalist groups has increased since 2015, with the sharpest increase occurring in 2018. As a result, by 2018 other white nationalist groups actually outnumbered traditional white supremacist groups. Nevertheless, the most important takeaway from Figure 3.2 is that the total number of all white nationalist groups decreased quite significantly after 2010, falling from 752 active groups in 2010 to 511 in 2018. This fact will undoubtedly come as a surprise to many political observers, as it would seem to contradict the conventional wisdom that Donald Trump's rise has coincided with an increase in the mobilization of white nationalist groups. Yet as we argue in Chapter 4, this decline is entirely consistent with our theoretical arguments concerning the mainstreaming of the WNM. The political mobilization of white racial extremists did not decline. Rather, their efforts were redirected to mainstream politics as a result of the opening of the political opportunity structure after the 2008 presidential election.

Racialized Narratives in the Rise of the White Nationalist Movement

Although there are no data on the number of white nationalist organizations and chapters prior to the 1990s,[17] by all accounts the WNM grew throughout the late 1970s and into the 1980s.[18] This growth was accompanied by the emergence of several charismatic leaders representing different factions of the movement. Yet it was also facilitated by the introduction of the internet in the 1980s, which greatly enhanced intramovement communication and reduced the costs of mobilization. This was especially helpful for the WNM because of the backlash movement members often experienced at public recruiting events. Indeed, white nationalists were among the first to effectively utilize the internet for mobilization.[19]

Most fundamentally, however, the growth of the WNM through the early 2000s was enabled by two sets of factors related to social movement mobilization. First, conventional politics became increasingly closed to white extremists after the victories of the CRM. Racial extremists were certainly unwelcome in the Democratic Party, which became disproportionately populated by racial minorities after the implementation of the Voting Rights Act. Yet white extremists were often just as unwelcome within the Republican Party as mainstream conservative gatekeepers tried to distance the party from right-wing extremism. One of the earliest and most visible examples occurred immediately after Barry Goldwater's defeat in 1964, when William Buckley led the purge of the John Birch Society from the mainstream of the conservative movement.[20] As time passed, white racial extremists became increasingly disenchanted with what they viewed to be unsympathetic Republican leaders, leaving them with few opportunities to pursue racist policy goals other than through participation in white nationalist organizations. This sentiment is reflected in the following passage from the Empire Knights of the Ku Klux Klan:

> Time was when parties stood for great principles. But today the difference between them is that of "tweedledum and tweedledee." One of the parties must be induced to champion great fundamental American principles that will hasten the development of our country; or else a new party must come into being. As the matter now stands we must cast our ballots for the right as it is most nearly represented and championed by men regardless of party.[21]

Equally important to the growth of the WNM in the pre-Obama years is that collective action frames, in the form of racialized political narratives so crucial to white identity formation, became increasingly powerful and effective tools for generating WRC. As affirmative action became widely practiced and welfare rolls and immigration rates increased throughout the 1970s–1990s, political narratives highlighting racial threats to whites' economic, cultural, and political standing became even more credible to whites generally, but to white nationalists in particular, representing an increase in what social movement scholars refer to as "frame resonance."[22] To better understand the variety of racialized political narratives used by white nationalist organizations, we closely analyzed the issue statements of thirty-seven white nationalist group websites in 2011.[23] Our sample consisted largely of Klan and neo-Nazi organizations, as they were the most likely to have detailed websites and have been the two largest categories of white supremacist groups since the 1990s. The time period for the analysis was chosen to coincide with the peak of white nationalist activity as well as to predate the emergence of Trump as a political figure.

Targeted Outgroups

The racial outgroups most likely to be referenced by white supremacist groups in their issue statements were Jews, blacks, and Latinx immigrants. The prominence of Jews in white supremacist rhetoric is not surprising, especially given the fact that the majority of the groups in our sample were either neo-Nazi (n = 8) or Klan (n = 21) organizations. Groups within these categories have a long tradition of anti-Semitism, especially neo-Nazis. Jews are generally seen by these groups as exerting a disproportionate amount of influence over (if not outright control of) the most important political, economic, and cultural institutions in the United States. The primary goal of Jews, according to white supremacist groups, is to maintain their political and economic power and advance the interests of Israel. As the American National Socialist Party declared:

> WE BELIEVE that the current government in America is run by Jews.
> WE BELIEVE that the Jews main goal is the total annihilation of the Aryan race, hertiage [sic], & culture.
> WE BELIEVE that Jews are a parasitic race and only wish world domination and the destruction of the Aryan race.

It is also not surprising that white supremacist groups have targeted blacks and Latinx immigrants as racial outgroups. Indeed, the resurgence of the Klan in the 1950s was a response to the CRM and racial desegregation. And although the targeting of Latinx immigrants is a more recent development within the WNM, there is a long tradition within the movement of opposing non-Aryan immigration from any country. In the 1920s, for example, the

Klan experienced its highest level of popularity largely due to its campaign against the "less desirable" immigrants from southern and eastern Europe. The targeting of Latinx immigrants by white supremacists is just the latest version of this form of racism.

One racial outgroup that is noticeably absent from white supremacist issue statements is Muslims. This is especially surprising given the rise of "Islamophobia" in the aftermath of the 9/11 terrorist attacks as well as the increasing correlation between attitudes toward blacks, Latinx immigrants, and Muslims that we documented in Chapter 2. Certainly Muslims have never been well-liked by white supremacists. Yet if this is the case, why were Muslims completely absent from white supremacist issue statements in 2011, well after the 9/11 attacks? One reason, perhaps, is that traditional white supremacists have always felt some degree of indifference toward Muslims because white supremacists and Muslims share a common enemy: Jews. This is especially the case for white supremacist groups inspired by Nazi ideology. Hitler and the Nazis often collaborated with Arab leaders during World War II, and Hitler was known to speak warmly toward the Arab world on occasion, in large part due to their common hatred of Jews.[24] Similar examples of pro-Muslim sentiment can occasionally be found throughout the history of the modern WNM. In 1985, one of the most well-known Klan leaders—Tom Metzger—was so impressed by Louis Farrakhan's anti-Semitic rhetoric at a rally in Los Angeles that he promptly contributed $100 to Farrakhan's organization, the Nation of Islam. And in one of the most chilling examples, longtime white supremacist organizer Billy Roper sent the following email to over fourteen hundred fellow National Alliance members while he watched the twin towers collapsing on the morning of September 11, 2001:

> The enemy of our enemy is, for now at least, our friends. We may not want them marrying our daughters, just as they would not want us marrying theirs. We may not want them in our societies, just as they would not want us in theirs. But anyone who is willing to drive a plane into a building to kill jews [sic] is alright [sic] with me. I wish our members had half as much testicular fortitude.[25]

Today there is no doubt that hostility toward Muslims as a racial outgroup is much more widespread among white racial extremists and that Muslims now occupy a place that is similar to those of blacks and Latinx immigrants within the extremist community. Yet the expression of anti-Muslim sentiment is most likely to originate from one of the many new alt-right or anti-Muslim organizations that have formed since 2011, rather than from the traditional white supremacist groups.

Varieties of Racial Threat Narratives

Table 3.1 presents examples of seven common racialized threat narratives, taken directly from the white supremacist websites in 2011. One of the most commonly used narratives by white nationalists is a demographic threat narrative in which policies such as immigration, interracial marriage, and the promotion of abortion are cited as contributing to the eventual "extinction" of the white race, or what some even refer to as "white genocide." Racialized economic threat narratives also have been commonly employed for years and come in a variety of forms. One of the most-cited economic threats claimed to originate from blacks is affirmative action, which white nationalists claim has contributed to the economic decline of the white working class. Latinx immigrants are blamed for taking jobs away from whites as well as contributing to depressed wages. Cultural threats are attributed to minorities as well as feminists, who are characterized as promoting an anti-Christian and anti-white agenda, with the aid of the (Jewish-controlled) media and entertainment industry. One of the most prominent racialized narratives, however, is that blacks and Latinx immigrants pose a security threat to whites. Both groups are often characterized as prone to violence and a significant source of violent crime, especially against whites. Yet these security threats can also extend to other types of physical threats, like the example in Table 3.1 in which the age-old fear of black men raping white women is connected to the spread of AIDS among whites.

Finally, many threat narratives reference the growing political power of minorities and the presence of minority officials in government, which white supremacists view as a violation of "divinely established laws" and a justification for rejecting the legitimacy of the U.S. government in its current form. As we show in the next section, the election of a black president (Obama) fueled a white nationalist backlash that led to a significant (although short-lived) increase in white nationalist activity. This backlash against the election of blacks to lower federal, state, and local offices had, however, been well underway prior to 2008. Although the Voting Rights Act was passed in 1965, many white-dominated state and local governments were able to effectively

Table 3.1 Varieties of Racialized Political Narratives Used by White Nationalist Groups

Racialized Threat Narratives	Representative Quote
Demographic	Our own Government Controlled media has said that the White Race is about to become extinct. (Rebel Brigade Knights of the KKK) Forced integration is deliberate and malicious genocide, particularly for a People like the White race, who are now a small minority in the world. (Aryan Nations 88)
Cultural	Since the fifties, minorities and feminists have been struggling to unseat white males and dismantle their culture; and they've executed the rout virtually unopposed, displaying the most frenzied and extensive example of bloodless cultural conquest in history. (White Aryan Resistance)
Economic (blacks)	"BLACKS" ARE CLIMBING the ladder of corporate America on the genes of their white ancestors, as Marxian Jews' affirmative-action quotas force whites to elevate the Negroid gene pool throughout whites' civilization. (White Aryan Resistance)
Economic (Latinx)	The Government is allowing all these illegal immigrants into our nation. While true Americans are having a hard time finding a job. The Government's pockets are getting fat off of cheap labor. America's unemployment rate is at an all time high; but our Government still refuses to build a Wall across our borders. (Rebel Brigade Knights of the KKK)
Security (blacks)	Out of the 35.3 percent of Whites with aids I can see that half of that percentage (if not close to all) came from blacks males raping white women. The studies show there is no case where White Males Rape Black women ... (White Brothers)
Security (Latinx)	DID YOU KNOW THAT ILLEGAL ALIENS KILL 12 AMERICANS EVERY DAY THATS 4,380 PER YEAR. ALSO 8 AMERICAN CHILDREN ARE SEXUALLY ABUSED BY ILLEGALS EVERY DAY THATS 2,920 PER YEAR. (Rebel Brigade Knights of the KKK)
Political	Every effort to wrest from White Men the management of its affairs in order to transfer it to the control of blacks or any other color, or to permit them to share in its control, is ... a violation of divinely established laws. (True Invisible Empire Traditionalist American Knights of the KKK) The Aryan Nations Knights was never intended to be a traditional klan organization which pays homage to or honors the current perverted American constitution, it's now decadent flag or the depraved governmental body full of Jews, Negros, Hispanics and sell out White traitors. (Aryan Nations Nights)

circumvent its full implementation by taking advantage of ostensibly "race neutral" election rules to prevent blacks and Latinxs from being elected to office.[26] It was not until the 1980s that the federal courts ruled that such practices were unlawful, paving the way for the election of black and Latinx elected officials in many communities where this had previously been impossible. At least two studies have found that once minorities began to be elected, this was likely to be followed by an increase in white nationalist organization activity.[27]

White Nationalism and the Obama Effect

The preceding analyses suggest that the rise of WRC was already underway by the early 2000s on the fringes of white society and that it was fueled by a variety of racialized political narratives that resonated among white racial extremists. However, perhaps no other single event served to reinforce the narrative of the supposed decline of whites' political power than Barack Obama's victory in the presidential election in 2008. As a result of Obama's election, several different reports documented a "new energy" among white nationalist groups that was directly attributable to the election of a black president and the fact "that there are more people who feel their voice isn't being represented."[28] David Duke, former grand wizard of the KKK and former presidential candidate from Louisiana, referred to Obama as a "visual aid" for the recruitment of white supremacists and predicted a surge in white hate group mobilization as a result of Obama's presence in the White House.[29] Indeed, on the day that Obama was elected in 2008, the most popular racist website on the internet—Stormfront—received so many hits that it had to temporarily shut down. The man who runs the website, Don Black (also a former grand wizard), commented that "people who had been a little more complacent and kind of upset became more motivated to do something."[30]

There is a good bit of evidence to support Don Black's assessment of Barack Obama's impact on the WNM. A number of studies have documented the effect of the 2008 election on racial resentment[31] and WRC.[32] Our theoretical framework presented in Chapter 2 highlights two conditions, beyond the presence of a preexisting WRC, which should increase the prospects for the translation of racial consciousness into political action. Both conditions seem to have been enhanced by Obama's election, and we discuss them in turn here.

Obama and White Racist Anger

First, we argued that WRC, accompanied by the generation of outgroup hostility, will often result in the experience of anger toward racial outgroups who are seen as the source of whites' grievances. In turn, this anger strengthens the motivation to participate in collective political action. We have already shown in Chapter 2 that there was a surge in outgroup hostility after the 2008 election. There also appears to have been an increase in anger among white racial extremists that is clearly associated with Obama's election. As we would expect, our analysis of white nationalist issue statements from 2011 found plenty of evidence of this anger. One of the clearest examples comes from the Knights of the Southern Cross Soldiers of the Ku Klux Klan in Virginia:

> By all rights Americans should be storming the White House and the Capitol buildings like a scene out of a Frankenstein movie, complete with pitchforks and torches screaming at the top of their lungs at the sheer lunacy that is being allowed to destroy this country of ours. We have a scene from the Three Stooges being played out daily by our incompetent government officials. We have an ass-kissing coward for a President who would rather suck face and bow to our enemies than destroy them and we have those capabilities or at least we used to.[33]

This new anger was not isolated to white nationalist activists. We also find evidence of a more general increase in government-directed anger among white racial extremists as a result of Obama's election. Figure 3.3 presents the results of a regression model that estimates the relationship between outgroup hostility (measured using the items described in Chapter 2) and the respondent's level of anger toward the federal government (controlling for party identification, ideology, economic evaluations, and other demographic variables). What makes this analysis so powerful is that the data for this analysis come from the ANES 2008–2009 panel study, and therefore the same individuals were interviewed at two points in time: one year prior to Obama's inauguration (January 2008) and again approximately four months into Obama's first term (May 2009). The results plotted in the figure clearly indicate that racial extremists experienced an increase in government-directed anger as a result of Obama's election. This is entirely consistent with the many reports of a "new energy" within the WNM after the election.

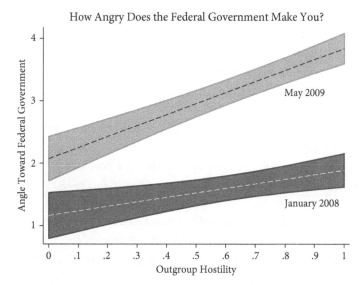

Figure 3.3 Predicted relationship between outgroup hostility and anger toward federal government, pre-post 2008 election

Source: American National Election Study Panel Study 2008–2009. See online Appendix for details of analyses.

The Political Opportunity Structure

Our theoretical framework also highlights the importance of the political opportunity structure,[34] which plays an important role in channeling the energy fueled by WRC into collective action. When conventional political institutions are perceived by group members to be closed to their group, we should expect to see (1) a larger share of aggrieved group members who opt out of conventional politics and (2) for those who are willing to absorb the costs of collective action, a greater preference for mobilization outside of conventional institutions. Even prior to the 2008 election, white racial extremists had become increasingly shut off from conventional politics. After the election of Obama, it appears that feelings of hopelessness only intensified. This was a common theme in white nationalist group narratives of political threats, which often cited the futility of the Republican Party as an avenue for redress (see Table 3.1). Yet as was the case for government-directed anger, there appears to have been a more general increase among white racial extremists in the perception that conventional politics was not a viable option.

We provide evidence of this fact in Figure 3.4. The figure presents the national trend in the ANES external political efficacy index, which has long been used by political scientists to measure citizen attitudes regarding the responsiveness of the federal government to their concerns.[35] The external efficacy index consists of the following two items:

"People like me don't have any say about what the government does."
(Agree, Disagree, Neither Agree/Disagree)
    "I don't think public officials care much what people like me think."
(Agree, Disagree, Neither Agree/Disagree)

The final index takes on five possible values: a value of 100 if the respondent agrees with both statements, a value of 0 if the respondent disagrees with both statements, and values of 25, 50, or 75 depending on the level of agreement, disagreement, or indifference across the two items. We estimated a

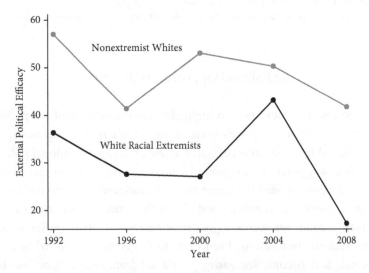

Figure 3.4 External political efficacy among white racists and nonracists, 1992–2008

Source: ANES Time Series Study, 1992–2008. Note: The values presented in the figure were generated based on a pooled regression analysis (ANES 1992–2016) of the ANES external efficacy index on a dichotomous indicator for white racists (and its interaction with a series of indicator variables for survey year), controlling for basic demographic variables (age, education level, gender, family income) and political attitudes (party identification and ideology). We then generated adjusted external efficacy scores by computing predicted values from this regression, holding all other variables constant at their mean. See online Appendix for details on measurement and estimation.

regression model of whites' external efficacy using the standard political and demographic predictors along with a dichotomous indicator for people who could be labeled "white racial extremists." This measure of racial extremists is slightly different than the measure described in Chapter 2 because we lack a measure of affect toward Muslims prior to 2004. Therefore, the measure that we used for this analysis is based on hostility toward blacks and Hispanics only.[36]

Figure 3.4 displays the trends in the efficacy index for racists and nonracists between 1992 and 2008, controlling for basic demographic variables, party identification, and ideology. The contrast in the trends is quite striking. Throughout the entire period, white racial extremists score lower on the external efficacy index, consistent with what we would expect if racial extremists view conventional politics as closed to their interests. Nonetheless, despite a brief increase in external efficacy in 2004 (perhaps in response to the threat posed by the 9/11 attacks), external efficacy among racial extremists plunged in 2008 to its lowest level throughout the entire 1992–2008 period.

Obama and White Nationalist Mobilization

The impact of Obama's election on white nationalist group activity can be seen by examining trends in white nationalist activity during the period preceding and immediately after Obama's election. Figure 3.5 presents trends for two groups of states classified as having high and low levels of outgroup hostility based on whites' responses to items measuring hostility toward blacks and Latinx immigrants from the 2010 CCES. We use the CCES for this analysis because unlike the ANES, the CCES is designed to include large samples for every state, thus allowing us to compute state-level outgroup hostility scores. As shown in the figure, the states with relatively high levels of outgroup hostility (defined as states with values above the median) experienced an increase in the rate change of white nationalist activity after Obama emerged as a national political figure. This was not the case in the states where outgroup hostility was relatively lower (i.e., state outgroup hostility scores below the median). Although Figure 3.5 presents data for the overall sample of white nationalist groups, we can look back at the bottom panel of Figure 3.2 to see that the increase in white nationalist groups was strongest among traditional white supremacist groups, which represent the

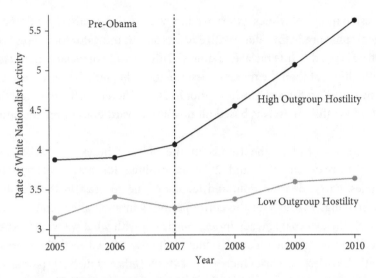

Figure 3.5 Trends in the mean rate of white nationalist activity across states with high and low outgroup hostility

Source: Southern Poverty Law Center, Intelligence Report (various years). State-level outgroup hostility scores were computed by the authors using data from the Cooperative Congressional Election Study. The rate of white nationalist activity is defined as the number of active white nationalist groups in a state per one million white residents. "High" and "low" outgroup hostility is defined based on the fifty-state median in 2010 (CCES).

most militant groups and those for which the costs of collective action are the highest due to the stigma associated with participation.

White Nationalists Go from the Fringe to the Mainstream

In many ways the dramatic rise in the number of white nationalist groups after Obama's emergence as a presidential candidate represented the continuation of a trend that had been underway for decades. For many years before that time, WNM leaders had been promulgating racialized political narratives of threats to white supremacy. These narratives increasingly resonated among racial extremists throughout the 1980s and 1990s as racial diversity steadily increased and black and Latinx political power continued to grow. Yet nothing could have contributed to the resonance of these narratives as much as the election of a black man to the office of president. Therefore, it is not surprising that Obama's election led to an acceleration of white nationalist activity.

Initially this new mobilization continued to be relegated to the fringe of American politics. To white extremists angered by Obama's election, the Republican Party appeared more than ever to be complicit in the political demise of white supremacy when prominent Republican leaders publicly celebrated Obama's victory as a welcome breakthrough for American democracy. As George W. Bush stated the day after the election, "No matter how they cast their ballots, all Americans can be proud of the history that was made yesterday," adding that Obama's "journey represents a triumph of the American story."[37]

Yet after 2010 a strange trend began to emerge: the number of white nationalist groups began to decline, and this has more or less continued ever since (see Figure 3.2). How can we explain this decline in white hate group activity? We have already seen the answer cannot be found in trends in racial attitudes, as the decrease in WNM activity predates the decline in outgroup hostility. In addition, in Chapter 2 we saw that the decline in outgroup hostility was largely concentrated on the left. A much more plausible explanation, we contend, is that the decline in white nationalist groups represents the beginning of the political mainstreaming of white racism. We provide evidence for this part of the story in Chapter 4.

4

The Mainstreaming of the White Nationalist Movement

Prior to 2009 the political opportunity structure provided few avenues for participation of racial extremists in conventional politics. As a result, the white nationalist movement (WNM) largely existed on the extremist fringe of American politics. Yet as Barack Obama assumed the presidency, the political opportunity structure began to change in important ways. One of the most important developments was the emergence of the Tea Party movement (TPM) as a protest movement with aspirations to impact electoral politics. The TPM provided an attractive alternative venue for many white racial extremists. The advent of the TPM coincided with an increase in the tactical trend within the WNM to move toward mainstream politics by softening its rhetoric and ridding itself of traditional symbols associated with white supremacist organizations. Various white nationalist organizations were also pursuing mainstreaming by aligning themselves with the emerging alt-right movement (ARM), whose leaders emphasized presenting their white supremacist ideology in terms designed to be appealing to a broader mainstream constituency. The ARM most especially emphasized that its primary goal was to promote white identity as a source of ingroup solidarity rather than espousing racism in the form of outgroup hostility.[1] The ARM's identitarian politics appealed especially to whites who were disenchanted with mainstream politics as not representing their concern that they were threatened by demographic diversification and cultural change in the broader society.[2]

In this chapter we show that these developments eventually led to the mobilization of a significant number of white racial extremists who had previously been inactive in conventional politics into the Republican Party through the TPM. Although the TPM eventually lost steam after its electoral successes in 2010 and 2012, this mobilization of racial extremists into electoral politics set the stage for Trump by providing him with a base of

Hard White, Richard C. Fording and Sanford F. Schram. Oxford University Press (2020). © Oxford University Press.
DOI: 10.1093/oso/9780197500484.001.0001

support among voters who were receptive to racist appeals. In this way the TPM and the ARM provided the bridge for white racial extremists to travel from the political fringe to the mainstream. This bridge helped facilitate a right-wing version of the coalition-building strategy of the antiglobalization left, often referred to as the "movement of movements."[3] As we show in this chapter, the white racial extremists' version of the movement of movements was to prove stunningly successful in broadening the appeal of their racist ideas.

Intramovement Competition and the Decline of White Nationalist Activity

As discussed in Chapter 3, after 2010 the number of white nationalist groups began to decline at a rapid rate and has more or less continued to do so ever since (see Figure 3.2). To better understand how and why this happened, we look to the social movement literature on interorganizational processes among social movement organizations (SMOs) within the same movement. In an important article, McCarthy and Zald coined the term "social movement industry" (SMI) to refer to the population of SMOs that share the same goals.[4] The use of the term "industry" was intentional, as McCarthy and Zald saw SMOs as analogous to economic firms within an industry. Perhaps the most important way that SMOs interact with one another within an SMI is through competition. SMOs compete with one another for both members and benefactors by offering a "product" in the form of goals and tactics.[5] As in economic firms, as competition within an SMI increases, this can have important effects on SMOs as they seek to adapt to their changing environment. Most important, as the number of SMOs increases within an SMI, competition among groups will eventually lead to a decrease in founding rates of new SMOs and an increase in the mortality of existing SMOs.[6] These insights help explain the decline of white supremacist groups since 2010. Although the election of Barack Obama may have initially served as a catalyst for the WNM through its effects on white racial consciousness (WRC) and out-group hostility, it also led to the birth of competing SMOs and an increase in competition within the white nationalist SMI. Much of the competition occurred over movement tactics and coincided with the increasing appeal of mainstream electoral tactics to combat the threat posed by Obama's election.

The White Nationalist Movement
and Electoral Politics Prior to Obama

Even prior to Obama's election, there were those within the WNM who felt that the movement's resources should be devoted to electoral politics. Among the earliest examples was George Lincoln Rockwell's American Nazi Party (ANP). After making an unsuccessful bid for governor of Virginia in 1965, Rockwell changed the name of the ANP to the National Socialist White People's Party (NSWPP), an obvious play on the name of the well-known African American organization and an attempt to soften the ANP's image. After Rockwell was assassinated, the NSWPP reemerged in the 1970s and began to run national socialist candidates for local office. One of the most successful efforts was made in a Milwaukee school board election, in which two NSWPP candidates each won approximately 20 percent of the vote.

The most well-known white nationalist to pursue electoral politics is David Duke. Duke resigned as grand wizard of the Knights of the Ku Klux Klan in 1980 to reboot the National Association for the Advancement of White People as a conventional interest group (although there was nothing conventional about it). Over the following years Duke made several high-profile runs for office and initially had some success. After winning a special election to the Louisiana state house in 1989, Duke ran for U.S. senator in 1990 and for governor in 1991. Although he failed to win either of these elections, he received a sizable share of the vote each time. In 1991 Duke lost in a runoff to Democrat Edwin Edwards but received 39 percent of the total vote and 55 percent of the white vote. Duke continued to run for various offices throughout the 1990s but never came close to matching the level of support he had achieved in the two earlier races. Despite these notable exceptions, WNM organizations generally rejected mainstream politics prior to the early 2000s, preferring to keep a lower profile on the extremist fringe until WRC developed to a point at which white nationalist candidates would be accepted.

The election of Obama and the subsequent backlash that it created caused many within the WNM to reconsider the utility of electoral politics, leading to an acceleration of mainstreaming efforts within the WNM. The movement of the WNM into electoral politics has taken two general forms. First, the number of white nationalists openly running for office has steadily increased since 2009. One of the most visible examples of this trend was the formation of the American Third Position (ATP) in 2009, a political party with a stated mission to "represent the political interests of White Americans." The ATP's goal was to unite disaffected racists by running white nationalist candidates for offices in every state.[7] Led by a team of prominent veterans of the WNM, the organization continues to exist but has fallen far short of its goals. ATP presidential candidate Merlin Miller was able to gain ballot access in just three states in 2012 (Colorado, New Jersey, and Tennessee), receiving a mere 2,703 votes. In 2013 the party changed its name to the American Freedom Party (AFP), and it has continued to run a handful of candidates under the AFP label, none of whom have won.

A far more significant form of mainstreaming has occurred through the participation of WNM members and other racial extremists in political organizations not explicitly founded on white nationalist principles. For some members of the WNM this strategy has been intentional. Movement strategists often refer to this tactic as "entryism," or the infiltration of movement members into another (often related) organization with the goal of influencing the direction of the target organization. For most white racial extremists, however, the decision to join these "white-friendly" political organizations and campaigns has certainly not been part of a coordinated strategy of entryism. Rather, it has most likely been driven by a combination of the increase in WRC caused by Obama's election and the efforts of political elites to capitalize on whites' outgroup hostility through implicit and explicit racist appeals.

In the decade prior to 2009 there were several examples of white nationalist groups penetrating conventional political parties and campaigns. For example, there are documented cases of known white nationalist activists running under the label of the Constitution Party (CP). Formerly known as the American Taxpayer Party before the name was changed in 1999, the CP quickly gained a reputation as the most far-right party in the country by the early 2000s. It was originally rebranded to serve as a vehicle for Pat Buchanan's presidential run in 2000, but Buchanan ultimately chose to run under the Reform Party (RP) label. Since its inception the CP has reflected a broad range of conservative positions, including support for an originalist interpretation of the Constitution; opposition to taxes, abortion, and gun control; and a staunch opposition to immigration. Despite losing Buchanan to the RP, the CP still managed to obtain ballot access in forty-one states in 2000 and received over 100,000 votes in each presidential election through 2016 (peaking at 404,000 in 2004). The RP ultimately crashed and burned after Buchanan's takeover, partly due to Buchanan's popularity among white nationalists and the controversies associated with their influx into the RP. Buchanan's supporters attempted to start their own party—the America First Party—in 2002. The party branded itself very similarly to the CP, including a strong nativist, anti-immigrant stance. However, it never really got off the ground because of disputes over the involvement of the self-declared leader of the militia movement at the time, Bo Gritz.[8]

The Tea Party Movement and Obama-Era Mainstreaming

In the years leading up to 2008, elements of the WNM had become increasingly more open to the pursuit of electoral politics, but this was certainly not the norm. Although it seems clear that racial extremists were angered by Obama's election in 2008, they still lacked an attractive mainstream vehicle to express their frustration. This quickly changed with the rise of the TPM. The TPM began as an antigovernment, antitax movement and can be traced to Ron Paul's 2008 presidential campaign, which featured "tea party" rallies across the country to protest government spending and taxation. However, the TPM as we know it today took off in 2009 soon after the election of Barack Obama as the first nonwhite president. Aided by well-financed, high-profile organizations such as the Koch Brothers' Americans for Prosperity, Freedom Works, and Tea Party Express, the number of local Tea Party chapters quickly grew in advance of the 2010 midterm election, transforming the TPM into a true grassroots movement. Indeed, based on data collected by the Institute for Research and Education on Human Rights (IREHR), at the peak of the movement in 2010 a total of 2,806 local Tea Party organizations (TPOs) existed in approximately one-third of the counties in the United States.[9] By 2010 most surveys estimated that Tea Party supporters comprised anywhere from 20 to 30 percent of the electorate, 45 to 55 percent of Republicans,[10] and a strong majority of active Republicans.[11]

The Tea Party Movement's Racist Roots

The TPM initially organized around a libertarian, antitax agenda, but it quickly became apparent that as the movement spread to the grassroots level, many supporters were drawn to it by a sense of hostility toward African Americans, Latinx immigrants and Muslims. Although many studies have

now documented these racist elements within the TPM, the most comprehensive treatment of this subject is provided by Christopher Parker and Matt
Barreto.[12] As Parker and Barreto show, Tea Party protests became well known
for the display of hateful signs targeting Barack Obama, often making explicit references to his race. There were also numerous reports of racist rhetoric directed at President Obama and minorities by Tea Party leaders. One
of the most publicized incidents involved an Arkansas Tea Party leader who
eventually had to resign her position after making a racist joke at a Tea Party
rally in 2012.[13] A speaker at a Tea Party anti-immigrant rally also drew national attention when he advocated racial purity in breeding at an event near
the Capitol in 2013, which was also attended by Senators Ted Cruz and Jeff
Sessions.[14] This led some political commentators to refer to TPM activists as
"neo-Klansman"[15] and to the TPM more generally as "racist madness."[16]

More generalizable evidence of the connection between Tea Party identification and racial extremism can be found in the public opinion literature,
in which studies have repeatedly shown that there is a direct link between
racial prejudice toward African Americans (variously measured) and identification with the Tea Party, even after controlling for party identification
and liberal-conservative ideology.[17] As Tope, Pickett, and Chiricos conclude
regarding their analysis of Tea Party support, "the results suggest that at least
to some degree, the Tea Party Movement is an outlet for mobilizing and
expressing racialized grievances which may have been symbolically magni-
fied by the election of the nation's first black President."[18] This conclusion is
echoed by Barreto et al., who find that "Tea Party sympathizers are not mainstream conservatives, but rather, they hold a strong sense of out-group anxiety and a concern over the social and demographic changes in America."[19]

In addition to prejudice toward African Americans, perhaps more than
any other issue Tea Party elites and activists were motivated by their hostility toward Latinx immigrants.[20] Echoing many of the narratives emphasized by white supremacists, Tea Party leaders called for a variety of
anti-immigrant policies, such as an end to all "welfare" services for undocumented immigrants, an end to "birthright citizenship," construction of a
border wall, and mass deportation. These proposals were often justified by
claims that the cost of undocumented immigration far exceeded its economic
benefits, largely due to the participation of undocumented immigrants in
government-funded healthcare and welfare programs. Another popular
narrative, which continues to be used by Donald Trump, alleges that undocumented immigrants are responsible for a significant number of violent

crimes. These narratives are often backed by statistics provided by the Center for Immigration Studies, a far-right think tank that has been labeled a "hate group" by the SPLC due to the frequency with which white supremacists use its reports to support their platforms. Although these narratives have been repeatedly debunked by research coming from both the left and the right (including the CATO Institute), they continue to resonate with racial extremists. The anti-immigrant efforts of Tea Party leaders have resulted in several policy successes since 2010, most notably the adoption of state anti-immigration laws and state and local laws that require local law enforcement to cooperate with the federal government in the apprehension and deportation of undocumented immigrants.

As discussed in Chapter 3, white supremacist groups have generally paid less attention to Muslims, being more concerned about Jews, blacks, and Latinx immigrants. The same cannot be said for the TPM, which has had many connections to the modern anti-Muslim movement over the years. The largest anti-Muslim "hate group" identified by the SPLC—ACT! for America—was founded in 2007 by conservative activist Brigette Gabriel, a former reporter for Pat Robertson's television show. ACT! garnered national attention in 2010 due to the controversy over the proposed construction of a mosque near the site of the former World Trade Center in New York City—dubbed the "Ground Zero Mosque." That same year, ACT! convened its first "Legislative Conference and Briefing" in Washington to promote opposition to the mosque as well as to Muslims more generally. The conference brought together anti-Muslim movement activists and prominent Tea Party leaders in Congress, including Michelle Bachman (R-MN) and Peter King (R-NY). King later received ACT!'s "Patriot Award" for his legislative efforts to fight radical Islam. Other prominent Tea Party–aligned leaders who have had ties with ACT! for America include Ted Cruz (R-TX), former House Speaker Newt Gingrich (R-GA), former vice-presidential nominee Sarah Palin, and former U.S. Army general Michael Flynn, who served as director of the Tea Party Patriots Super Pac in 2014.

The campaign against the Ground Zero Mosque soon became a focal point for local TPOs around the country and helped solidify the connection between the TPM and the anti-Muslim movement at the grassroots level. In New York the Brooklyn Tea Party held rallies to oppose the mosque on several occasions. At a 2010 gathering, its president declared, "Islam has an inherent aggressiveness and the Muslim American Society [the developers of the Sheepshead Bay mosque] are their warriors on the front line." Inspired by these protests in New York, local TPOs in Tennessee and Florida began a similar campaign to oppose mosques in the cities of Murfeesboro and Fort Lauderdale. In other communities, TPOs targeted local school boards and the use of public school textbooks that they claimed promoted Islam.

One of the most prominent voices within the anti-Muslim movement has been Pamela Geller, author of the prominent libertarian blog AtlasShugs.com. Geller used her platform to spread the false accusation that Barack Obama was actually a Muslim, along with many other anti-Muslim narratives. The accusation that Obama was a Muslim was especially popular within the Tea Party. By 2016, 44 percent of white Tea Party supporters still believed Obama was a Muslim, despite the fact that this lie had been refuted years earlier.[21] Geller has also been one of the most prominent promoters of the conspiracy theory known as "civilization jihad": the idea that the Muslim Brotherhood is plotting to infiltrate and subvert Western nations, including the United States, leading to the destruction of Western civilization. One of the primary vehicles for carrying out this cultural jihad, it is claimed, is the infiltration of sharia law into the American judicial system. Sarah Palin, one of the Tea Party's most prominent leaders, stated in 2011 that if sharia law is "allowed to govern in our country, it will be the downfall of America."[22] This narrative is widely believed by Tea Party supporters, and with the help of model legislation authored by the anti-Muslim Center for Security Policy, Tea Party leaders across the country have led the charge to pass anti-sharia legislation in several states, including Alabama, Arizona, Kansas, Louisiana, South Dakota, Tennessee, North Carolina, and Texas.

Tea Party Support and Outgroup Hostility: An Analysis of Public Opinion Data

Figure 4.1 presents the results of an analysis of survey data that provides systematic evidence of the nature and level of outgroup hostility within the TPM by examining the relationship between white attitudes toward several different outgroups and the strength of Tea Party support, based on data from the VOTER Survey. The top panel of Figure 4.1 presents the mean level of hostility toward blacks, Latinx immigrants, and Muslims, the three outgroups that we have argued form the basis of the new outgroup hostility that propelled Trump to victory (see Chapter 2). The sample for our analysis is restricted to approximately eighteen hundred white voters who

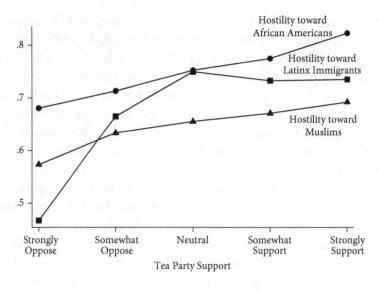

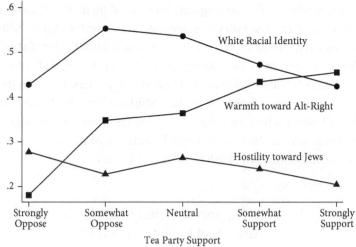

Figure 4.1 Racial attitudes among Republican identifiers by Tea Party support, 2011

Note: The data for this analysis are taken from the VOTER Survey. All variables are measured in 2011, with the exception of warmth toward the alt-right, which is measured in 2016. The two panels present the predicted level of each racial attitude based on a regression model that controls for party identification, ideology, age, gender, education level, and family income. Predictions were computed by holding each of these control variables constant at the mean value. The sample for the regression includes whites who identified as "Republican."

identified as Republican in 2011, the first year that the VOTER survey was administered. We examine the mean level of support for these three groups after controlling for several other variables that we might expect to be associated with racial attitudes, including the strength of Republican identification, ideology, age, gender, family income, and education level. Thus, the data presented in the figure represent the relationship between Tea Party support and outgroup hostility, independent of more general political orientations and demographics. The results clearly indicate that support for the Tea Party is positively related to hostility for each of these three racial outgroups. In other words, even among those who identify as Republican, those who identify strongly with the Tea Party display a level of outgroup hostility that is significantly higher than among Republicans who oppose the Tea Party. This relationship is also statistically significant for each outgroup.

The bottom panel provides further insight into the correlates of Tea Party support by examining the relationship between Tea Party support and three additional items in the VOTER Survey: the level of hostility toward Jews, the level of white racial identity ("How important is being white to your identity?"), and the level of warmth toward the ARM (measured in 2016). First, we find that Tea Party supporters were somewhat less likely to express hostility toward Jews, but this relationship was not statistically significant by conventional standards.[23] The lack of hostility toward Jews among TPM supporters is not surprising, as surveys have consistently found that Jews are now favorably viewed by most Americans.[24] Thus, building an electoral movement around anti-Semitism would simply not be viable. This finding also suggests that to the extent that white nationalists were drawn to the TPM, this attraction may have been limited to racial extremists whose racism is largely driven by hostility toward other groups, rather than Jews.

Second, we find that Tea Party support is unrelated to white racial identity. This finding is also important in that it suggests that the mobilization and mainstreaming of racism through the Tea Party was not directly driven by whites' attachment to their own racial group, consistent with our theoretical arguments regarding the origins of racially motivated political behavior in Chapter 2. Rather, TPM support appears to have been driven by hostility toward racial outgroups. Finally, we examine the relationship between Tea Party support (measured in 2011) and support for the ARM, based on a question that was administered to the same panel of respondents in the 2016 wave of the survey. As shown in the figure, support for the alt-right was significantly higher among strong Tea Party supporters than among Tea Party opponents—independent of ideology, partisanship, and respondent demographics. This suggests that there was considerable overlap in the constituency of both movements, thus supporting our argument that both the TPM and ARM served as important mechanisms to facilitate the mainstreaming of racism. And as we eventually show in the remaining chapters, both movements were absorbed into Trump's base.

The Broader Attraction of the Tea Party Movement

Given the strong association of Tea Party support with outgroup hostility, as well as the public display of that hostility at Tea Party events, the conventional narrative that has developed regarding the TPM is that it was essentially a racist movement from the very beginning. For some elements within the TPM, this may have been true. Yet our interpretation of the TPM is that for the most part, it was not racist by design but quickly evolved into a racist movement through its co-optation of white racial extremists and racial conservatives, including many of whom had previously identified with the WNM. Certainly many white extremists and conservatives were attracted to the TPM by its opposition to immigration and the election of a black president. But this interpretation is overly simplistic and ignores the social movement dynamics at play.

The TPM was founded on three core principles, none of which were explicitly related to race: fiscal responsibility, constitutionally limited government, and free market economics.[25] Indeed, we analyzed the mission statements of a geographically diverse sample of thirty-two TPOs and found very little mention of racial issues, including immigration. Parker and Barreto conducted a more formal analysis of the content of forty-two Tea Party websites in fifteen states and reached a similar conclusion. They found that only 5 percent of the content of the Tea Party websites contained text that they classified as related to "race/racism," and a mere 7 percent reflected text devoted to illegal immigration.[26] The movement eventually evolved to emphasize such issues, but that may have been as much a consequence of the eventual participation of white nationalists in the movement as it was a true cause of their participation. Nevertheless, it still begs the question: Why were white nationalists attracted to the Tea Party in the first place, especially in the early stages when the movement reflected a stronger emphasis on its core conservative principles? We believe the answer can be found in the ideological overlap of the

WNM and TPM on these ostensibly nonracial issues, along with the competitive advantage that the TPM had over WNM organizations due to the TPM's mainstream appeal. We address each possible explanation in turn.

Based on the content analysis of white nationalist issue statements described in Chapter 3, we found that the ideology of WNM organizations encompasses a far broader range of issues than most people probably realize. The core principles of the TPM, it turns out, are also core principles of the WNM. Table 4.1 summarizes some of the most important areas of ideological overlap between the WNM and the TPM on nonracial issues.

Like the TPM, white nationalists are strongly supportive of an originalist interpretation of the Constitution, which they believe has been distorted over the years for the purpose of undermining white supremacy. Many white nationalists, like the American National Socialists, also believe that they have a unique right to the preservation of an originalist interpretation because the Constitution was authored by their "Aryan founding fathers." For similar reasons, white nationalists also strongly oppose the growth of the power of the federal government, which they believe has been unfairly used to undermine the rights of white nationalists, especially their right to freely espouse what is now deemed "hate speech" and their right to own firearms to protect themselves from their enemies. WNM members also strongly oppose taxation, much like the TPM. However, unlike the TPM, which characterizes taxation as a general restriction of individual liberty, white nationalists see taxation as a tool to redistribute white economic advantage to minorities. Finally, many (but not all) WNM organizations identify as white *Christian* Americans and see Christianity as an integral part of the foundation of American democracy. This specific brand of nationalism is especially prominent among KKK groups and represents a strong area of ideological overlap with the TPM in the South. In sum, white nationalists were attracted to the TPM because of the latter's emphasis on these core, ostensibly nonracial values precisely because they believe that following these principles will have significant racial consequences that will benefit whites.

In addition to the prominent place of these white-friendly policies on the TPM's agenda, the TPM had a distinct competitive advantage over other SMOs competing within the white supremacist SMI, and this further encouraged the migration of white racial extremists into the TPM. Prior to the emergence of the TPM, the most ardent white racial extremists had few viable options for participating in the WNM beyond the traditional white supremacist groups, such as the Klan, neo-Nazi's, and other racist fringe

Table 4.1 Ideological Principles of White Nationalist and Tea Party
Organizations, 2011–2012

Ideological Principles	White Nationalist Position	Tea Party Position
Original intent (Constitution)	Uphold and defend the Constitution of the United States of America as it was originally created by the Aryan founding fathers who cultivated and created a WHITE HOMELAND! (American National Socialist Party)	Constitution First recognizes the need to educate the public and ourselves as to the intent of our Founders as they went about creating our Constitutional Republic and how they intended the Constitution to be interpreted and understood. (Constitution First Colorado)
Limited federal power	The crusade is on going to wake up the White Race -to reach out to people like us, to take command of our lives, to take the federal government's control out of our lives. The federal government is trying to take what freedom we have left; the right to own a gun and free speech; when these two go, its over. (Church of the National Knights of the Ku Klux Klan)	Americans, we have been asleep for far too long and have allowed the Federal Government to intrude and take over almost every aspects of our lives ... We can start in Oklahoma by having our Oklahoma State Legislatures join with the other 49 states to strongly re-enforce the limited powers granted to Federal Government by the people. (Oklahoma for Tea)
Taxation	Virtually all taxes today are directly, or indirectly, used to control and destroy the future of our race ... In short, the old adage applies. "The power to tax is the power to destroy." (White Aryan Resistance)	A constitutionally limited government, designed to protect the blessings of liberty, must be fiscally responsible or it must subject its citizenry to high levels of taxation that unjustly restrict the liberty our Constitution was designed to protect. (Forsyth Tea Party, Georgia)
Pro-Christian	America and its Christian Constitutional form of government must survive. (United White Knights of the KKK) Patriotism and Christianity are preeminently the moving principles of the Invisible Empire. The flag, the constitution and the Holy Bible are the keystone of the Order's principles. (White Camelia Knights of the KKK)	While government shall not endorse any particular religion, neither shall it prohibit nor restrict the private or public exercise thereof. Judeo-Christian beliefs and ethics are, and must remain, part of the foundation the United States of America. (The Common Sense Campaign, Alabama)

groups. Although there were occasional opportunities for electoral participation in white nationalist parties, these were relatively rare and uniformly
unsuccessful. Participation in explicit white supremacist groups was also
potentially costly because these groups are generally viewed as deviant and
dangerous and as such are often targeted by law enforcement. This was not
the case for the Tea Party. The Tea Party agenda was not explicitly racial, and
participation was widespread. Many candidates self-identified as Tea Party
members, and unlike white nationalist candidates, they often won. The electoral success of the TPM resulted in the formation of Tea Party caucuses in
Congress and in state legislatures across the country. This not only helped le-
gitimize the TPM but also offered an additional comparative advantage over
traditional white supremacist groups. The TPM offered racial extremists
an opportunity to advance their agenda by participating in conventional
politics due to the presence of sympathetic Tea Party candidates who were
getting elected to office. By joining the TPM, white racial extremists could
pursue their goal of mainstreaming their racist beliefs by electing Tea Party
candidates while avoiding being smeared as belonging to a fringe group that
focused exclusively and explicitly on the propagation of racist ideas. In this
sense, the Tea Party represented an appealing win-win situation for white racial extremists.

Although we cannot survey white nationalist group members directly,
the plausibility of the suggestion that the TPM competed for movement resources is evident in the most popular online forum for white supremacist
sympathizers, Stormfront.org. As early as 2009, WNM activists recognized
the opportunity that the TPM offered. In an effort to take advantage of this
opportunity, some movement leaders came together to form the Tea Party
Americans Coalition (TPAC). The idea behind the organization was, in its
own words, to create "a working group for serious white racialist activists
who want to coordinate our efforts and intervene for effect in Tea Party-
type events."[27] As one member of this group posted in support of TPAC on
Stormfront in June 2009,

> I recently joined the TPAC and it is a coalition. . . . We are trying to work
> with all groups and to get our message out using the tea party movement.
> If all WN's would join we would find some sort of organization and soli-
> darity. . . . The TPAC has given us a valuable tool to further the agenda of
> White Nationalism and to do alot more than just add two new members
> to a group of ten others which has yeilded [sic] no results. This approach

will NOT WORK. Study the history of the revolutionary movement here in this country. There were plenty of disagreements between the colonists but they banded together and worked together to achieve their goal. Independence!!! They sorted out the rest later as members of individual parties. That is a formula for success that cannot be denied. No matter the guise(sons of liberty or the militia) or the labels the king applied to them, from traitors to rebels, they were ALL colonists seeking control of their own destiny. We are ALL white nationalists and seek control of our own destiny.

In early 2013 a Stormfront user posed the following question to the group in the form of a poll: "Do you support the Tea Party?" The thread generated sixty-two responses, of which 34 percent said that they support a majority of the Tea Party agenda, while an additional 18 percent responded that they support some of it. Several users provided an explanation for their answers. One user discounted the Tea Party, essentially arguing that the movement was too watered down. This response is reproduced below and includes the user's unique signature (below the line), which reflects his unwillingness to compromise on the movement's goal's, as well his ideology of anti-Semitism.

I'm opposed to sellout oath-breakers and those who say America is a "blending pot" or "all inclusive." Rubio comes to mind.

_____

"Half-measures are only a delay tactic."

"The greatest trick the Jew ever pulled, was convincing the world he was human."

Yet some users responded that they believed the Tea Party provided a viable option for movement activists who are concerned about accomplishing the movement's racist goals:

I support the Tea Party because they actively advance some core ideals such as Reducing the size of the Federal Government, Reduced Federal spending, Adhere to the Constitution, etc. . . . The (National Socialist Movement) is not seriously engaged in any activity that has any chance of making meaningful change and, in fact, has become the preferred standard for "Whacko Extremist" whenever the subject of race comes up. Unless we can integrate the many groups who have similar goals, the browning/loss of America will continue unabated.

Another member expressed a similar sentiment:

> I support the stated ideals of the Tea Party movement. Like any movement (including ours) it can be watered down or sidelined. We need to be more inclusive of like-minded groups in order to achieve any level of success. Armed conflict is an immediate fail. We are currently marginalized as radical fringe when, in fact, the majority of Americans believe most of what we know to be the truth. We have been demonized by the mainstream to the point that people won't even consider the message because of the messenger. The magic can only occur when we can both remain true to our beliefs and also become the mainstream.

These posts are entirely consistent with our arguments concerning the broad range of incentives offered to white supremacists by the TPM. They clearly indicate that in addition to the TPM's anti-immigration stance, at least some white supremacists were attracted to the TPM by issues that are not explicitly tied to race, such as reducing federal spending and more generally, federal power. We suspect that this also extends to social issues, such as opposition to abortion and LGBT rights. These themes were also prominent in the white nationalist issue statements we analyzed. These posts also make it very clear that white nationalist activists are aware that they are highly stigmatized as "white supremacist" activists, which comes at some personal cost and which they also recognize as counterproductive to movement success. Finally, and most significantly, these activists seem to have believed that the TPM could be successful in advancing white nationalist goals. To the extent that these views reflect a broader group of white supremacist activists, it seems quite plausible that the TPM absorbed at least some energy from the WNM.

Empirical Evidence of Mainstreaming

We have shown in Figure 4.1 that whites with high levels of outgroup hostility were significantly more likely to support the Tea Party. Yet did white nationalists actually respond to this messaging by redirecting their energy and support to the Tea Party? Although there is much anecdotal evidence to support our interpretation of the TPM's effects on the WNM, in this section we present several empirical analyses that provide more generalizable evidence of mainstreaming. Since we cannot observe the attitudes of individual white nationalist activists directly, as we would in a survey, we instead must rely on evidence that is less direct to test our arguments. First, we examine geographic and temporal trends in WNM activity and how these trends were related to changes in the local political environment. We expect that where opportunities for participation in less costly forms of collective action are made available, such as local TP chapters, white nationalists will be more likely to redirect their energy into those activities. This should result in a decrease in WNM activity in areas where this has occurred.

While this analysis relies on data on the behavior of actual white nationalist organizations, it suffers from the weaknesses inherent in the use of aggregate level (rather than individual level) data. Therefore, we supplement these analyses of white nationalist group activity with analyses of survey data on the political behavior of white racial extremists who may or may not be members of white nationalist organizations.

The Tea Party Movement and the Co-optation of the Klan

We begin with an analysis of county level data on white nationalist activity that links the decline in WNM groups to Tea Party activity during the peak years of the TPM. For our statistical estimation we rely on a technique known as *survival analysis*, which is designed to estimate the effect of various factors on the duration of time that a case in the sample "survives" (i.e., remains active). In our case, we wish to estimate the extent to which the emergence of TPOs throughout the country was related to the survival of white nationalist organizations. Specifically, we estimate the effect of the number of TPOs on WNM organizational "death," which we measure as the year in which an active white nationalist group ceased to be active (defined as at least two consecutive years of inactivity). We focus on one of the largest and most notorious categories of white supremacist groups: the Ku Klux Klan. Our sample consists of all Klan chapters (550) that were active for at least one year during the period 2008–2017, thus spanning the period both before and after the peak years of TPM activity. We are interested in testing the hypothesis that the death of a KKK chapter was positively related to the presence of the number of TPOs in the surrounding community (defined as being located in the same county). To estimate the relationship between Tea Party presence and KKK death, we also control for several other variables, which we

THE MAINSTREAMING OF THE WHITE NATIONALIST MOVEMENT   89

measure at the county level (the percentage of the population that is black and Hispanic, real per capita income, county population size, and the average Republican vote share over the entire analysis period).[28]

Figure 4.2 provides a graphical summary of the results of the analysis. The figure presents the relationship between the number of TPOs in a county and the predicted hazard ratio, which measures the risk of KKK death. Unfortunately we do not have precise information on the exact timing of the formation of these TPOs. We simply know that they existed at some point during the period when the TPM was active. We defined this period of peak TPM activity as occurring from 2010 to 2014. We then estimated the relationship between the number of TPOs and KKK survival for two different periods: (1) 2010–2014, when the TPM was most active, and (2) the remaining years in the sample (2008–2009, 2015–2017), when many of these TPOs were either not yet established (2008–2009) or were in decline or defunct.[29]

For the period 2010–2014, we see that there was a positive (and statistically significant) relationship between the number of TPOs and the risk of KKK death. This suggests that at least for KKK chapters, their decline was most likely to occur in counties where the Tea Party was most active, perhaps due to the alternative form of collective action that the TPM provided to pursue white nationalist goals. The figure also presents the relationship between the number of TPOs and KKK chapter death during the period in which the TPM was not active. As can be seen, there is no relationship during this period. This result allows us to rule out the possibility that the effect we see for the 2010–2014 period was due to preexisting differences between Tea Party counties and non–Tea Party counties and thus provides stronger evidence that the effect of TPOs in our analysis is causal in nature.

Next we turn to individual level survey data to more closely examine the extent to which the TPM attracted white racial extremists to mainstream politics. While white nationalist activists cannot be identified in these data, studying the behavior of the broader population of racial extremists captures disaffected whites as well as the smaller number of racial extremists active within the WNM. Our analysis relies on data from the 2010 CCES, which is based on a large, nationally representative sample that includes respondents from every congressional district. We focus on white Republican identifiers who were confirmed to be registered voters, which leaves us with a sample of approximately eleven thousand respondents.

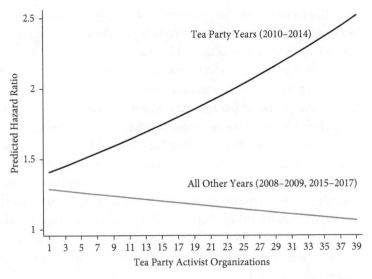

Figure 4.2　Predicted hazard of KKK chapter death, by number of TPOs

Note: The figure presents the predicted hazard ratio of KKK organizational death by the number of TPOs in a county based on a Cox proportional hazards model, which controls for per capita income, the employment rate, the percentage of the population that is black and Hispanic, total population size, and the percentage of the vote cast for Obama in 2008 (all measured at the county level).
Tea Party data are provided by Rory McVeigh and were originally collected and geocoded by the Institute for Research and Education on Human Rights (see Rory McVeigh, Kraig Beyerlein, Burrel Vann Jr., and Priyamvada Trivedic, "Educational Segregation, Tea Party Organizations, and Battles over Distributive Justice," *American Sociological Review* 79, 4 (2014): 630–52).

Unfortunately the 2010 CCES did not include any items measuring attitudes toward Muslims. Therefore we created a measure of white racial extremists based on people's attitudes toward African Americans and Latinos only. We used two items from the racial resentment scale, which ask respondents how strongly they agree or disagree with the following statements:

(1) The Irish, Italians, Jews, and many other minorities overcame prejudice and worked their way up. Blacks should do the same without any special favors.

(2) Generations of slavery and discrimination have created conditions that make it difficult for blacks to work their way out of the lower class.

In addition, we constructed an anti–Latinx immigrant scale based on responses to three immigration policy items. "What do you think the U.S. government should do about immigration?"

(1) "Grant legal status to all illegal immigrants who have held jobs and paid taxes for at least 3 years, and not been convicted of any felony crimes." (Yes-No)

(2) "Increase the number of border patrols on the U.S.-Mexican border." (Yes-No)

(3) "Allow police to question anyone they think may be in the country illegally." (Yes-No)

For this analysis we identify white racial extremists as whites who chose the response that reflected the maximum level of hostility for each of these five survey questions regarding African Americans and Latinos. Since the number of items used for this measure is far fewer than the number of items used for our outgroup hostility scale described in Chapter 2, it is easier for whites to achieve the maximum score and be identified as "racial extremists." This results in a larger percentage of the population (23 percent) being designated as white racial extremist than what we reported in our analyses in Chapter 2. Although we continue to refer to this group of voters as extremists, this group undoubtedly includes many whites who would be more aptly characterized as "racial conservatives."

We begin by examining the relationship between the presence of local TPOs and the respondent's level of participation in the 2010 midterm. To measure participation, we constructed an index based on the sum of affirmative responses to four standard items in the CCES, which asked respondents if they (1) attended a political meeting, rally, or speech; (2) wore a campaign button or posted a yard sign or bumper sticker; (3) worked for a political party or candidate; and (4) contributed money to a specific candidate. The top panel of Figure 4.3 presents the results of a regression model that examines the relationship between local Tea Party activity and the respondent's level of political participation in the 2010 midterm. The results presented are based on models that control for several other factors that might be related to campaign participation, including the respondent's age, education level, income, party identification ideology, and attitudes toward several issues known to be important to conservatives (abortion, gun rights, government spending, and gay rights; see the online Appendix for details: https://rcfording.com/research/HardWhite).We estimate the relationship separately for racial extremists and nonextremists based on the definition previously described. Previously we saw that the presence of local TPOs was significantly associated with a decline in the mobilization of the KKK. Our expectation is that where the TPM was active, it would help serve as the bridge from the fringe to the electoral mainstream, and therefore white racial extremists would be more likely to participate in the midterm campaign.

The results are consistent with our expectations. White racial extremists living in counties where TPOs were relatively numerous were significantly more likely to participate in the 2010 campaign than racial extremists in counties with no TPM activity. This was not the case for nonextremists, as the relationship between local TPOs and campaign participation was statistically insignificant. In combination with our analysis of KKK demobilization, this provides support for our claim that of one of the most important mechanisms through which the TPM attracted white racial extremists and white racial conservatives was that they were mobilized away from the fringe into the mainstream of electoral politics.

The strength of the preceding analysis is that it shows that both the demobilization of the KKK and the electoral mobilization of racial extremists occurred in counties where the TPM was active. One weakness, though, is that we cannot know that it was support for the TPM that actually motivated white racial extremists to participate in electoral politics. We address this issue in the analysis presented in the bottom panel of Figure 4.3. Here we replicate the analysis presented in the top panel, but instead of relying on the local presence of TPOs, we instead examine how campaign participation was related to the respondent's level of support for the TPM. Our expectation is that if white racial extremists were truly inspired by the TPM, their level of support for the TPM would be positively related to participation in the 2010 campaign. We should not, however, expect to see such a relationship among nonextremists.

The results clearly demonstrate the importance of support for the Tea Party in pulling white racial extremists into electoral politics. As we have shown previously, outgroup hostility overall has a negative effect on political participation and turnout. This is not surprising. As we saw in Chapter 3, white racial extremists exhibited much lower levels of political efficacy than nonracial extremists. Yet what is striking about the results presented in the figure is that even after controlling for the standard predictors of political participation, support for the Tea Party actually flips this relationship: white racial extremists actually exhibited higher levels of political participation in 2010 if they were enthusiastic about the Tea Party. These results further support our explanation for the political mainstreaming of white racial extremists and WNM activists. White extremists were attracted to the Tea Party in no small

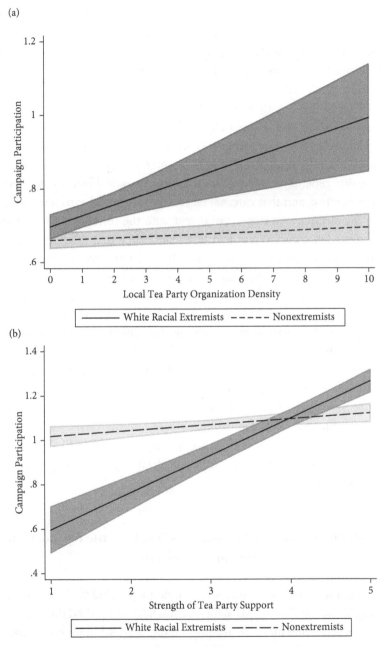

Figure 4.3 Relationship between political participation, local Tea Party activity, and Tea Party support among racial extremists and nonextremists. (A) Campaign participation and local Tea Party activity. (B) Campaign participation and Tea Party support

part because it emphasized issues that were of concern to them; they felt that the TPM provided a promising venue for mainstreaming their racist beliefs. Where Tea Party candidates emphasized the concerns about outgroups, white racial extremists were mobilized to participate in politics and vote in elections. The Tea Party was therefore critical in mainstreaming racism.

If this was the case, then we would also expect that white racial extremists would come to feel more politically efficacious because they believed TP candidates and representatives were more likely to care about what "people like me" think. Recall that in Chapter 3 we showed how white racial extremists generally exhibited lower levels of political efficacy than nonracial extremists, and that external efficacy among racial extremists plunged after the election of Obama, consistent with the interpretation that white extremists felt dejected and had little confidence that the federal government would be responsive to their interests. Our mainstreaming thesis, however, suggests that due to the nature of the Tea Party agenda and the success of Tea Party candidates in the 2010 midterm election, the level of external efficacy among white racists should have increased after 2010. Figure 4.4 updates this analysis by presenting the same trends we examined in Chapter 3 but now including values through 2016. The post-2008 trend is exactly as we would expect. Between 2008 and 2012 white racial extremists became more efficacious, while efficacy levels among nonextremists fell. This cannot be explained as simply due to differences in partisanship or other demographic traits between extremists and nonextremists, as our analysis explicitly controls for these differences. Rather, it is most likely due to the success of the TPM in moving the agenda of white nationalists into the political mainstream.

Mainstreaming White Nationalism Lays the Foundation for the Rise of Trump

The election of Barack Obama set in motion a political backlash that had a lasting impact on the WNM. Many analysts have recognized the importance of Obama's election for racial attitudes among whites, but we know relatively little concerning how those attitudes were translated into action within the WNM. As we have shown, the immediate reaction was a surge in WNM among traditional white supremacist organizations. Yet one of the most important consequences of Obama's election was the subsequent change

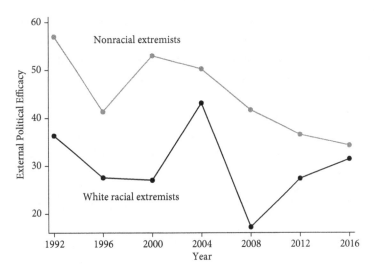

Figure 4.4 Trends in external political efficacy among racial extremists and nonextremists, 1992–2016

Note: The values presented in the figure were generated based on a pooled regression analysis (ANES 1992–2016) of the ANES external efficacy index on a dichotomous indicator for white racists (and its interaction with a series of indicator variables for survey year), controlling for basic demographic variables (age, education level, gender, family income) and political attitudes (party identification and ideology). We then generated adjusted external efficacy scores by computing predicted values from this regression, holding all other variables constant at their mean.

in the political opportunity structure and its effects on the political behavior of white racial extremists. Whether through the intentional strategy of entryism or simply in response to the appeal of the Tea Party message, white racial extremists and conservatives flocked to the Tea Party after its launch in 2009. Their participation likely contributed to an even greater emphasis on explicitly racial issues within the TPM and certainly contributed to its electoral success. As a result, white racial extremists felt more politically empowered than they had for decades.

After the re-election of Obama, the TPM began to fade as it became absorbed into the Republican Party. This left an opening for a strong national figure to capitalize on this mobilization, and Donald Trump took full advantage. Returning to Figure 4.4, we see that the level of external efficacy among white racial extremists continued to increase after 2012, and by 2016 the efficacy gap between racists and nonracists had closed. Since the Tea Party had largely disappeared by 2016, it seems more than likely that the 2012–2016 increase in efficacy among white racial extremists can be attributed to the emergence of Trump as a national spokesperson for their community. In the next chapter we trace the history of Trump's connections with the WNM and how he employed a campaign strategy that relied heavily on the racialized political narratives of the movement. He emphasized a variety of political, economic, and cultural threats to whites originating from the three most salient racial outgroups: African Americans, Latinx immigrants, and Muslims. He accentuated white outgroup hostility, ultimately winning the White House in the process and accelerating the mainstreaming of racism in American politics.

5

A Leader Normalizes White Extremist Rhetoric

Trump 2016 Presidential Campaign Speeches Mainstream Outgroup Hostility

The Tea Party movement (TPM) was a major advance in the effort to inject outgroup hostility into mainstream politics.[1] By 2012 the Tea Party Caucus in Congress had grown to include ninety-three members and was a significant force in Congress.[2] The most impressive display of its power occurred in 2015 when caucus leaders chased Speaker John Boehner (R-OH) from office on the grounds that he was willing to compromise with President Obama, especially on social welfare spending and taxes. Despite these successes the caucus was less than a coherent bloc, and its leadership was diffuse. Some leaders, like Rep. Michelle Bachmann (R-MN), were at first quite popular and created a buzz only to fizzle, such as when Bachmann's extreme views and erratic statements ended up not working for her in her home district. The Tea Party (TP) was also divided over fiscal and social issues. Most TP members in Congress seemed more interested in pursuing the TPM's fiscal goals, as demonstrated by their insistence on shutting down the government over the debt ceiling debate. To many within the movement, it appeared that fiscal issues had taken precedence over addressing TPM supporters' growing outrage over demographic diversification, immigration, and what they perceived as an antiwhite bias reflected in President Obama's policy agenda.

As the TP started to flounder inside the halls of Congress, so too did the movement begin to lose steam at the grassroots level. In what might be the only systematic study of trends in the activity of local Tea Party organizations (TPOs), political scientist Jeffrey Berry collected data on a sample of local TPOs and found that as of 2017, no new organizations had formed since 2013, and approximately 40 percent of the chapters formed between 2009 and 2013 had ceased to exist.[3] Given the trajectory of the movement, as 2016

Hard White, Richard C. Fording and Sanford F. Schram. Oxford University Press (2020). © Oxford University Press.
DOI: 10.1093/oso/9780197500484.001.0001

approached, many racial extremists were once again in search of an attractive vehicle for pursuing their goals.

For some racial extremists, the answer would be found in the emerging alt-right movement (ARM). Indeed, as discussed in the previous chapter, there seems to have been a good deal of overlap between TP supporters and ARM supporters. Nonetheless, even as the ARM undoubtedly tried to maintain a more mainstream image, its explicit call for white separatism ensured that it would remain closer to the fringe than to the mainstream of American politics. Like the TPM, the ARM had also lacked a national leader who could be viable in electoral politics. Therefore, it was clear from the beginning that the ARM would never be successful in penetrating mainstream politics on its own. Yet the broader white nationalist movement (WNM) had tasted victory with the electoral successes of the TPM and by 2015 was hungry for more. The stage was thus set for Donald Trump to swoop in and capitalize on the mobilization of outgroup hostility, which is exactly what he did.[4]

The Rise of Trump as a White Nationalist Leader

In many ways Trump was the ideal candidate for mainstreaming racialized narratives of white resentment. His own personality as it developed over the years was basically one of resentment, directed at people who were richer, smarter, more popular, or especially sexier than he was.[5] His revenge was best demonstrated on a weekly basis for years as he played the successful businessman who got to say "you're fired" to celebrities (though often has-beens) on his popular television show *Celebrity Apprentice*. Trump was almost never depicted positively by others, say as a kind and loving person, but instead was most often characterized as a desperate striver. He shared resentment with his emerging political base (though his resentments were not always racialized). Therefore, Trump fit the mold of a leader of a movement founded on resentment even if he had not spent years toiling as an organizer and leader of a white nationalist organization.

Not all white nationalists embraced Trump straight away as their natural leader even if they shared his sense of resentment toward mainstream society. Yet by 2016 most white racial extremists had come around and overwhelmingly swung their support solidly in his direction.[6] This support solidified into an impenetrable base when Steve Bannon, the editor of the right-wing populist news site Breitbart, became chairman of Trump's campaign in

August 2016.[7] Bannon had previously interviewed Trump multiple times in recorded conversations for *Breitbart News Daily* radio broadcasts.[8] These interviews are revealing in that one can hear Bannon tutoring Trump more than questioning him. It was as if Trump were being groomed to assume leadership of the emerging right-wing populist movement. Ultimately, Bannon would prove to be critical in navigating Trump's 2016 presidential campaign to victory and pushing its white nationalist agenda in the White House.

From its inception, Trump's campaign was indebted to the WNM. It built on the resentment that the movement was articulating regarding how whites saw themselves as under assault in a changing society. This resentment crystallized in reaction to Obama's presidency, and Trump shared that resentment. While as a candidate he opportunistically chose to align himself with this movement to give himself a needed base of support, it was a base he felt at home with given his own personal racist past and proclivity to increasingly express hostility to outgroups he saw as threatening to the position of whites in American society. It was like coming home; his father had been accused of attending a KKK rally, and he and his father had more clearly denied rental units to African Americans.[9] More to the point, Trump's personal history is littered with racist comments and actions. Trump might have been operating opportunistically in pursuing the birther conspiracy and his quest for a white nationalist base of supporters, but he was comfortable doing so, not just as the charlatan he was but as the racist he had always been.

Yet Trump did not just take the support of racial extremists; he returned the favor. He provided much-needed leadership for the entire range of racially inspired movements in the post-Obama era: traditional white supremacists, the emerging ARM, the racist wing of the TPM, and the growing anti-Muslim movement. And in the process he created a coalition of racial extremists united under the ideology of Trump's outgroup hostility: animus toward African Americans, Latinx immigrants, and Muslims. He was older and more prominent than either Bannon or Richard Spencer and put a recognizable face on this new brand of white nationalism. As a result, he effectively mainstreamed its ideas, especially with use of his racially charged rhetoric targeting these outgroups. And he continues to do this even as president. It cannot get more mainstream than that. Daryl Johnson, a former government official responsible for tracking right-wing extremism, has commented on Trump's racialized narratives designed to stoke outgroup hostility toward African Americans and the Latinx and Muslim populations:

Building a border wall, deporting immigrants, a travel ban on Muslim countries—these are themes discussed on white-nationalist message boards and websites for years, now being endorsed and talked about at the highest levels of the government. He's retweeted messages about Muslims from conspiracy sites. What keeps these groups energized and active is the fact that the administration has mainstreamed their message and tried to put it forth as policy.[10]

The remainder of this chapter focuses on one of the most important mechanisms that Trump used to mobilize more mainstream racial conservatives and more rabid white racial extremists around his candidacy in 2016 and which he has continued to use throughout his first term as president: incendiary, racialized political narratives that promote the development and intensification of white racial consciousness (WRC). This strategy was not entirely original, echoing the rhetoric of hatemongers of the past, at home and abroad, from white supremacists to fascists, neo-Nazis, and Hitler himself.[11] Indeed, we show that the use of racialized rhetoric was a key to the success of the TPM in co-opting white racial extremists in 2010. Trump centered his candidacy for the presidency on the use of hatemongering racialized rhetoric. Although the case can be made that race-baiting had long been established as a core practice of the Republican Party in the post–civil rights era,[12] we show that Trump was distinctive in his use of racialized rhetoric, compared to his 2016 primary opponents and also to the Republican nominee who preceded him in 2012, Mitt Romney. His use of racialized rhetoric did not abate during the general election. The evidence suggests that Trump's 2016 candidacy had superseded all prior efforts to make white nationalist rhetoric mainstream, stoking outgroup hostility in the public and doing so on the grandest stage possible, a presidential campaign.

The Tea Party Movement and the Use of Racialized Appeals

In Chapter 4 we argued that the TPM attracted racial extremists and conservatives in part because of its association with issues important to the advancement of white nationalist goals. There were likely several mechanisms through which racial extremists were drawn to the movement. The racist agenda of the TP was regularly on display at TP protests, and these events often provided highly visible cues to racial extremists and conservatives that their participation was welcome. TPOs also had a strong online presence. And as Theda Skocpol and Vanessa Williamson have noted,[13] the TPM greatly benefited from coverage on the news source of choice for the extreme right, Fox News. Yet none of these mechanisms could have led to the electoral mobilization of white extremists if TP political candidates had not been so effective in articulating the goals of racial extremists through racialized appeals embedded in their campaign rhetoric.

Although considerable scholarly attention has been devoted to understanding the sources of TP support among the mass public, relatively less has been paid to how TP elites—candidates and elected officials—differed from their Democratic and (non–Tea Party) Republican colleagues. A handful of studies have examined the distinctiveness of TP representatives by exploring the differences in roll call voting behavior in Congress. These studies have generally found that TP representatives' voting behavior closely resembles that of non-TP Republican colleagues, at least with respect to legislation that falls along the traditional left-right dimension.[14] Bryan Gervais and Irwin Morris however extended the study of TP distinctiveness to support for civil rights legislation and found that TP representatives were significantly less likely to support bills classified as pro–civil rights by the Leadership Council on Civil and Human Rights.[15] This finding aligns with the research on the importance of racial resentment in mass support for the TPM. Yet this analysis fails to provide a mechanism for the mobilization of racial extremism that led to the election of TP representatives in the 2010 election. That mechanism can be found, we argue, in racialized appeals in TP candidate rhetoric.

To test this proposition we conducted a detailed content analysis of the issue platforms of all candidates for the U.S. House in 2010. To collect these data we first downloaded candidate issue statements from the websites of 847 congressional candidates who competed in the general election, using the Federal Election Commission's historical campaign website archive. A total of 175 candidates were identified as "Tea Party" candidates based on national news media sources that collected endorsements by several national TPOs.[16] We collected text for an additional 262 non–Tea Party Republicans and 410 Democrats.

To analyze the text we first created a dictionary of words and phrases that we believed reflected explicit and implicit references to African Americans, Latinx immigrants, and Muslims. To develop this list we first analyzed the texts using terms that explicitly identify each group, such as "African

Americans," "blacks," "immigrants," "Mexican," "Hispanic," "Muslim," and "Islam." Based on an analysis of TP rhetoric and the text of presidential candidate speeches, we identified many other words and phrases that tended to cluster together with the more explicit terms. Finally, once the complete list of terms was compiled for each outgroup, we created subcategories designed to capture references to racial outgroups that were either positive, negative, or neutral. The complete lists of terms for each racial outgroup are presented in Table 5.1.

For Latinx immigrants, we coded references to immigrants as "documented" or "undocumented" as positive. We also included references to immigration reform, such as the "pathway to citizenship," as positive. Negative references to Latinx immigrants described them as "legal" or "illegal" and framed immigrants as criminal, a security threat, overflowing our borders, or in need of deportation. Negative references to Muslims were coded as those made to the "radical" nature of Islam and its threat to U.S. security through terrorism. Neutral references were those made to various countries within the Middle East and the foreign policy challenges they pose to the United States. Finally, we coded positive references to African Americans as those that emphasize structural factors—such as poverty and discrimination—as a barrier to achieving racial equality. Negative references were coded as those that use the dog-whistle frames of welfare and crime as strategies to appeal to white racial extremists and conservatives. One important limitation of our approach is that we must assume that all of these terms are equally representative of positive or negative tone. For example, references to gang members and drugs in relationship to Latinx immigrants are arguably much more negative in tone than saying immigrants take away jobs. Yet with this limitation in mind, this tone analysis can add substantially to the evidence of whether the TP distinctively invoked racialized threat narratives that stoked white outgroup hostility.

Based on this dictionary of terms, we conducted an automated content analysis to measure the frequency with which the congressional candidates used these terms in their issue platforms in 2010. The results of our content analyses are presented in Figure 5.1. For each racial outgroup the figure presents measures of rhetorical emphasis for (1) terms that we considered reflected positive or neutral references to each racial group (represented by the gray bar) and (2) terms that we considered reflected a more negative tone (represented by the black bar). To measure rhetorical emphasis, we relied on a commonly used metric in the field of communication studies known

Table 5.1 Racial Outgroup Dictionary: Positive, Neutral, and Negative Terms

LATINX IMMIGRANTS	MUSLIMS	AFRICAN AMERICANS
Negative	**Radical Islamic Terrorism**	**Crime and Welfare**
ILLEGAL_IMMIGRANT	*TERROR*	POLICE
OPEN_BORDER	ISIS	LAW_ENFORCEMENT
MASSIVE_INFLOW_OF_REFUGEES	RADICAL_ISLAM	WELFARE
BUILD_A_WALL	*DEFEAT_ISIS*	CRIMINAL
MAKE_AMERICA_SAFE	WORLD_TRADE	SHOT
SANCTUARY_CITIES	MAKE_AMERICA_SAFE	CHICAGO
CRIMINAL_ALIENS	THREAT	*FOOD_STAMP(S)*
GANG	AL_QAIDA	MAKE_AMERICA_SAFE
SAN_FRANCISCO	SAN_BERNARDINO	LAW_AND_ORDER
STOP_THE_DRUGS	SALUTING_ONE_AMERICAN_FLAG	VIOLENT_CRIME
SECURE_AND_DEFEND	*DELIVER_JUSTICE*	SHOT_IN_CHICAGO
KATE_STEINLE	SAFE_COUNTRY	BROKEN_CRIMINAL_JUSTICE_SYSTEM
JOBS_TO_MEXICO	DEATH_AND_DESTRUCTION	STOP_THE_DRUGS
DEPORT	**Middle East—Foreign Policy**	RISING_CRIME
GANG_MEMBER	IRAN	REDUCE_SURGING_CRIME
Positive or Neutral	MIDDLE_EAST	CRIMINAL_ENTERPRISE
BORDER	*NUCLEAR_WEAPON*	**Neutral**
LATINOS	ISLAM	*AFRICAN_AMERICAN*
FOREIGN	IRAQ	RACIAL
MEXICO	ISRAEL	*DEPARTMENT_OF_JUSTICE*
UNDOCUMENTED	SYRIA	*CRIMINAL_JUSTICE_SYSTEM*
AMERICAN_CITIZENS	WAR_IN_IRAQ	FAILING_SCHOOLS
BORDER_PATROL	WEAPONS	*INNER_CITY*
PATH_TO_CITIZENSHIP	*IRAN_DEAL*	YOUNG_AFRICAN
AMERICAN_AND_HISPANIC	BIN_LADEN	*JUSTICE_DEPARTMENT*
ACROSS_THE_BORDER	SAUDI_ARABIA	YOUNG_AFRICAN

Continued

Table 5.1 *Continued*

LATINX IMMIGRANTS	MUSLIMS	AFRICAN AMERICANS
ICE_AND_BORDER_PATROL	*INCREASE_IN_SYRIAN_REFUGEES*	**Poverty and Discrimination**
COMING_INTO_OUR_COUNTRY	*REBUILD_OUR_MILITARY*	JUSTICE
DOCUMENTED	END_THE_WAR_IN_IRAQ	CIVIL_RIGHTS
	FOREIGN_COUNTRIES	DISCRIMINATION
	IRAQ_WAR	LIVE_IN_POVERTY
	IRAQ_AND_SYRIA	*SLAVERY*
	GULF_STATES	NEGLECTED_PART_OF_THIS_NATION
	PATH_TO_NUCLEAR_WEAPONS	RACIAL_DISCRIMINATION

Note: Italicized terms represent cases in which multiple terms with the same meaning were collapsed into a single item. Details are available in the online Appendix.

as "Total Document Frequency by Inverse Document Frequency" or TD-IDF.[17] We measured the TD-IDF based on the candidate issue platforms for each of the three party groups: Democrats, non-Tea Party Republicans, and Tea Party Republicans. To help provide a benchmark for our analysis, we also analyzed issue statements from the white supremacist websites that we described in Chapters 3 and 4, using the same dictionary of terms.

In addition to the level of emphasis of positive and negative terms used by candidates as represented by the height of the bars in the figure, we also measured the relative balance of positive and negative emphasis for each candidate. This is important, as there may be systematic differences in the degree a candidate placed on negative terms relative to positive or neutral terms, and vice versa. To measure the positive-negative balance of rhetorical emphasis, for each party group we computed the ratio of the TD-IDF score for positive or neutral terms to the TD-IDF score for negative terms. That ratio value is presented atop the gray bars in each graph. Values greater than 1.0 thus reflect a more positive balance of tone, values less than 1.0 reflect a more negative balance, and a value of exactly 1.0 reflects equal emphasis on positive and negative terms. We expect that TP candidates and to a lesser extent non–Tea Party Republicans referenced these racial groups in ways that were

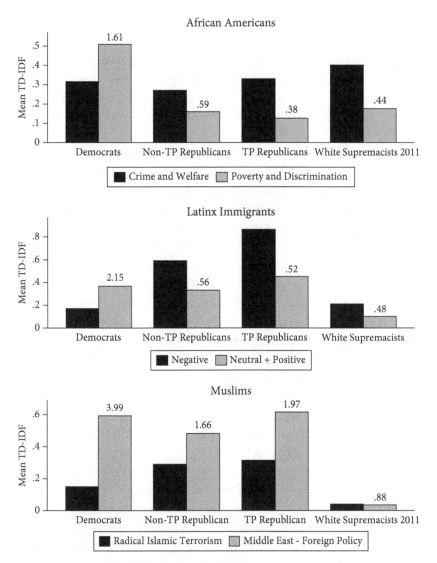

Figure 5.1 Content analysis results for 2010 House candidate emphasis on racial outgroups, by party

Note: The bars in each plot present the degree to which House candidates utilized negative terms (black) or positive/neutral terms (gray) related to African Americans, Latinx immigrants, or Muslims (see Table 5.1). The value above each gray bar represents the balance of positive/neutral and negative rhetorical emphasis, calculated as the ratio of the TD-IDF score for positive/neutral rhetoric to the TD-IDF score for negative rhetoric.

generally less positive than Democrats did. We also expect that the results for white supremacist groups will most closely resemble those of the TP.

The results generally support the conclusion that TP candidates were distinctive in their use of negative, racialized appeals in their campaign rhetoric compared to other candidates. For terms related to African Americans, Democratic candidates were the mostly likely to employ references to poverty and discrimination. In addition, Democrats were the only group for whom the balance of terms leaned more heavily toward poverty and discrimination. In other words, both groups of Republican candidates as well as white supremacists were significantly more likely to use text related to crime and welfare than text referencing poverty and discrimination. Interestingly, white supremacists exhibited the strongest level of emphasis on crime and welfare terms of any group, but the positive-negative balance of rhetoric was nearly identical to what we observed for TP candidates.

The results were very similar for Latinx immigrants. Once again, Democratic candidates were the only group to emphasize positive or neutral terms more than negative terms. Tea Party candidates displayed the strongest level of emphasis on negative terms, and the positive-negative balance was only slightly less negative than among white supremacists. The results for rhetoric related to Muslims were somewhat less consistent. All three candidate groups were more likely to use Muslim-related terms that we classified as neutral (i.e., related generally to the Middle East or foreign policy) than negative terms referencing the "radical" aspects of Islam and its threat to U.S. security. As with the other two racial groups, Democratic candidates were the group most likely to rely on neutral terms rather than negative terms. And once again, white supremacists reflected the most negative balance of tone. Yet there are two aspects of the results for Muslims that stand out.

First, white supremacists rarely used any language referencing Muslims. This should not come as a surprise given our findings reported in Chapter 3. As we discussed, one reason may be that many white supremacists are somewhat cross-pressured in their attitudes toward Muslims, in part because they view Muslims as allies in the fight against Jews. A second major difference in the results for Muslims is that there is not much difference in the balance of tone between Tea Party Republicans and non–Tea Party Republicans. As the party that was responsible for both Iraq wars as well as the war in Afghanistan, Republicans have consistently taken a more hawkish position on Middle East foreign policy as a means to combat terrorism. Tea Party Republicans, at least in the early years of the TPM, apparently saw nothing to gain by characterizing Muslims as any more of a threat than did non–TP Republicans. Nevertheless, the result of our content analysis of House candidates is resoundingly clear: TP candidates used negative, racialized terms far more than other candidates.

Did White Racial Extremists Respond to the Tea Party's Racialized Appeals?

We have shown that TP candidates were mainstream "pioneers" of sorts in the use of racialized appeals in the post-Obama era. Did this work? Was this an important mechanism in the movement of white racial extremists from the fringe to the electoral mainstream? The answer to this question is certainly important to our understanding of the TP's success. It is just as important, we believe, for our understanding of Trump's success in 2016. As we argue later in this chapter, Trump was clearly influenced by the electoral success of the TPM and adopted its strategy of highly charged, racialized appeals to outgroup hostility. If this rhetorical strategy contributed to the electoral successes of TP candidates, then there was good reason for Trump to follow suit and make it the cornerstone of his own candidacy.

To examine the extent to which the TPM attracted white racial extremists to electoral politics, we again turn to individual level survey data. Our analysis relies on data from the 2010 Cooperative Congressional Election Study (CCES), which we utilized in Chapter 4 to establish the connection between TPO density and the participation of white racial extremists in the 2010 campaign. The sample consist of white respondents who were confirmed to be registered voters, which leaves us with a sample of approximately 21,000 respondents.

The question we ask is this: Did the racialized rhetoric of TP candidates attract white racial extremists to the TPM? We measured support for the TPM using the same measure of TP support utilized in Chapter 4. This indicator ranges from 1 (strongly oppose) to 5 (strongly support). We measured TP candidate outgroup emphasis by computing for each TP candidate the TD-IDF score for negative rhetoric. For House districts in which a TP candidate ran in the general election, we then assigned the outgroup negativity score for that candidate to all CCES respondents who resided in that candidate's district. In districts where a TP candidate did not run, a value of 0 was assigned. We expect that exposure to negative outgroup rhetoric by

TP candidates will have a positive effect on support for the TP among white racial extremists (defined as in Chapter 4), and that this effect will be significantly stronger than the effect estimated for nonextremists in the voting public.

Figure 5.2 presents the results of a regression model that examines the effect of TP candidate rhetoric on TP favorability for both racial extremists and nonracial extremists. The results are consistent with our expectations regarding the mobilizing effect of TP candidates through the rhetoric of outgroup hostility. For white racial extremists, TP favorability increases with the degree of negative rhetoric by TP candidates, and this relationship is statistically significant (p < .05). Although the slope of the relationship for nonracial conservatives is negative, it is not statistically significant. This provides important confirmation of one of the most important potential mechanisms through which the TPM attracted white racial extremists and white racial conservatives more broadly. And as we eventually show, it was no less successful for Trump in 2016.[18]

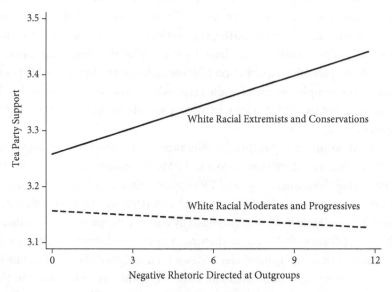

Figure 5.2 The relationship between Tea Party candidate outgroup rhetoric and support for the Tea Party, 2010

Imitating White Nationalist Tropes: Donald Trump and the Rhetoric of Outgroup Hostility

For all its success, the TP was fading by the time the 2016 presidential election campaign commenced. Trump nonetheless was able to make its rhetoric of outgroup hostility the centerpiece of his campaign. At the beginning of Trump's declared presidential candidacy, shock was a common response. Trump was widely dismissed as beyond the pale, not just as unqualified but also as uncouth. He said things that no normal politician would say, and he said them in an unvarnished way. He was ineptly but quite consciously stating the concerns of the base of white nationalist supporters he aspired to build his campaign on. This was obvious from the beginning, when during his campaign announcement in Trump Tower he spoke to a crowd filled with paid audience members placed there to make him look more popular than he was at the time.[19] Trump did not yet have throngs of supporters, but he was working his way up to that with an incendiary speech that energized whites who were glad to see a presidential candidate say the outrageous things he did about Mexicans, Muslims, and others. Trump was like no other on that day and has been so all the days since. For white extremists in particular, it was nothing less than a godsend that there was now a mainstream candidate for the highest office in the land who was saying the kinds of hateful things they had been saying or thinking for a long time. While white extremists had been busy making themselves and their rhetoric more palatable to a broader white audience, Trump was taking their hateful rhetoric and placing it at the center of his presidential campaign.

In Chapter 3 we documented how racialized threat narratives that were prominent among white supremacist groups began to influence more mainstream groups like the TP. Trump was building on this mainstreaming and adapting it to the changing political environment, especially to address anxiety about immigration and terrorism. In mainstreaming white extremist threat narratives about outgroups, Trump was following suit when he came to focus on the three targeted groups of African Americans and the Latinx and Muslim populations as personifying racialized threats.

As a result, Trump commonly invoked the hateful language of the racialized threat narratives that we have associated with extremist groups. At first it was jarring, like his announcement speech, but it became commonplace, especially at his rallies, where he went off script often when he saw how his crowd reacted to his hateful rhetoric. One 2016 campaign speech directed at African Americans was quite noteworthy in this regard. On August 16, 2016, Trump spoke to a largely white audience in a suburb of Lansing, Michigan, but the speech was an appeal to African Americans for their votes. As odd as that setting was for such an appeal for black votes, Trump made the whole pitch much stranger when he went off script to say: "You're living in poverty, your schools are no good, you have no jobs, 58 percent of your youth is unemployed—what the hell do you have to lose"?[20] Trump asked a question of blacks but stared straight at his largely white audience. The rhetoric invoked racial stereotypes for a white audience under the guise of directing a plaintive question to blacks that nonetheless implied they themselves were responsible for high poverty rates, failing schools, and extensive youth unemployment.

Regarding Latinx immigration, Trump constantly lied about the issue using numerous racialized threat narratives. Trump's rally speech on August 31, 2016, in Phoenix, Arizona, began with a painful but misleading litany of murders of white Americans by illegal immigrants, failing to point out that the rate at which illegal immigrants commit violent crimes is below that of U.S. citizens. Then Trump went on to focus on jobs and the failure of Democrats to protect American workers from the effects of illegal immigration:

> While there are many illegal immigrants in our country who are good people, many, many, this doesn't change the fact that most illegal immigrants are lower skilled workers with less education, who compete directly against vulnerable American workers, and that these illegal workers draw much more out from the system than they can ever possibly pay back.
>
> And they're hurting a lot of our people that cannot get jobs under any circumstances.
>
> But these facts are never reported. Instead, the media and my opponent discuss one thing and only one thing, the needs of people living here illegally. In many cases, by the way, they're treated better than our vets.
>
> Not going to happen anymore, folks. November 8th. Not going to happen anymore.

Trump added to his lies about immigration a bit later in his speech when he said:

Hillary Clinton has pledged amnesty in her first 100 days, and her plan will provide Obamacare, Social Security, and Medicare for illegal immigrants, breaking the federal budget.

On top of that she promises uncontrolled, low-skilled immigration that continues to reduce jobs and wages for American workers, and especially for African-American and Hispanic workers within our country. Our citizens.

Most incredibly, because to me this is unbelievable, we have no idea who these people are, where they come from. I always say Trojan Horse. Watch what's going to happen, folks. It's not going to be pretty.

This includes her plan to bring in 620,000 new refugees from Syria and that region over a short period of time. And even yesterday, when you were watching the news, you saw thousands and thousands of people coming in from Syria. What is wrong with our politicians, our leaders if we can call them that. What the hell are we doing?[21]

Trump continued to emphasize throughout the campaign that Clinton was for "open borders" and that that would lead to a deluge of immigrants coming in and taking jobs away from American citizens, killing innocent people, intensifying the drug epidemic, and engaging in more gang violence. The threat to ordinary Americans (read white), Trump insisted, was real, even if his facts were not.

On Muslims, Trump pushed the terrorist threat among other racialized narratives designed to demonize Muslims as a threat to white America. He sometimes had to exploit tragedies unrelated to Muslim immigration to make his hateful point. In early June, after the mass shooting that left forty-nine dead at an Orlando, Florida, gay nightclub, Trump stated:

We need to respond to this attack on America as one united people, with force, purpose, and determination. But the current politically correct response cripples our ability to talk and to think and act clearly. We're not acting clearly. We're not talking clearly. We have problems.

If we don't get tough and if we don't get smart, and fast, we're not going to have our country anymore. There will be nothing, absolutely nothing left.

The killer, whose name I will not use or ever say, was born an Afghan, of Afghan parents, who immigrated to the United States. His father published support for the Afghan Taliban, a regime who murder those who don't share radical views. And they murder plenty. The father even said he was running for president of Afghanistan.

The bottom line is that the only reason the killer was in America in the first place was because we allowed his family to come here. That is a fact and it's a fact we need to talk about.

We have a dysfunctional immigration system which does not permit us to know who we let into our country and it does not permit us to protect our citizens properly.[22]

These are but three examples among many that demonstrate how Trump boldly invoked racialized threat narratives in ways distinctive for a presidential candidate in the post–civil rights era. Trump took the racialized narratives of white extremists and, just as the TP candidates for Congress had done, he mainstreamed those racialized narratives into conventional electoral campaigning. He targeted the three outgroups that whites had come to be most concerned about in the current period; Africans Americans now were joined by the Latinx and Muslim populations as the groups to be demonized as personifying threats to white America. Trump willingly focused on these three groups and repeatedly told outrageous stories about them in order to stoke outgroup hostility among his supporters.

A Systematic Analysis of Trump's Rhetoric

The distinctiveness of Trump's rhetoric regarding outgroups can be systematically documented quantitatively by comparing Trump's use of racialized rhetoric to that of other presidential candidates and political groups. We collected speeches on all presidential candidates from the 2016 presidential campaign, along with speeches by Barack Obama and Mitt Romney in 2012, from the American Presidency Project campaign speech archive housed at the University of California at Santa Barbara. This sample includes 74 speeches from Donald Trump, 85 speeches from Mitt Romney in 2012, 87 speeches from Hillary Clinton, 37 speeches from Barack Obama in 2012, and 109 speeches from the other Republican and Democratic presidential candidates who ran in 2016.[23] While this sample of speeches is not exhaustive, it is representative because candidate speeches tend to be highly repetitive.

We utilized automated content analysis to examine the text of the speeches, using the racial outgroups dictionary summarized in Table 5.1 that we applied to the campaign rhetoric of 2010 House candidates. As with the analysis of the House candidates, we examined rhetoric that we coded as referring to African Americans, Latinx immigrants, and Muslims for four groups of speeches from the 2016 campaign: (1) Donald Trump (n = 74), (2) the other Republican presidential candidates from 2016 (n = 42), (3) Hillary Clinton (n = 88), and (4) the other Democratic candidates from 2016 (n = 75). To add additional perspective, we also added Mitt Romney's campaign speeches from 2012 (n = 88). As done in the analysis of House candidates, we computed the TD-IDF scores for the level of emphasis of positive and negative terms as well as the balance of positive and negative terms (based on the ratio of the TD-IDF scores for the two categories). Our expectation is that Trump was not only the most likely to use outgroup-relevant rhetoric that is negative in tone but also displayed the most negative balance of rhetoric.

Figure 5.3 presents the results of our content analysis of presidential candidate speeches. As was the case in our analysis of House candidates, Democrats (Clinton and the other Democrats in 2016) were always more likely to emphasize the positive or neutral terms than the negative terms. And in all cases, Democrats were far more likely to reflect a positive balance of rhetoric than any of the Republicans. Yet the most important takeaway from Figure 5.3 is not the general distinctiveness of Democrats and Republicans, but the degree to which Trump stands apart from all of the other candidates, even those within his own party.

For each of the three racial outgroups, Trump was far more likely to use negative rhetoric than any of the other candidates. The only group for which a candidate or candidate group came close to matching Trump was Muslims, when the other 2016 Republican candidates reacted to Trump's rise throughout the primaries by ramping up their emphasis on "radical Islamic terrorism." This is not unexpected, as the demonization of Muslims was consistent with the Republican Party's history of taking a hawkish position concerning the War on Terror, both at home and abroad. We also saw some similarity in Muslim-related rhetoric between TP and non-TP candidates. Yet neither Mitt Romney nor the other Republican candidates in 2016 seemed willing to "go there" when it came to African Americans and Latinx immigrants. And in the case of Muslims, both Romney in 2012 and the other Republicans in 2016 actually ended up using neutral terms more frequently than negative terms. Romney and the other Republicans were also more likely

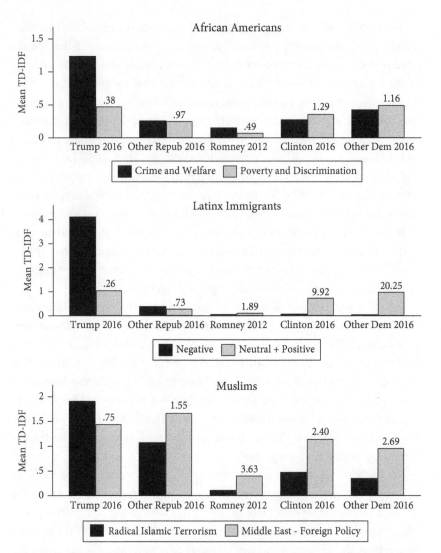

Figure 5.3 Trump's rhetorical emphasis on racial outgroups compared to other candidates and political groups

Note: The bars in each plot present the degree to which presidential candidate speeches utilized negative terms (black) or positive/neutral terms (gray) related to African Americans, Latinx immigrants, or Muslims (see Table 5.1). The value above each gray bar represents the balance of positive/neutral and negative rhetorical emphasis, calculated as the ratio of the TD-IDF score for positive/neutral rhetoric to the TD-IDF score for negative rhetoric.

to use positive rather than negative rhetoric for Latinx immigrants in comparison to Trump. But perhaps the more striking finding for Romney and Trump's 2016 Republican challengers is that they hardly spoke about Latinx immigrants at all (evident from the height of the bars in Figure 5.3). Finally, according to this content analysis Romney more than anybody else looked more like Trump when it came to African Americans; however, this is not too surprising. The emphasis on crime and welfare by Republican nominees has been part of the Republican playbook since Nixon's 1968 campaign.

Thus far, our content analysis has found that Trump was for more likely to use rhetoric that tends to cast racial outgroups in a negative light. Yet simple dictionary analyses such as this are somewhat unsatisfying, in the sense that they simply code the use of these terms and tell us very little about the rhetorical context in which the terms were used. We next present the results of an additional analysis that attempts to provide a more nuanced picture of Trump's rhetoric of outgroup hostility, compared to other recent presidential candidates. The strategy for this analysis is straightforward. We simply extracted the words and phrases that were most likely to co-occur within close proximity to explicit references to the three racial outgroups. For the purpose of this analysis, "close proximity" is defined as occurring within the same sentence. In other words, when using terms explicitly referencing the three racial groups, what other terms were most likely to be used in the same sentence?

To conduct this analysis we specified words that identify the targeted groups as follows:

(1) black, blacks, African = "black"
(2) Muslim, Muslims, Islam, Islamic = "Islam"
(3) immigrant, immigrants, immigration = "immigrants"

We scored the number of times these words were paired with specific racial outgroup terms across all of the speeches and then calculated the results for Trump, the other Republicans in 2016, and the Democrats in 2016. These results are presented in Table 5.2. Regarding the "immigration" rubric, Trump once again stands out. The top co-occurring terms for immigration for Democrats are words like "reform," "comprehensive," "families," "parents," and "citizenship," while for Trump the top co-occurring terms are "illegal," "criminal," "stop," and "border." In this regard, his Republican opponents fall

Table 5.2 Co-occurrence Analysis of Outgroup References for Trump, Democrats, and Republicans

AFRICAN AMERICANS		
DEMOCRATS	REPUBLICANS	TRUMP
WHITE	POVERTY	HISPANIC
WOMEN	SCHOOLS	POVERTY
YOUNG	WHITE	CITIES
NATIVE	RATE	CHILDREN
LATINOS	POOR	COMMUNITY
MEN	LIVE	COMMUNITIES
PERCENT	INCREASED	LIVE
LIVES	RICH	JOB
POLICE	STUDENTS	CRIME
ISLAM	CITIES	SCHOOL
MATTER	PROUD	EDUCATION
COMMUNITY	NUMBER	YOUNG

LATINX IMMIGRANTS		
DEMOCRATS	REPUBLICANS	TRUMP
REFORM	ILLEGAL	ILLEGAL
COMPREHENSIVE	WORKERS	CRIMINAL
FAMILIES	LEGAL	RADICAL
PARENTS	SYSTEM	SECURITY
NATION	NUMBER	STOP
PATH	LAWS	PLAN
GRANDPARENTS	JOBS	TRADE
CITIZENSHIP	WORKER	END
WOMEN	LAW	COUNTRIES
ECONOMY	LABOR	BORDERS
UNDOCUMENTED	RACE	DEPORTED
ISLAM	MILLION	CITIZENS

MUSLIMS		
DEMOCRATS	REPUBLICANS	TRUMP
ISIS	RADICAL	RADICAL
NATIONS	TERRORISM	TERRORISM
GROUND	THREAT	TERRORISTS
BLACK	DEFEAT	IMMIGRATION

Table 5.2 *Continued*

FIGHT	ISIS	ISIS
WOMEN	TERRORISTS	SUPPORT
COALITION	EAST	DEFEAT
TROOPS	FIGHT	POLICY
IMMIGRATION	MIDDLE	PLAN
SUPPORT	STATE	BORDERS
KING	DESTROY	TERRORIST
LATINOS	GROUPS	EAST

Note: For each explicit mention of a racial group, the table contains the top twelve words that occurred most frequently in the same sentence.

somewhere between the Democrats and Trump, with their top co-occurring terms including "illegal" but also "legal," "workers," and "jobs."

The differences are less visible in this analysis for the "Islam" category, with Trump not having co-occurring words that are much different than the other Republicans; however, both Trump and the Republicans were distinct from the Democrats. Regarding Islam, the Republicans and Trump had most frequently co-occurring words like "radical," "terrorism," and "ISIS," while the Democrats' most frequent terms also paired Islam with "ISIS" but never "radical" or "terrorism." We find similar co-occurrences for "black," with the Republicans and Trump most frequently pairing it with poverty and related terms but the Democrats most frequently pairing it with "white," as if to emphasize race relations as opposed to the "black problem" that conservatives are prone to emphasize. For Democrats, talking about blacks was most often in the context of discussing what to do about race relations between blacks and whites. For Republicans and Trump, talking about blacks was more about how to address problems of crime and poverty.

Overall, in combination with the analysis of rhetorical emphasis and tone, the co-occurrence analysis of specific terms provides additional evidence of Trump's distinctiveness in importing what once were extremist racialized threat narratives into presidential campaign discourse. He did so by focusing on the three outgroups of African Americans and the Latinx and Muslim populations that the white racial extremists had come to target and discussing them in a negative tone that emphasized them as personifying threats to whites. Trump talked about the three groups considerably more than other candidates and groups we examined. He talked about them positively as well as negatively, but mostly negatively, at a rate that surpassed the other candidates and groups we examined. While Trump talked more harshly about all three of the targeted outgroups, our findings suggest he was especially aggressive in his language regarding Latinx immigration, even if he also used harsh demonizing rhetoric about African Americans concerning issues of crime and poverty and about Muslims over terrorism.

Trump's Rhetoric Mainstreams White Extremism

The foregoing analysis provides strong empirical evidence that as a presidential candidate Trump helped mainstream the inflammatory rhetoric associated with white outgroup hostility. In doing so, Trump was following his white nationalist base as much as they may have come to take cues from him. The rhetoric they expressed in the years preceding Trump's political ascendancy became his own. He built on that movement and invoked their discourse. And he continued the targeting of African Americans and the Latinx and Muslim populations perhaps even more aggressively as president. Trump had gained the presidency by mainstreaming white nationalist rhetoric, and once he had made his bed he had to lie down with the racists. His mainstreaming of the racialized threat narratives of white extremists had also gotten him a loyal base of support among anxious whites more generally, and he became all the more committed to stoking white anxiety on a regular basis in order to keep his base of supporters agitated on his behalf. Trump mainstreamed white extremism and accentuated the white mainstream's outgroup hostility. If Trump ever wanted to turn away from a politics of outgroup hostility, he never seemed to indicate that, and over time his political fortunes came to rest squarely on remaining committed to a politics of hate. It became irrelevant whether this interloper was himself the racist he seemed to be; now his political fortunes were tied to talking like one. Trump's political predicament therefore now fated him to intensify his mainstreaming of racial threat narratives designed to stoke outgroup hostility. This was his own Faustian bargain, made with the likes of Steve Bannon, the alt-right, and white nationalists more generally. Trump chose to align with them, they with him, and both with the need to feed the monster of white outgroup hostility that they had unleashed on mainstream politics.

We can see now that the 2016 campaign was a watershed for mainstreaming the rhetoric of white hate in the post–civil rights era. The hateful rhetoric of white extremism has since been increasingly mainstreamed into conventional U.S. politics, in no small part due to Trump's willingness to incessantly invoke racialized threat narratives that agitate his base of resentful white supporters. As president Trump continued to emphasize the racialized threat narratives that stoked outgroup hostility toward African Americans and the Latinx and Muslim populations. Trump's authoritarianism and sexism, combined with his racism, helped make him persistently popular with his base of disproportionately older, male supporters, but not with others.[24] The intense appeal to a narrow slice of the mass public over time forced Trump to double down and go back to the well of hate repeatedly. The result was ongoing dissemination of the racialized threat narratives that once largely languished on the web pages of white extremist groups. Mainstreaming racism was pursued as an alternative to diluting a message that could appeal to the mainstream. As a result, more mainstream whites became open to thinking in racialized terms of outgroup hostility, while more fringe white nationalists became more active in mainstream politics. The watershed of the 2016 election marked a point from which it seemed there was no turning back, at least for Trump and perhaps for American politics more generally. The politics of hate seemed something now entirely potent and could not be avoided.

Daryl Johnson, the official who had responsibility for tracking right-wing extremism during the Obama administration, provides a good perspective on which to end this chapter on Trump's role in taking the final steps to mainstream the racialized threat narratives of white nationalists and other extremists. Johnson wrote a controversial report on right-wing extremism in 2009 when he was in the Office of Intelligence and Analysis at the U.S. Department of Homeland Security.[25] The report warned of the threat of white nationalist extremism, but Republicans protested that Johnson was persecuting conservatives. Johnson lost his job, and the Obama administration retracted the report. Ten years on, Johnson says that the threat has only increased and in fact has become more mainstream. Johnson says, "When you have a president mainstreaming your ideas, a president who seems to lend tacit support to you, it gives you a license to misbehave,"[26] "Stochastic terrorism" is the buzz word bloggers use to explain how Trump's rantings end up encouraging some white nationalists to just go off and commit mass murder. In this context, Trump's hammering away at racialized threat narratives does more than mainstream hateful rhetoric; it is an instigation, intended or not, to white terrorist attacks, which have been increasing in frequency during Trump's presidency.[27] Stochastic terrorism might be one horrific result of Trump's hateful rhetoric, but another is the less violent but politically more potent legitimating of white resentment toward outgroups. Mainstreaming hate is never just words; they are fuel being poured on the fire of white resentment, now a thoroughly common practice in contemporary American politics.

6

From Tracking to Trolling to Tribalism

Stoking Outgroup Hostility in a Transformed Media Landscape

As we have shown, the mainstreaming of racism has been facilitated by a confluence of forces and actors, involving changes in both structure and agency. White racial extremism had been fomenting for decades, but it was not mainstreamed in the post–civil rights era until there were changes in the political opportunity structure, instigated by the election of a black president (Barack Obama) who was then countered by the rise of a popular protest movement that proved to be attractive to white racial extremists (i.e., the Tea Party). Only then did white extremists come out of the woodwork and off the sidelines to pursue electoral politics, with a passion not seen in many years. And as we argued in Chapter 5, Donald Trump was essential to this process as a prominent politician who effectively disseminated racialized threat narratives that stoked outgroup hostility.

Yet the mainstreaming of racism via ramping up people's outgroup hostility is not solely the result of changes in structure and agency; it is the result of their dynamic relationship. The changed political opportunity structure created an opening for someone like Trump; however, an additional reason Trump was effective in stoking outgroup hostility was that he was adept at operating in a changed information environment. As we saw in the previous chapter, Trump regularly used explicit appeals to outgroup hostility in his campaign speeches to both reinforce and appeal to white racial consciousness (WRC). In the past such candidates had been unable to gain traction because so many voters were repelled by their racism. Indeed, a large literature in political science has documented this phenomenon; candidates who use explicit racial appeals are soundly rejected by voters.[1] By all accounts, Trump's explicit racist appeals should have doomed his candidacy.[2] In this chapter we argue that one important reason this did not happen is that

Hard White, Richard C. Fording and Sanford F. Schram. Oxford University Press (2020). © Oxford University Press.
DOI: 10.1093/oso/9780197500484.001.0001

Trump's candidacy occurred within a much different information environment, and Trump took full advantage of it.

Today's information environment is skewed toward exacerbating resentments and widening divisions, encouraging people to stay in their silos and only communicate with the like-minded; the internet intensifies political tribalism.[3] Trump is the perfect demagogue for this environment. He has become our first Twitter president. He regularly tweets away with racist abandon in order to keep his white nationalist base with him.[4] He is our first internet president, having won office with an aggressive digital campaign that profiled people based on their internet use and then fed them customized ads tailored to their emotional makeup.[5] He is also our first cable news president. Trump is essentially married to Fox News, the cable TV network that was created two decades ago by Rupert Murdoch and Roger Ailes specifically to propagandize for conservatism.[6] Fox News operates as state TV for Trump, who does not just benefit from Fox's slavish commentary on his political ascendance but evidently relies on Fox News to find out what his own government is doing and then incessantly retweets their often slanted and misleading news reports. He makes policy decisions based on Fox News misinformation, sometimes provided over the phone by Fox News personalities such as Sean Hannity, Lou Dobbs, and Tucker Carlson. Most significant for our purposes is that some of Trump's most racially inflammatory statements, stressed in his speeches at his rallies, are inspired by the propaganda disseminated by Fox News.[7] In other words, there is a new divisive information environment in which Trump has situated himself and which he continues to exploit to ramp up outgroup hostility and keep his base of white supporters agitated and unwavering in their loyalty.

In this chapter we provide evidence of how Trump exploited this closed circle of communication to build and keep a base of supporters. We present empirical evidence of how Trump's approach to campaigning, especially his campaign organization's use of social media, exploited the changed information environment to win the 2016 election by spreading fake news, sowing division, and activating white racial resentment. We further show the critical role Fox News has played in insulating his strongest supporters from other sources of information that would otherwise call out Trump's inflammatory narratives as dishonest and racist. Our conclusion is that Trump effectively exploited today's changing information landscape to pollute public discourse and thereby accelerate the mainstreaming of racism.

From Tracking to Trolling

Tribalism is a real problem in the transformed information environment. People today are becoming increasingly distrustful of information, especially when the source is not associated with their side of the partisan divide.[8] Partisan cable news channels, hate radio, and internet blogs and web pages have helped fuel this politicization of news sources. Prominent among these sources has been the Fox News Channel on cable television, which became Trump's main media ally, working on a daily basis to defend his lies and outrageous statements. Many Fox News officials and onscreen personalities became Trump's personal advisers.[9] Yet the changing media landscape has meant that others could be counted on to pump up Trump's incendiary messaging. The most important outlets were Sinclair Broadcast Group television stations, internet sources like Breitbart News, mainstream radio show hosts such as Rush Limbaugh and Glen Beck, hate radio shows via Clear Channel (now iHeartMedia), and other nodes in this hatemongering "right-wing media ecosystem" dedicated to stirring up support for extreme right-wing and racist politicians and policies.[10] The Trump campaign did not create this environment, but it did take advantage of it. This loosely allied media community helped to intensify the distrust of news sources and accelerate the spread of fake news, especially that focused on stoking outgroup hostility toward African Americans and the Latinx and Muslim populations.

Donald Trump was more than well-suited for this environment. While it is a truism that all politicians lie to garner support, Trump's lying was on an entirely different level. He spewed a constant blizzard of lies that suggested he was willing to say anything to rally people to his side.[11] His campaign rallies featured his giving not so much a speech as a kind of political performance in which his lying was most commonly focused on ginning up hatred in real time among his disenchanted white supporters.[12] Trump improvised his speeches depending on how agitated his audience became in response to his inflammatory rhetoric. In Chapter 5 we showed that his speeches distinctively targeted outgroups much more than his fellow Republican primary opponents. Trump railed against what he called the "fake news" of the mainstream media but actually ran a propagandist campaign himself that used lies about targeted outgroups designed to stoke white hostility. He did this not just at rallies but also via Twitter, his preferred method of communication on social media. Twitter suited him because tweets are short and more often than not exclamatory, without much analysis or factual documentation.

Trump's tweets were almost always fact free, and he especially loved to re-tweet without confirming the claims of other people, including white nationalists who pushed deceitful accusations about outgroups.[13] These lies and fake news were most likely to work with uninformed whites who did not have contact with the targeted outgroups (see Chapter 7).

Trump's incendiary style of campaigning was buttressed by a digital cam-paign that was smartly designed to exploit the transformed media landscape. Trump's digital campaign was headed by Brad Parscale, who has defended the campaign's use of digital profiling to tap into people's emotions and mo-bilize votes for Trump. Parscale highlights that the campaign made it a pri-ority to use social media, Facebook in particular, to mobilize nonvoters in swing states based on emotional appeals tailored to people's digital profiles. In his prominent *PBS Frontline* interview Parscale states:

> I would say we had a few different targets that were very important, and I'd say one was low propensity to turn out Trump voters. You had a lot of Trump people and Trump supporters that maybe only showed up one or two of the last four elections, not because they didn't care about this country—they love it. They're just hardworking middle-class Americans who on that day their kids had basketball camp, or they have to pick three kids up from school; it's like, "I don't have time to get over there." A lot of people live hour to hour, paycheck to paycheck in this country, and some of them struggle just to put food on the table, and sometimes the thought of getting out to vote feels disconnected for them.[14]

He emphasizes that conservative voters were already emotional and that this is why the campaign focused on emotions and could not be held responsible for any fake news that was implicated:

> They're emotional about [the issues]. Maybe they're emotional about them. But to determine an algorithm that takes a conservative value and lump it into an emotion and say "because they're emotional about it means it's wrong" is not right. [Y]ou can't use an algorithm. You can't weed out fake news by emotion.

He insists that it was perfectly normal politics that the campaign's pre-ferred method of targeting people was through customized ads, largely via

Facebook, on the basis of their emotional profile (as established by their internet use):

> All politics are about people and their emotions. I mean, the Trump campaign doesn't do anything any other campaign don't. Yes, do we care about the emotions of the people who vote for us, and we want to see them have a better life? Yeah. I don't—that's an odd statement. You don't think Hillary Clinton wanted to make people feel very excited and hopeful for her? You don't think Obama wanted to bring hope and change? What is hope and change? Those are—I mean, "hope" is a word of emotion, right? That's an emotion, right? That was a key word of his campaign was "hope," right, and that emotion. We ran an extremely minuscule amount of money into persuasion. I would say out of $90 million, less than a million bucks maybe, I mean, into persuasion. . . . Most of our ads money was focused on GOTV [Get Out the Vote], which is getting out our vote, and raising money. The thought process you're saying here is that customize had an effect on persuasion is just not—is false. I don't know if I've proven that you can actually show an ad on Facebook and change someone's mind. I haven't seen data to show that I could do that.

Parscale denies that the Trump campaign's digital operation sought to deceive the nonvoters it targeted in swing states to support Trump and oppose Clinton. Instead, he emphasizes that the Trump effort was a breakthrough in digital campaign operations because it successfully tailored advertisements to individuals based on their internet use. While Obama's digital operation had accelerated the use of the internet in presidential campaigns, the Trump 2016 campaign was both more sophisticated and more troubling.[15] The major distinction is that the Trump campaign profiled people based on their internet use so as to feed them customized ads tailored to their emotional makeup, most often posted on people's own personal Facebook pages. The ads the Trump campaign ran were often what have been called "dark posts," which are invisible to everyone but the targeted individual on whose Facebook timeline they are posted.[16] Dark posts also are not identified by source (something that Facebook now no longer allows given the controversies associated with the Trump operation). The campaign ads were, as Parscale has noted, most often designed to run so "only the people we want to see it, see it."[17]

Posting fabricated, negative dark posts to individuals would amount to a specific form of what people have come to refer to as trolling, in which someone intentionally intends to antagonize or agitate the person being targeted. Parscale disputes that the Trump campaign engaged in trolling in this sense, either to gin up the white vote or to depress the black vote;[18] however, key Cambridge Analytica staffer Brittany Kaiser says they did.[19] All told, Trump's campaign ran 5.9 million customized Facebook ads tailored to pushing people's emotional buttons. By contrast, the Clinton campaign ran a paltry 66,000 Facebook ads (approximately).[20]

The Trump digital campaign has to be declared a success. It seems to have been nothing less than brilliant regarding the focus on mobilizing "low propensity to turnout" Trump voters, especially in swing states. In fact, we show in Chapter 9 that the Trump campaign was successful in mobilizing these voters on the basis of their outgroup hostility. Parscale might want to disassociate the digital campaign from efforts to stoke hate; he instead emphasizes that the digital ads were based on Trump's tweets, as if to suggest they were not controversial.[21] Yet Trump's tweets are often highly incendiary and racist, targeting outgroups. The customized ad tailored to people's digital profiles pushed emotional buttons based on Trump's incendiary tweets about outgroups. It was a successful campaign, but one grounded in preying upon people's worst instincts.

The Trump digital effort becomes even more controversial when we include the fact that it relied on the now-repudiated firm Cambridge Analytica (CA). Cambridge Analytica was tied to Steve Bannon, who at one point also headed Breitbart News and then eventually the Trump campaign. Cambridge Analytica was prominently involved in winning the Brexit vote for England to leave the European Union. Investigations have since shown that its techniques were highly manipulative. It used what it called "psychographics" (as opposed to demographics) to profile people based on their internet use and then systematically tailor misleading information to them, largely via Facebook. Alex Hern (2019) quotes the CA whistle-blower Christopher Wylie:

At a certain point, psychometric targeting moves into the realm of dog-whistle campaigning. Images of walls proved to be really effective in campaigning around immigration, for instance. "Conscientious people like structure, so for them, a solution to immigration should be orderly, and a wall embodied that. You can create messaging that doesn't make sense to some people but makes so much sense to other people. If you show that image, some people wouldn't get that that's about immigration, and others immediately would get that." The actual issues, for Wylie, are simply the "plain white toast" of politics, waiting for the actual flavour to be loaded on. "No one wants plain white toast." The job of the data, he says, is to "learn the particular flavour or spice" that will make that toast appealing. that really as simple as slightly hokey-sounding appeals to love of order, or fear of the other?[22]

After Wylie testified in March 2018 before the British Parliament, CA was revealed to have had a long-standing approach to campaigns that was scurrilous if not criminal; its modus operandi was to use highly deceptive campaign ads designed to deceive particular groups by preying on their emotions.[23] Wylie also testified before the U.S. Senate in May 2018, emphasizing that these techniques were deployed in the CA efforts to assist the Trump campaign.[24] By then an undercover investigation by a television news team in Britain had produced a video that captured CA head Alexander Nix boasting to prospective governmental clients that in fact CA "worked beyond the scenes" to set up political opponents to its clients who could be bribed.[25] It was soon revealed that CA had an established pattern of working on elections in less-developed countries to deceive voters, stoke fear, and suppress opposition turnout. Now the head of the company was recorded promising illegality to go with its questionable campaign tactics. It was a full-service elections firm in the worst possible understanding of that term. In other words, CA did not limit itself to harvesting internet data on millions of people without their consent. It went beyond using the data to deceive people into supporting or opposing various candidates and policies, often seeking to depress the votes of opponents. It engaged in outright criminal activity. Shortly after video surfaced and went viral, Nix was suspended from his own company. Then in May, CA closed its doors. Nonetheless, the CA saga highlights that the Trump campaign was in one way or another associated with some very questionable, technologically innovative, but nonetheless propagandistic microtargeting.[26] This kind of campaigning exploits the transformed media landscape to sow division and amp up resentments. In the case of the Trump campaign, it was outgroup hostility that was inflamed, mobilizing disaffected whites while suppressing the votes of blacks.

Trump's Gaslighting

The Trump internet campaign was a sophisticated social media operation that was ethically suspect if not actually illegal. It was focused on targeting specific forms of misinformation to people who would be predisposed to act accordingly. We should not overlook that the Trump digital operation was therefore first and foremost a propaganda campaign, in the traditional sense of misinformation designed to mislead the public into supporting a candidate, party, or cause. Trump's campaign may be considered pathbreaking; however, its emphasis on propaganda makes it arguably a throwback. Propaganda is designed not to promote democracy but instead to undermine the ideal that an informed public makes the key public decisions as to who should rule over them and on what grounds.[27]

The broader context of politics in the United States also made this approach all the more acceptable. First, campaigns were getting better all the time in using the new means of messaging and targeting. The Obama campaign resulted in books that took the reader inside the "victory lab" to learn how they targeted voters so successfully.[28] Obama's targeting was profoundly less sophisticated than what the Trump people did; but it also was far less focused on identifying whom it could deceive with propagandistic appeals, misinformation, and the like.[29] Second, American politics had for some time endured increasing polarization and growing tribalism.[30] Political adversaries were morphing into enemies. Politics was becoming more like war. In war, propagandizing against the enemy is considered patriotic. Demonizing the other side as not human makes it easier to justify killing them. Politics was becoming more and more like that, if not entirely so, as political divisions widened in the United States and across the globe, especially on issues related to globalization, such as demographic diversification, multiculturalism, and immigration. Under these conditions, people become less open to hearing what the other side has to say. They become increasingly distrustful of information, often only believing factual claims from specific sources. In these times of tribalistic politics, news from particular sources can be more readily dismissed as untrustworthy; it becomes "fake news" even if it is actually factually correct.

Trump clearly sought to take advantage of the transformed media landscape, exploiting division to make his outrageous lies about various public issues seem to be true because dissenters could be dismissed as untrustworthy purveyors of fake news. There were at least two dimensions to this systematic attempt to assert outrageous lies and dismiss criticism as coming from unreliable sources. In all of this Trump was pursuing the same classic propaganda strategy that authoritarians like the Nazis under Adolf Hitler used.[31] The first part of the strategy is to insist your most outrageous lies are true and to never correct them. If these lies can survive criticism, then your whole program is beyond reproach. Trump arguably told more and bigger lies than any major party candidate in the history of presidential campaigns. And he almost never took back any of these lies. Even his five-year insistence that Barack Obama was not born in the United States was finally blamed incorrectly on Hillary Clinton as the source. Trump has continued to lie with increasing frequency as president without losing the support of his base. It is a proven strategy for him.

The lies are believed or not by supporters. Some do not know better; the targeting has identified them as vulnerable to deception. Others know better but cynically support or tolerate the lying because they want the political and policy gains the propaganda campaign gets them. In both cases, the propaganda campaign can go forward, in part because its critics are dismissed as unreliable. Trump, like Hitler and other authoritarian propagandists before him, has consistently railed against the mainstream media as not just partisan or biased but "enemies of the people." There is psychological projection involved in this dimension of the strategy. It is the mainstream media, not the propagandist, who are a threat to democracy; they are the ones undermining democracy with lies, misinformation, and fake news designed to deceive the public. The smearing of the press is important for Trump, as it was for Hitler and other authoritarians seeking unchallenged power. The smearing insulates the big lies of the propaganda campaign from criticism by undermining alternative sources of information. Along the way, facts, science, and even the very idea of truth come under suspicion.

Trump consciously lied and dismissed his critics as the ones who were a threat to democracy. He did this constantly on the campaign trail and has continued doing it as president. It is in this specific way that Trump has been practicing a classic form of propaganda, in that his campaign deflected criticism and projected it back on his opponents, especially those in the mainstream media.[32] Trump was turning the tables when he insulated his base from taking seriously criticisms from the mainstream media by labeling them the "enemies of the people" who reported "fake news." This was classic "gaslighting," where people are led to doubt their criticisms and the sources they relied on. The result was to reduce people's willingness to question

Trump's outrageous claims about not just outgroups but also even basic events and facts like the size of crowds and fundamental political practices like registering people to vote. Trump exploited a transformed media environment to lie about matters large and small, but especially to gin up hostility toward outgroups as his main campaign focus. Nothing was safe from his fog of deception. Along the way, his gaslighting reinforced the lie that not he, but other sources of information like the mainstream media, were the real threat to democracy.

The turning of the tables involved a second side to this gaslighting strategy beyond labeling the mainstream media as purveyors of fake news: disseminating fake news to activate some voters and deactivate others. Trump irresponsibly painted all the mainstream media with the broad brush of "fake news," when they were actually using facts to counter his lies and misstatements. All the while, the Trump campaign used CA and other surrogates to actually spread fake news. It was a classic propaganda strategy to accuse his opponents of committing the wrongs he himself was committing.[33]

Swimming in a Sea of Fake News

Context matters. It is a big reason that Trump's propaganda campaign was not dismissed as the outrageously irresponsible assault on democracy that it was. People were already becoming inured to purveyors of misinformation playing fast and loose with the facts. Fake news was becoming a big business on the internet. People were making money lying about products as well as events. The internet was like an unregulated Wild West of exchange in information. Politics was already being assimilated to these market practices. Political advertising was no different than any other kind of marketing (as Parscale pointed out when asked how a political novice could run such a successful digital campaign). Yet there was more. Politics was becoming more polarized; parties were becoming more tribalistic.[34] More and more questionable practices were acceptable if it meant one's side could win. Consciously spreading lies became more common, as did the proliferation of outrageous conspiracy theories that blamed opponents for just about anything. Rumors about the most outrageous lies often went viral. The Clintons trafficked children, ate babies, and killed Vincent Foster (their one-time appointee and a longtime colleague who committed suicide). Michelle Obama was a man, and Barack Obama of course was a Muslim born in Kenya who was snuck into Hawaii so he could someday claim to be a U.S. citizen when running for the presidency. The Trump campaign rose up in a sea of fake news. His presidency ran on fake news that especially targeted outgroups who were seen as threatening to his white supporters. What made it all different was that Trump did not seek to promote the truth to combat fake news. Instead, he and his operatives sought to weaponize fake news.

There is scant explicit evidence that the fake news spread on Donald Trump's behalf, whether by his own campaign organization, CA, or even the Russians' Internet Research Agency (which was investigated by Special Prosecutor Robert Mueller), actually won the election for Trump. Part of the problem in evaluating this proposition is that Trump's digital campaign in 2016 left few footprints, given that its customized ads tailored to people's digital profiles disappeared from the internet after they were posted and seen.[35] There are no studies that can document the effect of the trolling for Trump on the election. We do not know if, for instance, fake news disseminated by the Trump campaign, CA, and even the Russians either influenced the vote for Trump or suppressed the Clinton vote, though we do know they all tried hard. Yet on the general issue of fake news and its influence on voters, we do have some empirical evidence. A study by Hunt Alcott and Matthew Gentzkow shows that fake news in favor of Trump was shared via social media during the election campaign over thirty million times, which was quadruple the rate for Clinton.[36] Yet Alcott and Gentzkow think television was much more influential than social media in influencing the vote.

Another study, by Richard Gunther, Paul Beck, and Eric Nisbet, gets even closer to producing compelling evidence that fake news helped Trump win the election.[37] They write: "Our analysis leads us to the conclusion that fake news most likely did have a substantial impact on the voting decisions of a strategically important set of voters—those who voted for Barack Obama in 2012." Given that Trump's margin of victory in key battleground states was quite small, Clinton's failure to get all the votes that went to Obama in 2012 was critical in flipping these states and giving Trump a victory in the electoral college. Gunther and his colleagues conducted a YouGov survey with a nationally representative sample of voters that indicated that 77 percent of Obama voters supported Clinton. Approximately "10 percent of the former Obama voters cast ballots for Trump in 2016; 4 percent switched to minor parties; and 8 percent did not vote." They find that belief in fake news was associated with defecting.

To test the effect of fake news on these defectors, the researchers asked respondents about three fake news statements. Two of these were negative statements about Clinton and one was a positive statement involving Trump. All three were widely disseminated through social media and were picked up by the broadcast media as well. The first is the claim that "Hillary Clinton is in very poor health due to a serious illness." Twenty-five percent of all respondents believed that this was "definitely true" or "probably true," as did 12 percent of former Obama supporters.

The second is the statement that "Pope Francis endorsed Donald Trump for president prior to the election." About 10 percent of the national sample and 8 percent of Obama supporters thought this statement was true. The third stated that "during her time as U.S. Secretary of State, Hillary Clinton approved weapon sales to Islamic jihadists, including ISIS." Thirty-five percent of the national sample believed that Clinton had sold weapons to ISIS, as did 20 percent of former Obama voters. Researchers found a strong statistical relationship between belief in these fake news stories and vote choice in the 2016 election by former Obama supporters. Among those who believed none of the three fake news stories, 89 percent cast ballots for Hillary Clinton in 2016; among those who believed one fake news item, this level of electoral support fell to 61 percent; but among those who had voted for Obama in 2012 and believed two or all three of these false assertions, only 17 percent voted for Clinton. These findings hold with appropriate statistical controls. This is not evidence that targeted fake news disseminated by the Trump campaign, CA, or the Russians turned Obama voters away from Clinton. Instead, this analysis provides evidence that regardless of the source, fake news may have done that. The Trump campaign was swimming in a sea of fake news. The point here is that the Trump campaign did not try to go against the tide; instead it went with it. And that tidal wave depressed the vote for Clinton.

What effect did fake news have on Trump supporters? To examine this question we analyzed a December 2016 Ipsos Poll done in collaboration with Buzzfeed that examined people's belief in fake news and their support for Trump. The survey sampled 3,015 people, asking them about their familiarity with the top-performing real and fake news headlines (as posted, commented upon, and shared on Facebook). Respondents were also queried about their sources of political information and their support for Trump in the 2016 presidential election. The fake news headlines were about things that were demonstrably false, like the headline about that fictitious endorsement: "Pope Francis Shocks the World, Endorses Trump, Releases

Statement." The real headlines included the following: "Donald Trump on Refusing Presidential Salary: 'I'm not taking it.'" Consistent with other studies, most people indicated they had never seen the false (aka "fake news") headlines. But depending on the fake headline, between 10 and 25 percent indicated they had seen it. And most of those who said they had seen a headline thought it was accurate. Real news headlines were recognized by 10 to 60 percent of those queried, depending on the headline, and most who had seen a real headline indicated they thought it was accurate.

We calculated a net score for each person indicating the extent to which he or she believed real news compared to fake news by subtracting each respondent's believability score for fake news from the score for real news. Our analyses yielded two important findings concerning voters' susceptibility to fake news. First, we found that relying on Fox News as a major news source had a negative and statistically significant effect on a person's belief that real news, compared to fake news, was accurate. This effect was significant even in multivariate analyses that control for respondent political orientation and demographics (partisanship, age, education, income, gender, employment, region of residence, and race) The magnitude of the Fox effect, compared to the effects of consumption of other news sources, is displayed in Figure 6.1. The only other news source to have a negative effect on believing real news relative to fake news was *Vox*, which interestingly is a decidedly liberal news source on the internet. Nonetheless, Fox News was right up there with *Vox* in having an audience that was more likely to believe fake news (but with a much larger audience compared to *Vox*). People who relied on the *New York Times* for their news, however, had significantly higher net scores indicating belief in real over fake news.

Second, the people who were more likely to believe in fake news were also more likely to support Trump, again even after controlling for respondent partisanship and other demographics. This result is displayed in Figure 6.2. The figure displays the predicted probability that a respondent supported Trump by three categories of believability of fake news: whether the respondent was more likely, equally likely, or less likely to believe fake news over real news. In our analysis we allowed the effect of fake news believability to vary by respondent party identification, coded simply Democrat, Independent, and Republican. The figure indicates that believing fake news over real news was associated with support for Trump for all three party groups, but the effect was particularly decisive for Independents.

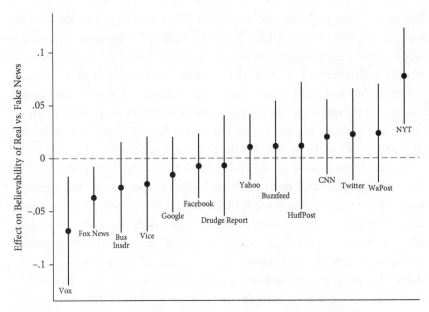

Figure 6.1 Effect of source of news on belief in real vs. fake news, 2016

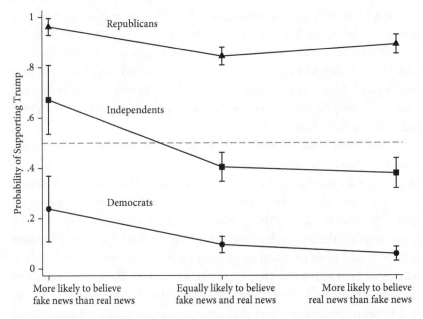

Figure 6.2 Relationship between belief in fake news (vs. real news) and support Trump

Trump therefore seems to have clearly benefited from the fake news that spread so easily in the transformed media landscape, including the insulated environment provided by Fox News. Fox News viewers were especially more likely to believe fake news (even if it was Trump who constantly directed that term of opprobrium at his critics), and people who were more likely to believe fake news were significantly more likely to support Trump. It therefore seems straightforward that Trump supporters were much more likely to rely on Fox News than people who did not support Trump. This fact is confirmed in Figure 6.3, which presents the difference in the average use of various media sources between Trump supporters and people who did not support Trump. For example, for Fox News the figure shows the difference in the mean use of Fox by Trump supporters minus the mean use of Fox by non-Trump supporters. Values that are highly positive indicate Trump supporters are more likely to rely on that source. Negative values mean that non-Trump supporters are more likely to rely on that source than Trump supporters.

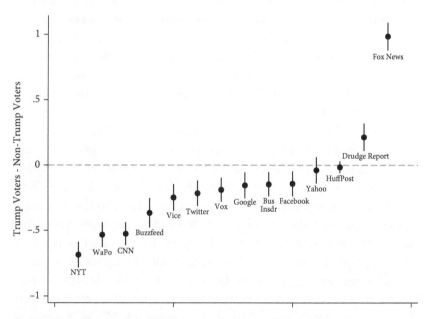

Figure 6.3 Difference between Trump supporters and non-Trump supporters in use of major news sources

Note: The figure presents the difference between Trump supporters and non-Trump supporters in their mean usage of various news media sources. Positive values indicate Trump supporters are more likely to use a source, while negative values indicate that non-Trump supporters are more likely to use a source.

Most of the values for the media sources reported in Figure 6.3 are negative. Only two media sources have positive mean differences: the Drudge Report and Fox News. And Fox News is the highest by far, indicating that it was much more highly preferred as a news source by Trump supporters than by nonsupporters.

Fox News Insulates Outgroup Hostility

It seems then that Fox News helped to solidify Trump's base. Fox News viewers were more likely to believe fake news, and Trump supporters were more likely than other voters to rely on Fox News. Yet even more troubling is the way Fox News has operated in the transformed media landscape to help sustain white outgroup hostility.

We have noted that today's changing media landscape encourages a tribalism or "my-side bias" wherein people listen only to the sources that reinforce their preexisting biases.[38] Fox News has been a major contributor in creating the separate "right-wing media ecosystem" that insulates viewers from countervailing facts.[39] Fox News has been perhaps the most critical among the conservative news sources in helping develop this insulated environment.[40] The result is that viewers come to be cut off from disconfirming information that might lead them to question the biased reporting they are receiving.[41] We have evidence of this insulating effect when it comes to outgroup hostility. There is research that indicates that since 2016, Fox News has devoted significant attention to stories that focus on racial outgroups. For example, McBeth and Lybecker compared Fox News coverage of stories related to sanctuary cities to coverage from Breitbart News, CNN, and the *New York Times*.[42] Between 2015 and 2017 Breitbart (3,150) and Fox (638) ran far more stories on sanctuary cities than did CNN (97) and the *New York Times* (78). Breitbart and Fox were also far more likely to cover stories that reflected racialized political narratives of white victimization by Latinx immigrants, such as the murder of Kate Steinle. There is also considerable evidence that Fox promotes a variety of other types of racialized narratives, often promulgated by white supremacists, through its coverage of African Americans and the criminal justice system[43] and its characterization of Muslims.[44] The focus on racial outgroups appears to have only increased during Trump's presidency. As prominent conservative commentator and former Fox News

contributor Bill Kristol recently observed, the network has undeniably esca-
lated its "whipping up of ethnic resentments, racial resentments, and the
deep state."

There is good reason to suspect that the disproportionate focus on racist
narratives by conservative media outlets such as Fox News has had an important effect on Americans' racial attitudes and in the process, their support for Trump. One possibility is that repeated exposure to these messages
through conservative media has led to an increase in outgroup hostility. For
example, Gil de Zúñiga, Correa, and Valenzuela found that those who are
frequent viewers of Fox News are significantly more likely to exhibit higher
levels of hostility toward Mexican immigrants.[45] More recently, Rene Flores
found that attitudes toward Latinx immigrants worsened after being exposed
to coverage of Trump's campaign speeches.[46] Although all of the major
networks have covered Trump's racist rhetoric, Fox News has devoted considerably more attention to Trump's speeches, and unlike most media outlets,
which have characterized Trump's rhetoric as "racist," Fox has strongly
defended Trump's racist rhetoric as justified.[47]

Yet the expectation that Fox News viewership has led to an increase in
outgroup hostility on the right seems inconsistent with recent trends in racial attitudes. As we showed in Chapter 2, the mean level of outgroup hostility peaked in 2012 for the white public overall and declined somewhat
by the 2016 election. We also failed to see an increase in the population of
racial extremists and conservatives, despite the endless coverage of Trump's
campaign messages throughout 2016. Does this mean that greater exposure to racialized political narratives had no effect? One possibility is that
rather than leading to an increase in outgroup hostility, exposure to conservative news outlets, such as Fox News, did not necessarily persuade many
viewers to become more hostile toward racial outgroups but rather led to a
strengthening and reinforcement of outgroup hostility and a resistance to
counternarratives that Trump's rhetoric was racist. This expectation is entirely consistent with the larger literature on the consequences of selective
consumption of partisan media and represents an important type of media
effect.[48]

To explore this question we examined data from the VOTER Survey, focusing on the panel of white respondents interviewed in 2011 and again
in 2016, a sample of 3,118 respondents. They were asked questions that
enabled us to see if their outgroup hostility toward African Americans,

Latinx immigrants, and Muslims (as measured in Chapter 2) had changed. The data also allow us to measure respondents' degree of Fox News consumption. This measure is based on responses in 2011 to questions asking whether they watched five different Fox News programs: *Fox and Friends, Fox News Sunday, O'Reilly Factor, Hannity,* and *Fox Special Report with Brett Baier.* Fox News consumption was measured as 0 = does not watch any of the shows, 1 = watches one to four of the shows, 2 = watches all five of the shows.

Figure 6.4 presents a series of graphs indicating the level of change for four dependent variables: change in the outgroup hostility index, change in racial resentment scale, change in hostility toward immigrants scale, and change in coldness toward Muslims (feeling thermometer, reverse-scaled). The graphs plot the predicted change in these racial attitudes by Fox News consumption for strong Republican identifiers. The results are based on additional controls for age, education, family income, and religious affiliation and are presented for men and women separately.[49]

We find that Fox News consumption did in fact have a statistically significant effect on outgroup hostility for these Republican respondents. Among male Fox viewers, outgroup hostility actually increased during the 2011–2016 period. Among female Fox viewers there was no statistically significant change. The fact that the effect is stronger for men than for women raises questions about why this is the case. Fox's audience tends to be slightly more male than female; 45 percent of Fox viewers are over fifty-five years of age; and the audience as a whole has an overwhelming, almost all white racial makeup.[50] There is also reason to believe its programming appeals most especially to angry males.[51]

For those who did not watch Fox at all, the level of outgroup hostility actually decreased from 2011 to 2016. These effects are strongest for affect toward Latinx immigrants and Muslims and less for racial resentment. It is not clear why Fox News consumption did not have as great an effect on changes in racial resentment as it did for hostility toward immigrants and Muslims. One possibility is that most whites are very familiar with African Americans as a group and that racial resentment may thus be more resistant to change in the face of new information. In any case, we find strong evidence that Fox News consumption may have helped insulate strong Republican identifiers from effects of the counternarratives presented by other media sources—what Trump termed "fake news"—which depicted Trump's incendiary appeals as factually suspect and even racist. As a result, while these counternarratives

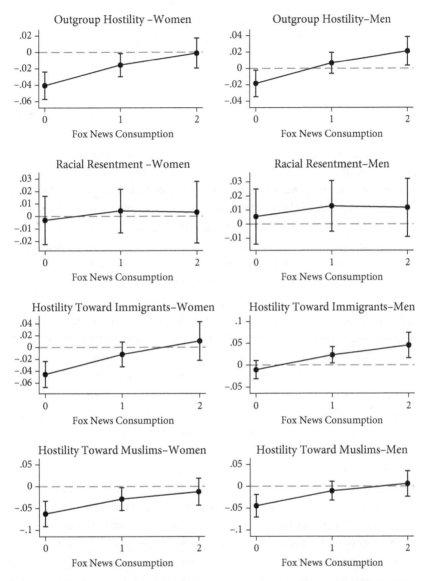

Figure 6.4 Effect of Fox News consumption on the change in outgroup hostility, 2011–2016, by gender

may have contributed to an anti-Trump, pro-outgroup backlash among many Americans, many of Trump's supporters were effectively inoculated from these counternarratives. Fox News provided a safe space for Trump to stoke their outgroup hostility without challenge.

The Transformed Media Landscape Enables the Mainstreaming of Racism

The evidence we present in this chapter makes a strong case that Trump effectively exploited the changing media landscape to stoke outgroup hostility among his supporters. The growing prominence in the mass media of cable news channels like Fox News and the nearly all-pervasive presence of Facebook and Twitter on social media have changed how people get their political information. This transformed information environment encourages division and sows the seeds of resentment as people silo, situating themselves in isolated information bubbles where they only hear from like-minded members of their political tribe and fact-free assertions often go unchallenged. Such a transformed media landscape gives an advantage to the demagogue who uses propaganda. It has proven an ideal environment for a politician like Trump, who centered his campaigning on tapping into people's emotions independent of the facts. Trump's politicking from the start of the 2016 presidential campaign cycle was centered on stoking white people's outgroup hostility. His campaign focused more crucially on mobilizing disaffected nonvoters in swing states to come into the election and vote for him based on specific emotional appeals tailored to their concerns about outgroups. The Trump digital campaign used sophisticated profiling techniques on social media, Facebook in particular, to achieve this specific objective. And with allies in the mass media, like Fox News, Trump could continue to sustain high levels of outgroup hostility among his supporters, especially the less informed ones, even as mainstream media criticism mounted.

As we show in our analyses of survey data in later chapters, Trump's success in mobilizing disaffected whites was in fact concentrated in swing states. The targeting of disaffected, low-information voters who were more vulnerable to emotional appeals that triggered their hostility toward outgroups was to prove crucial in enabling Trump to win the electoral college while losing the popular vote to Clinton. This was to prove critical in how Trump was able to win the election, despite winning approximately the same percentage of votes as Mitt Romney. As we document in discussing Trump's strategy of inflaming outgroup hostility, Trump traded additional votes from disaffected whites in key swing states for fewer votes among racial moderates and racial liberals in Democratic states that he was destined to lose regardless of his strategy.

7

Preying More Than Pandering

The Case of the Low-Information Voters

As the previous chapter suggests, the mainstreaming of racism today has been greatly facilitated by the changed media environment and how it enhances the effectiveness of racialized appeals. Our research reported in the prior chapters provides evidence that the Trump campaign explicitly chose to emphasize mobilizing white voters by inflaming their hostility toward racial outgroups, in particular African Americans, Latinos, and Muslims. In doing this, the Trump campaign was keen to appeal to the bloc of voters it called the "persuadables."[1] Yet as we noted in the previous chapter, Brad Parscale, the head of the Trump digital campaign, emphasized that the focus was not on trying to convince voters to switch allegiance but rather to mobilize disaffected nonvoters and to do so not with facts and reasoning but with emotional appeals. A logical target group would be the less informed, not only because they are more likely to be inactive but because they would be less likely to challenge Trump's fact-free, inflammatory claims about outgroups. In this chapter we document how even before Trump rose in the polls high enough to become the lead candidate for the Republican Party nomination, he already was polling high among the uninformed, who it turns out were also very likely to have high levels of outgroup hostility.

To be sure, Trump's largely all-white coalition had its own kind of diversity. His coalition included many people who were not so much ignorant about political matters as "willfully ignorant" about the dangers of supporting a candidate like Trump. They joined with others to support him in spite of his profligate lying, reliance on outlandish conspiracy theories, constant name-calling, and smearing of his opponents, in addition to his continual efforts to stoke outgroup hostility among his core base of supporters. The willfully ignorant chose not to know or care about the dangers of such a candidate. Many of these voters likely supported Trump for partisan, ideological, and public policy reasons, such as abortion, tax cuts, deregulation, and other standard conservative positions. As difficult as it could be, they would bend

Hard White, Richard C. Fording and Sanford F. Schram. Oxford University Press (2020). © Oxford University Press.
DOI: 10.1093/oso/9780197500484.001.0001

over backwards to tolerate the underside of Trump's candidacy by screening out his willingness to fan the flames of hatred. True believers and cynics joined in their support of Trump.

As his campaign progressed Trump lost support among establishment Republicans, conservative intellectuals, and public policy experts who normally sided with the Republican Party (a.k.a., "Never Trumpers"). It is necessary to consider the possibility that a nontrivial portion of Trump's support came about by replacing lost supporters of the traditional Republican coalition with pro-Trump people who were not previously active in the Republican Party or even electoral politics overall. A significant part of this replacement process concerned swapping out voters by education. In acceleration of an ongoing trend for Republican presidential candidates, Trump lost votes among the educated and gained support among the less educated, what Thomas Edsall has called "the great democratic inversion."[2] Whereas Romney eked out a slight majority of support in 2012 from white college-educated voters, Trump trailed among college-educated whites throughout the 2016 campaign (increasingly so), while winning the non-college-educated vote.

The issue of education points to the larger question of how knowledgeable Trump supporters are about politics and how much interest they have in relying on ideas for making their political choices. One uncomfortable issue that tends to get pushed aside is whether a distinctive number of Trump's white supporters were people we call "low-information voters," that is, people who were largely ignorant about public affairs and politics. Trump presented himself in ways that appealed to people who were uninformed, especially by talking in overly simplistic terms. This further reinforced the idea that he was the candidate of the people who resented being looked down upon. At the same time, Trump's critics often sought to avoid being labeled elitists who look down on ordinary people, thereby justifying the rage Trump supporters have against the establishment. The snobbery problem was highlighted when Hillary Clinton spoke at a New York City LGBTQ gala right after Labor Day at the height of the 2016 campaign. In what became a rallying cry for Trump's base, she said that half of his supporters could be put in a "basket of deplorables."[3] Clinton may have been furtively gesturing to survey research that indicated about half of Trump's supporters harbored high levels of racial resentment, feared Muslim immigrants as potentially violent, and thought President Barack Obama was actually Muslim.[4] Yet it proved to be a tone-deaf statement that reinforced the idea that Clinton was part of what people like Steve Bannon called the "Washington cartel" of political elites who did not understand the problems of ordinary people and had no interest in changing public policies to address them. Clinton in fact subsequently was forced to apologize for her statement.[5] Nonetheless, since Trump's election, further research has indicated that in fact Trump supporters on average were less intelligent than Clinton supporters.[6]

In this chapter we show that all of these distinctive features of Trump's base—in particular their tendency to be less educated and racially resentful and to display relatively low levels of political information—are connected through their mutual relationship with an important yet understudied psychological trait in election research: a low need for cognition.[7] As we have already shown, Trump attracted a disproportionate share of racially resentful voters. Yet those who are susceptible to negative outgroup stereotypes also tend to display a low need for cognition. This combination of traits has not only led Trump's core supporters to be susceptible to Trump's strategy of inducing outgroup-directed anger through rhetoric rooted in distortions and lies but also has played a critical role in Trump's success by further insulating his base from alternative narratives from mainstream media that might otherwise persuade Trump's supporters he is a liar and a racist.

Research on Trump Supporters: Deplorables and Others

Initial research on who supported Trump pointed to a wide variety of factors. Beyond the common factors of party and ideology, there were other issues associated with Trump's distinctive campaign. For instance, there was research indicating that authoritarianism led to support for Trump as a strong leader who would impose needed solutions on society.[8] Other research indicated that sexism played a role among Trump supporters.[9] Yet relatively quickly debate arose about whether race or class was the more important factor in energizing support for Trump.[10] Thomas Edsall's "democratic inversion" suggested that the Trump candidacy acted as a magnet for low-educated voters who swung away from the Democratic to the Republican Party.[11] Yet other research cast doubt on the idea that there were many "Trump Democrats."[12] Still other research indicated that economic anxiety, while pervasive in the general public after the Great Recession, was not as significant a predictor of Trump support as racial and ethnic anxieties.[13] Further, while Trump support drew heavily from selected segments of the white working class, research indicates that Trump supporters had slightly higher incomes than the nation as a whole, and many of his supporters came from the middle and upper classes, as had been the case with prior Republican presidential nominees.[14] In other words, the research generally showed that Trump support stemmed more from social-cultural anxieties, especially associated with antipathy to foreigners and nonwhites.[15]

The issue of whether racial or economic concerns were more significant can be misleading. These factors can be interrelated. Ronald Inglehart and Pippa Norris have presented evidence supporting the argument that objective economic conditions and subjective anxieties about one's economic prospects can heighten anxieties about cultural and demographic changes that lead to opposition to various "outgroups" like Mexican immigrants, Muslim refugees, and resident nonwhites.[16] A related question raised by Inglehart and Norris is the extent to which Trump's support is a continuation of preexisting trends related to the rise of right-wing populist movements in the United States over time and around the developed world:

> The evidence examined in this study suggests that the rise of populist parties reflects, above all, a reaction against a wide range of rapid cultural changes that seem to be eroding the basic values and customs of Western societies. Long-term processes of generational change during the late twentieth century have catalyzed culture wars, for these changes are particularly alarming to the less educated and older groups in these countries. It is not an either/or story, for the two sets of changes may reinforce each other in part—but the evidence in this study suggests that it would be a mistake to attribute the rise of populism directly to economic inequality alone. Psychological factors seem to play a more important role. Older birth cohorts and less-educated groups support populist parties and leaders that defend traditional cultural values and emphasize nationalistic and xenophobia appeals, rejecting outsiders, and upholding old-fashioned gender roles. Populists support charismatic leaders, reflecting a deep mistrust of the "establishment" and mainstream parties who are led nowadays by educated elites with progressive cultural views on moral issues.[17]

While Inglehart and Norris's were more general, their characterization of populist supporters reacting to defend traditional cultural values from the threat of outgroups resonates with prominent understandings emerging in the empirical research about who supported Trump. While many Trump supporters were less educated, they were also not poor and as economically anxious as some research has suggested. Instead, as we show, less informed voters, whether they were less educated or not, were more likely to have high levels of outgroup hostility and to support Trump. Consistent with the Trump campaign's strategy, trolling low-information voters in order to stoke their outgroup hostility was just the right strategy for the pool of voters already open to supporting Trump.

Low-Information Voters, the Need for Cognition, and the Emotional Basis for Trump Support

In 1991 Samuel Popkin coined the term "low-information voters," using it in a way quite different than we do in our analysis. For Popkin, it was an important social science term for understanding how a sizable portion of the electorate relies on limited information to make rational choices in the polling booth.[18] More recently, right-wing, hate-radio commentator Rush Limbaugh used the term in his own way to hammer away at the idea that Democrats won elections by preying upon the lack of knowledge of vulnerable "low-information voters" who do not consider all the relevant news sources (especially his radio show). For Limbaugh, these liberal voters remain in the dark about the major political issues. Limbaugh was no doubt blowing a dog-whistle about nonwhites.[19] Limbaugh essentially inverted Popkin's term for his own political purposes. Conceptually, our use of the term aligns more with Limbaugh's but points in the opposite direction politically. He saw liberals as ignorant. We are focusing here on how a portion of Trump's supporters fell into the category of being uninformed. Actually, available survey data indicate that a larger percentage of African Americans and Latinos score low in political knowledge than whites; nonetheless, a sizable contingent of white survey respondents could be similarly categorized.[20] In any case, it could very well be that Trump disproportionately drew support from whites with relatively low levels of political information.

There is good reason to suspect that people with low levels of political knowledge may also have what social psychologists call a low need for cognition (NFC).[21] John Cacioppo and Richard Petty first introduced the NFC scale in 1982. The purpose of the scale is to provide a deeper understanding of how individuals "derive meaning, adopt positions, and solve problems" in their attempts to make sense of the world.[22] Those with a high need for cognition naturally seek and reflect on information when evaluating stimuli and events in the world. They have a positive attitude toward tasks that require reasoning and effortful thinking and are therefore more likely to invest the time and resources to do so when evaluating complex issues. Those with a low need for cognition, on the other hand, find little reward in the collection and evaluation of new information when it comes to problem solving and the consideration of competing issue positions. They are more likely to rely on cognitive shortcuts, such as "experts" or "celebrities" (such as Donald Trump) for cues. They are also more likely to rely on stereotypes as a cognitive shortcut, and for this reason we expect that low NFC may provide the mechanism linking low-information voters to outgroup hostility. Finally, low NFC voters may compensate by relying more on a need for affect to make their candidate choices. [23] Absent an NFC and possessing a paucity of political knowledge, voters then become vulnerable to relying on how they feel about the prevailing political climate, various political controversies, and other emotional reactions in deciding whom to support. A lack of political knowledge and a de-emphasis on cognitive processing create an opening for emotions rooted in outgroup hostility to predominate in the decision-making process.

Given the foregoing, it is distinctly possible that Trump attracted a relatively high number of low-information, low NFC white voters compared to his opponent, Hillary Clinton, and his predecessor as the Republican nominee, Mitt Romney. Further, given their lack of information and low levels of reliance on cognitive processing, Trump's supporters may therefore have relied more on emotions in their vote decisions, making them more vulnerable to acting on fears and anxieties regarding Mexican immigrants, Muslim refugees, African Americans, and even President Obama. And with emotions replacing facts and reasoning, this base of supporters for Trump may well have been more willing to ignore his deficiencies as a candidate and vulnerable to not being able to challenge his consistent misstatements, untruths, and outright lies. We turn to survey data to examine the extent to which the data support these hypotheses.

An Empirical Test

The data for our analysis come from the 2016 ANES Pilot Study, which was conducted by researchers at Stanford University in late January 2016. The sample consists of twelve hundred adults who were chosen in a manner that provided a nationally representative sample based on age, race, gender, and education. Our primary interest lies in examining the relationship between an individual's NFC, level of political knowledge, outgroup hostility, and support for Trump. The survey allows us to measure all of these variables.

The 2016 ANES contains two items from the NFC scale that have been found to be reliable indicators of NFC. For each item, respondents were asked if they "(1) strongly agree," "(2) agree," "(3) neither agree nor disagree," "(4) disagree," or "(5) strongly disagree" with the following statements:

Item 1: "Thinking is not my idea of fun."
Item 2: "I would rather do something that requires little thought than something that is sure to challenge my thinking abilities."

We summed the scores (1–5) from these two indicators to create a version (albeit limited) of the NFC scale for our analysis of Trump support. The final index ranges from 2 to 10. Since those with high NFC enjoy the process of gathering and evaluating information, we would naturally expect that they display a higher level of political knowledge than those with low NFC. We can test this proposition by constructing a simple political knowledge scale from the following two items asked of all respondents in the 2016 ANES:

Item 1: "For how many years is a United States Senator elected—that is, how many years are there in one full term of office for a U.S. Senator?" [Correct answer: 6]
Item 2: On which of the following does the U.S. federal government currently spend the least?
Foreign aid [Correct answer]
Medicare
National defense
Social Security

For each respondent, our political knowledge scale was constructed by summing the number of correct answers across the two items. Approximately 46 percent of the sample received a score of 0 (both answers incorrect), 33 percent a score of 1, and 22 percent a score of 2 (both answers correct). As we would expect, it turns out that NFC and political knowledge are strongly correlated. Among those who scored a 0 on the political knowledge scale (i.e., answered both questions incorrectly), approximately half scored in the lowest third of the NFC scale, while only 15 percent were classified as high NFC respondents (a score of 9 or 10). In contrast, only 7 percent of those who scored a 2 on the political knowledge scale (i.e., answered both questions correctly) were classified as falling in the lower third of the NFC distribution, while 93 percent scored in the middle or upper third of the NFC distribution. Thus, it seems that this basic disposition, one's need for cognition, has a lot to do with one's level of political knowledge.

What does this have to do with the election? To answer this question, we examined two "feeling thermometer" measures of support, one for Donald Trump and one for Hillary Clinton. As in previous chapters, we limit our analysis to whites. Respondents were asked to rate each candidate on a 0–100 scale, where 100 reflects a "very warm or favorable feeling," 50 indicates "no feeling at all," and 0 reflects a "very cold or unfavorable feeling." We examined the relationship between each of the feeling thermometer scores and the NFC and political knowledge scales. The main results from the regression analyses are displayed in the Figure 7.1. In each graph, the Y-axis represents the predicted feeling thermometer score for Clinton and Trump for each category of NFC (upper panel) and political knowledge (lower panel). These values were generated from regression models which control for partisanship, ideology, education, income, religion, gender, and age. Thus, the differences we see across the levels of NFC and political knowledge in the feeling thermometer scores are not due to these other factors, as they are fixed at the mean value in the sample for all of these calculations. In each case, the pattern is clear. Among the respondents with relatively high NFC and political knowledge, there is practically no preference for one candidate over the other. However, as we move left along the X-axis to those with low NFC and political knowledge, a clear preference for Trump emerges. The advantage for Trump over Clinton is more than twenty points among those with low NFC or low political knowledge. Thus, compared to respondents with a high NFC and high political knowledge, low-information voters seem to exhibit significantly stronger support for Trump over Clinton.

This difference between low-information voters and those we designate as high-information voters is statistically significant for both analyses. Yet is this difference substantively significant? It is difficult to translate the magnitude of this difference in support into votes because the ANES survey was conducted in January, before the parties had chosen their nominees. We can, however, compare the magnitude of the difference in support between low- and high-information voters to the differences seen for other subgroups

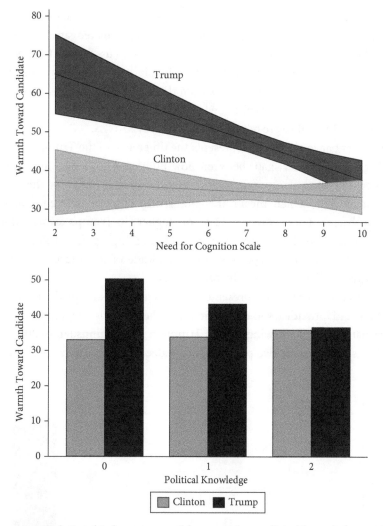

Figure 7.1 Relationship between need for cognition, political knowledge, and support for Donald Trump and Hillary Clinton

that we generally believe to be politically meaningful. In addition, we can compare the difference in the Trump advantage between high- and low-information voters to the equivalent difference in 2012, when Republican nominee Mitt Romney ran against Barack Obama.

To generate these comparisons, we computed a new variable, which we call the "feeling thermometer gap," by subtracting the Clinton feeling

thermometer score from the Trump feeling thermometer score. We then
estimated the relationship between the feeling thermometer gap and our political knowledge scale, as well as the control variables used in the first regression model (partisanship, ideology, education, income, religion, gender, and
age). Figure 7.2 presents the results from this analysis. We limited our analysis to the effects of political knowledge because the items needed to construct the NFC scale were not included in the 2012 ANES.

The first bar in the figure represents the difference in the Trump-Clinton
feeling thermometer gap between low-political-knowledge and high-
political-knowledge respondents in 2016. The specific value for this comparison is 20.2, which means that the Trump-Clinton difference in the
feeling thermometer score is 20.2 points higher (in Trump's favor) among
low-political-knowledge supporters than among high-political-knowledge
voters. This value thus represents the magnitude of the effect of political
knowledge on Trump support in our analysis.

The second comparison presented in the figure is perhaps the most important and provides some insight into whether this tendency of low-
information voters to swing toward Trump in 2016 is unusual. In 2012 the
ANES asked the same two political knowledge questions in its pre-election

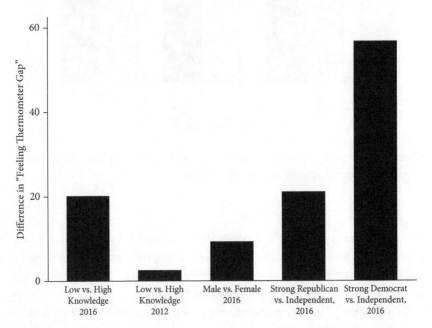

Figure 7.2 Difference in feeling thermometer gap between different subgroups

survey, allowing us to replicate our 2016 analysis using 2012 data. Our analysis of 2012 data yields a very different result. The Romney-Obama feeling thermometer gap was only 2.6 points higher (in Romney's favor) among low-information voters than among high-information voters. This difference was not statistically significant. Thus, not only did low-information voters decidedly favor Trump in 2016, our 2012 results suggest that the concentration of low-information voters in the Trump camp was not based on a general tendency of low-information voters to support the Republican nominee.

The remainder of the figure reports the difference in the feeling thermometer gap across other pairs of subgroups. The Trump-Clinton feeling thermometer gap was 9.3 points higher among men (in Trump's favor) than among women. In other words, being a low-information voter (rather than a high-information voter) is more important in affecting one's relative support for Trump over Clinton than one's gender. Of course this survey was conducted in January, and we know that Trump's support among women declined after that. Nevertheless, the fact that the effect of political knowledge is as good a predictor of Trump support as gender is both surprising and impressive. The final two bars in Figure 7.2 present (1) the effect of moving from Independent to strong Republican on the 7-point partisanship scale, and (2) the effect of moving from strong Democrat to Independent on the same scale. This results in respective increases of 21.1 and 56 points in the Trump-Clinton difference. The effect of moving from Independent to strong Republican is nearly identical to the effect of political knowledge (20.2 points). Yet there is a much larger effect moving from strong Democrat to Independent.

Lack of Information Creates an Opening to Support Trump Based on Fear and Hate

Our data show that low-information voters, defined as those with low NFC or low level of political knowledge, were significantly more likely than high-NFC or high-knowledge respondents to indicate warm feelings toward Trump. These findings raise a final question: What exactly was the mechanism at work in producing the relationship between low NFC/knowledge and Trump support? We conducted an additional analysis of the 2016 ANES data that we believe sheds light on this question.[24]

Based on our analysis of the many attitudinal items in the ANES data, we find that political knowledge exerts its influence on support for Trump through its effect on several more specific attitudes and issue positions related to racial resentment, fear of Muslims, opposition to immigration, and the economy. Using path analysis techniques, we determined that approximately 85 percent of the effect of political knowledge on support for Trump flows through the following six items, each of which is significantly related to support for Trump over Clinton: (1) the belief that Barack Obama is Muslim, (2) the belief that whites are losing jobs to minorities, (3) the belief that Muslims are violent, (4) support for immigration restrictions, (5) "racial resentment" against blacks, and (6) the belief that the economy has worsened over the previous year. The relative magnitude of these indirect effects of political knowledge is displayed in Figure 7.3. The fact that the effect of political knowledge works almost exclusively through these six variables will be unsurprising to many.

These pathways of influence represent some of the most important themes in Trump's campaign speeches throughout the campaign. These findings

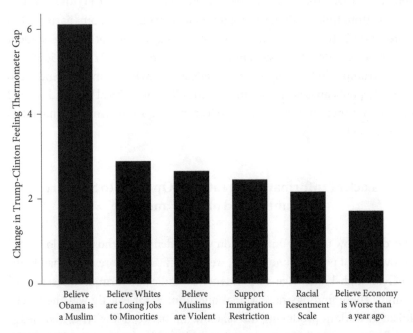

Figure 7.3 Decomposition of effect of political knowledge on Trump-Clinton feeling thermometer gap

also point to how low-information voters were prone to relying on emotional concerns in their evaluation of Trump versus Clinton. The fact that low-information voters were attracted to Trump for these reasons also helps explain why they continue to support him in the face of so many other mistruths. If they are willing to believe that Barack Obama is a Muslim, that Muslims are inherently violent, and that the economy actually worsened during 2015, for example, why wouldn't they believe that the election was "rigged" against Trump? At the same time, many of Trump's supporters refused to express concern about whether Trump colluded with the Russians in trying to influence the election. Was this because they were uninformed or were emotionally committed to his success as president?

It is possible that people's high levels of resentment made them impervious to facts; however, consistent with the overall thesis we have been examining in the prior chapters, it is also possible that their informational and cognitive deficits concerning politics made them vulnerable to having their resentments stoked by a campaign that preyed upon their emotions. Either way, the fact remains that voters with low levels of political information and a low NFC supported Trump on the basis of social and economic anxieties about refugees, immigrants, African Americans, and the presidency of Barack Obama.

Low-Information Voters and the Threat
to Inclusive Democracy

The United States has been called a democratic experiment, something that is a project in the making, as yet not fully realized and the potential of which is contingent upon the willingness of the people to take on the responsibility of being independent thinkers who can practice "eternal vigilance," as Thomas Jefferson emphasized.[25] Writing originally in 1835 for a French readership, Alexis de Tocqueville, an ambivalent and not entirely unfriendly critic of Jeffersonian democracy, insightfully noted upon visiting the United S in the early days of the Republic that a historical push to egalitarianism would engender a preference for democratic government, making the United States reflective of a global trend.[26] He worried that egalitarianism would lead to a devaluation of standards regarding many things, including ideas and critical judgment. The country's laudable impulses to realize a more egalitarian and democratic society risked enabling a populace that would worship the "idol of equality" to the point of becoming vulnerable to the "tyranny of the ma-jority" and by extension a disdain for independent critical thought. Under these conditions, people would dismiss being told by others what to think only to ironically end up following the crowd thoughtlessly.

While the egalitarianism Tocqueville found in U.S. political culture can promote both a healthy anti-elitism and an unhealthy reluctance to think in-dependently, the country's political culture has also included an equally con-tradictory tendency toward an individualism that from another direction can work to reinforce the reluctance to be influenced by the ideas of others. At the turn of the twentieth century, William James added a critical per-spective to the analysis of American political culture by suggesting that the country's tendency to allow for excessive individualism led people at times to practice a "certain blindness" toward others, especially those less fortunate than themselves.[27] Our individualistic culture encouraged people to not care about or feel the need to know about public problems and issues if they did not impinge on their own situations.

In other words, from the founding of the country right through to today, positive and negative strands of our political culture have produced low-information voters who may lack sensitivity toward others different from themselves. In fact, they may be especially vulnerable to being manipulated by a virulent strain of politics, what Richard Hofstadter called "the paranoid style of American politics."[28] The paranoid style was for Hofstadter a recur-rent political practice throughout the modern era across the Western world. It traded in conspiracy theories about how foreign elements were conspiring to take over society. Telescoping a long view of history across centuries and countries, Hofstadter wrote:

This glimpse across a long span of time emboldens me to make the conjecture—it is no more than that—that a mentality disposed to see the world in this way may be a persistent psychic phenomenon, more or less constantly affecting a modest minority of the population. But certain re-ligious traditions, certain social structures and national inheritances, cer-tain historical catastrophes or frustrations may be conducive to the release of such psychic energies, and to situations in which they can more readily be built into mass movements or political parties. In American experience ethnic and religious conflict have plainly been a major focus for militant and suspicious minds of this sort, but class conflicts also can mobilize such energies. Perhaps the central situation conducive to the diffusion of the paranoid tendency is a confrontation of opposed interests which are (or are felt to be) totally irreconcilable, and thus by nature not susceptible to the normal political processes of bargain and compromise. The situation becomes worse when the representatives of a particular social interest—perhaps because of the very unrealistic and unrealizable nature of its demands—are shut out of the political process. Having no access to political bargaining or the making of decisions, they find their original conception that the world of power is sinister and malicious fully confirmed. . . . We are all sufferers from history, but the paranoid is a double sufferer, since he is afflicted not only by the real world, with the rest of us, but by his fantasies as well.[29]

Hofstadter was reminding us that ignorance about history can make people vulnerable to being manipulated into believing the most outlandish conspiracy theories about others plotting to take over the government and everything else.

It is breathtaking to see how in this day and age we have witnessed Donald Trump coming into the White House by practicing the paranoid style of American politics perhaps better than any other politician who has ever appeared on the political scene. He uses conspiracy theories daily to stoke white outgroup hostility and fuel resentments among his core supporters, many of whom possess a low NFC and are without much understanding of the basic workings of the constitutional system. And he has demonstrated his willingness to exploit people's gullibility to sow division even as president. He knows no limits. He uses these stories to try to consolidate his grip on power, such as when he spews outrageous lies about Democrats and their wealthy supporters encouraging illegal immigrants to come to the United States and vote en masse and thereby help Democrats rig our elections. He has toyed with the idea of encouraging his supporters to demand that he get more than two terms as president or even become president for life. His fear-mongering often leads to supporters taking things into their own hands, as in the mass shooting in El Paso, Texas, in August 2019.[30] Yet the conspiracy theories lead to more mundane misbehavior as well, like when some Trump supporters committed voter fraud because they feared Clinton supporters were stealing the election by doing the same.[31] Whether it is mass shootings or election fraud, low-information voters are perhaps the most vulnerable to being manipulated into acting on the basis of their fears and anxieties. They risk becoming pawns of a candidate like Trump, responding to his conspiracy theories irrespective of whether doing so will actually be any good for them individually or for us as a society collectively.

The paradigmatic example of Trump as the quintessential practitioner of the paranoid style of American politics occurred in the final week of the 2016 campaign in a major television advertisement (see https://www.youtube.com/watch?v=vST61W4bGm8#action=share).[32] The ad includes the less than subtle dog-whistle that Hillary Clinton is a pawn of an international elite of global financiers led by Jews like George Soros, the international investment entrepreneur and social justice activist; Janet Yellen, the chair of the U.S. Federal Reserve; and Lloyd Blankfien, the chief executive officer of the prominent Wall Street Firm Goldman Sachs. Trump argues that Clinton and others in Washington take their marching orders from this international cabal keen to ruin the U.S. economy, take away our jobs, and undermine everything that is good about our country. Only by electing him can we prevent this foreign foe from invading us and destroying our way of life. It is disturbing to see this perfect pitch rendition of the typical anti-Semitic conspiracy theory fear-mongering by a presidential candidate. While it is classic paranoid conspiracy theorizing, it is actually unprecedented to have a presidential candidate espousing such theorizing so explicitly and then even more shockingly winning the election.

We should always be keen to remind people that Trump's support comes from a diversity of sources; some of his supporters are more informed than others, and some have given serious thought to supporting his candidacy, while others have relied more on emotion and are responding to his constant barrage of incendiary lies. Some of Trump's supporters are not actually ignorant but instead willfully ignorant, choosing to evince a certain blindness (as James called it) in the name of backing a flawed candidate who speaks to their resentments. Nonetheless, our data indicate that among his supporters there have been low-information voters who, as our analysis has shown, overall were much more likely to prefer him over Clinton and much more than such voters supported Romney in 2012. Trump was very much the candidate of low-information voters (even as he was popular with others as well). His candidacy in no small part thrived on the low information levels and lack of interest in ideas of a significant block of his supporters. As he himself stated at one point after a primary victory: "I love the poorly-educated."[33] And they have loved him back, sometimes with less reasoning than at others, sometimes more based on his emotional appeals than on much reasoning at all, making them all the more vulnerable to manipulation. Love is just as powerful an emotion as hate, and both can be manipulated, especially when people are not relying on sound political knowledge or do not rely very much on ideas for thinking about politics. Love for the candidate and hate toward outgroups combine to make a base of supporters prone to political manipulation.

Our research in this chapter suggests that low-information voters were early on predisposed to vote for Trump; it also suggests that campaign efforts helped seal the deal. Our analysis in the previous chapter shows that the Trump campaign did indeed troll low-information voters on the internet, via social media, by profiling them and then exposing them to fake news stories, conspiracy theories, and lies about his opponent, Hillary Clinton.[34]

In conclusion, the foregoing findings provide empirical evidence for the hypothesis that Trump distinctively attracted unprecedented levels of support from low-information voters. His campaign exploited the void of facts and reasoning among these voters, which made them more vulnerable to relying on emotions, fear, anxiety, hate, and rage about Mexican immigrants, Muslim refugees, and African American citizens, as well as their disdain for the first African American president, Barack Obama. Given their low levels of political knowledge and their low NFC, these voters were more vulnerable to responding to emotional appeals that exploited their fears and anxieties regarding these outgroups. As a result, these Trump supporters were in a position of not wanting or being able to question Trump's seemingly unprecedented campaign of misstatements, untruths, and lies about the targets of his hateful rhetoric.

The implications of our analysis for our political system are worth pondering. In 2012 former Supreme Court associate justice David Souter responded to a question about the importance of civic education from a woman in the audience with remarks that are pertinent to our analysis:

> Franklin was asked by someone I think on the streets of Philadelphia shortly after the 1787 convention adjourned in what kind of government the constitution would give us if it was adopted. Franklin's famous answer was "a republic, if you can keep it." You can't keep it in ignorance. I don't worry about our losing republican government in the United States because I'm afraid of a foreign invasion. I don't worry about it because I think there is going to be a coup by the military as has happened in some other places. What I worry about is that when problems are not addressed, people will not know who is responsible. And when the problems get bad enough, as

they might do, for example, with another serious terrorist attack, as they might do with another financial meltdown, some one person will come forward and say, "Give me total power and I will solve this problem." That is how the Roman republic fell. Augustus became emperor not because he arrested the Roman senate. He became emperor because he promised he would solve problems that were not being solved. . . . That is the way democracy dies. And if something is not done to improve the level of civic knowledge, that is what you should worry about at night.[35]

As we document in the remaining chapters, Trump's surprising victory was in no small part enabled by support from low-information voters. This result is disconcerting in many ways, but perhaps most profoundly for what it says about threats to the country's aspirations to become an inclusive democracy. People who lack information and disdain critical thinking often rely on their feelings and emotions, acting on the basis of fear and anxiety, hate and rage, to demand political change that they often rightly deserve. Yet when elites manipulate those emotions by directing them against convenient scapegoats, they can ride to political victory on the backs of irrational political hysteria. When that happens, their manufactured popular mandate comes with no real democratic accountability, for the people have authorized elites to act on the basis of how their emotions were exploited. Without sufficient political knowledge and a willingness to engage in critical thinking, emotionally manipulated voters lose their ability to enforce democratic accountability. A manipulated populism replaces democracy.[36] As Justice Souter warned, "This is how democracy dies." It is also how the dream of an inclusive democracy dies. Trump feeds his low-information voters messages of hate and anger about African Americans, Muslims, and the Latinx population. He exploits people's information deficits and pushes them to rely on emotional concerns about outgroups. This has proven to be a winning electoral strategy and in the process has helped to mainstream racism in U.S. politics.

8

The Critical Role of Outgroup Hostility
in the 2016 Election

Donald Trump's base strategy in the 2016 election was to intensify outgroup hostility among the white population. Such a presidential campaign, if successful, could not but accelerate the ongoing mainstreaming of racism in America. Further, any candidate who won the highest office in the land through such a campaign would likely feel committed to continuing to stoke the fires of outgroup hostility, just as Trump has done since assuming office (see Chapter 1). Yet the success of such efforts very much depends on whether attitudes toward outgroups were in fact a critical factor in determining whites' vote choices in the 2016 presidential election. In this chapter we present the results of an extensive series of analyses of recent presidential elections to show that this was very much the case. In the process we contribute to our understanding of the 2016 election and Trump's rise to power in several important ways.

First and foremost, we confirm prior research showing that outgroup hostility was the most important predictor of support for Trump in both the primary and general elections. The strength of this effect not only rivaled that of party identification but was far stronger than it had been in 2012 and generally as strong as or stronger than its effect in 2008, when Barack Obama was first elected. Second, we provide evidence that clarifies the relative validity of the two most prominent competing explanations in the elections literature for Trump's unwavering support among the white working class: the role of white racial identity and economic anxiety. We show that the effect of white outgroup attitudes far outweighed the importance of white ingroup attitudes (i.e., white identity) and economic anxiety. This is important because like many self-declared white nationalists, many Trump supporters have insisted that their vote for Trump was not grounded in racism, instead insisting that their support for Trump was based on what they felt was the need for white people to stand up for themselves due to threats to whites' economic status.[1]

Hard White, Richard C. Fording and Sanford F. Schram. Oxford University Press (2020). © Oxford University Press.
DOI: 10.1093/oso/9780197500484.001.0001

The 2016 election was not as much a "white identity" election as it was an outgroup hostility election.[2]

In addition, we show that the 2016 election was not simply a "white backlash" election in the sense that Trump's victory was due to simply an increase in outgroup hostility.[3] Instead, our findings indicate that the unprecedented importance of outgroup hostility in the 2016 election was based on the fact that outgroup hostility not only became more polarized but also became more politicized in a rather specific way: through the unusually strong attraction of racial conservatives and extremists to Donald Trump's campaign. Finally, we conclude by arguing that one of the most important mechanisms connecting outgroup hostility to support for Trump was his ability to generate an unusually large degree of partisan-directed anger and enthusiasm in 2016 among racial extremists and conservatives.

Outgroup Hostility and Candidate Preference in 2016

How exactly were racial attitudes related to vote choice in 2016? We explore this question through an analysis of 2016 survey data from the ANES and VOTER surveys. The dependent variable for our analysis is a dichotomous indicator of vote choice (1 = Trump, 0 = Clinton or other candidate). As we discussed in Chapter 2, a number of studies have found evidence that the component attitudes that comprise our measure of outgroup hostility—racial resentment, hostility toward immigrants and Muslims—had a significant effect on support for Trump in 2016.[4] Therefore we expect that our measure of outgroup hostility will be strongly related to Trump support. We are more interested in how the effect of outgroup hostility fares compared to other explanations offered to account for Trump's support among white voters.

In addition to racial hostility, many analysts have argued that support for Donald Trump in 2016 was driven by the growing importance of white racial identity (WRI) among white voters. Although there is extensive literature on the importance of group identity for understanding the political behavior of racial minorities, far less effort has been devoted to the study of white identity. One important reason for this is that historically, measures of white identity have often been found to be unrelated to political attitudes and behavior.[5] This finding is generally consistent with theories of intergroup relations that suggest group identity should be less salient among dominant groups.[6]

More recently, scholars have revisited the effects of WRI on whites' political behavior and have found that in the post-Obama period, WRI has become far more relevant to understanding whites' political behavior and especially opposition to black candidates in biracial contests.[7] Although 2016 did not feature a black candidate on the ticket, white identity emerged as a significant predictor of Trump support in some post-election analyses, even after controlling for attitudes toward racial and ethnic minority groups and economic evaluations.[8]

Ingroup attitudes have been variously defined and measured within the literature. Our operationalization focuses on the "intragroup ethnocentrism" dimension, which stresses the importance of ingroup "cohesion" and "devotion."[9] Specifically, we rely on a single question available in both the ANES (2012 and 2016) and VOTER (2016) surveys: "How important is being white to your identity?" This measure has been used to measure white identity in several recent studies and has the advantage of being available for both 2012 and 2016 in the ANES, thus allowing us to observe changes in the effects of white identity over time.[10] There are five possible response categories for the white identity item, ranging from "not at all important" to "very important." Based on our theoretical arguments regarding the greater causal proximity of outgroup hostility to political behavior (see Chapter 2), we expect that the effect of outgroup hostility will be significantly stronger than the effect of WRI.

In addition to WRI, one of the most widely accepted explanations for Trump's victory is economic anxiety experienced by the white working class since the 2008 recession.[11] To test the importance of economic anxiety in the 2016 election, we included the standard measures of sociotropic and pocketbook economic pessimism used by election scholars. We also included the modern sexism scale and a social issues scale consisting of items measuring the degree of conservatism on policies toward abortion, same-sex marriage, and transgender rights. Finally, we included standard controls commonly used in studies of voting behavior: party identification, ideology, frequency of church attendance, union status, marital status, education, family income, gender, and age.[12] To facilitate comparisons of effects we rescaled the following variables to range from 0 to 1: outgroup hostility, WRI, modern sexism, and the social issues scale.

The results of our analyses of ANES and VOTER data are displayed in Table 8.1. To save space, we do not report the results for the control variables (but the full results can be found in our online Appendix). The first two columns (Model 1) present results for our preferred specification, which estimates the

Table 8.1 Logistic Regression Results for Effect of Racial Attitudes on Support for Trump

Independent Variables	Model 1 Outgroup Hostility		Model 2 Substitute Individual Group Affect Items	
	ANES	VOTER	ANES	VOTER
White racial identity	0.049	−0.273	0.127	−0.172
	(0.311)	(0.182)	(0.326)	(0.180)
Outgroup hostility	5.482**	4.626**	—	—
	(0.817)	(0.358)		
Sexism scale	2.684**	1.340**	2.725**	1.338**
	(0.709)	(0.275)	(0.775)	(0.284)
Social issues scale	1.435**	1.509**	1.482**	1.371**
	(0.577)	(0.240)	(0.594)	(0.252)
Specific outgroup affect items				
Racial resentment	—	—	2.438**	1.913**
			(0.599)	(0.315)
Immigrant scale	—	—	1.848**	3.484**
			(0.871)	(0.333)
Muslim (FT)	—	—	1.256*	0.750**
			(0.536)	(0.251)
Blacks (FT)	—	—	−0.215	−0.527
			(0.885)	(0.360)
Hispanics (FT)	—	—	0.488	−0.757*
			(1.013)	(0.385)
Asians (FT)	—	—	−0.918	−0.138
			(0.885)	(0.398)
Jews (FT)	—	—	−0.551	−0.738*
			(0.709)	(0.347)
Party identification				
Strong Repub vs. strong Dem	4.508**	5.109**	4.338**	5.029**
	(0.663)	(0.384)	(0.640)	(0.394)
Economic evaluation (national)				
Much better vs. much worse	3.079**	0.167	3.375**	0.217
	(0.782)	(0.176)	(0.887)	(0.180)
Economic evaluation (personal)				
Much better vs. much worse	.760*	1.073**	0.723*	0.958**
	(0.368)	(0.189)	(0.366)	(0.195)

Continued

Table 8.1 *Continued*

Independent Variables	Model 1 Outgroup Hostility		Model 2 Substitute Individual Group Affect Items	
	ANES	VOTER	ANES	VOTER
Education (baseline ≤ H.S.)				
College degree	−0.211	−0.278	−0.205	−0.220
	(0.293)	(0.488)	(0.292)	(0.486)
Graduate degree	−0.286	−0.295	−0.310	−0.177
	(0.310)	(0.460)	(0.321)	(0.464)
Sample size	2,055	5,365	2,045	5,233

Note: The results reported in the table are based on analyses of the ANES 2016 Time Series Study (ANES) and the 2016 Voter Study Group Survey (VOTER). Cell entries are logit coefficients with standard errors in parentheses. In addition to the variables reported in the table, all models also included controls for ideology, church attendance, marital status, union status, family income, age, and gender. The sample for all models consists of white respondents only. The full results are presented in our online Appendix.

$^{*}p < .05$, $^{**}p < .01$

effects of racial attitudes through the inclusion of both our measure of outgroup hostility and the WRI scale. We begin by summarizing the results for the major alternatives to outgroup hostility that have been offered as explanations for Trump's support among white voters. Consistent with recently published research, support for Trump was significantly related to the modern sexism scale,[13] as well as our social issues scale. This was true for both the ANES and VOTER datasets. The effects of economic pessimism were more uneven. For the ANES, only national economic evaluations were significantly related to vote choice, while only personal (pocketbook) evaluations were significant predictors of Trump support in the VOTER data. Somewhat surprisingly, the effect of respondent education level was insignificant in both models, suggesting that our attitudinal variables fully mediate the widely reported strong effect of education seen in bivariate analyses of Trump support.[14]

Next we turn to the effects of racial attitudes. As expected, the coefficient for outgroup hostility is positive and highly significant for both datasets (see columns 1 and 2). Perhaps more interesting is the impressive magnitude of this effect. Indeed, our estimates for 2016 suggest that the effect of outgroup hostility was substantively larger than the effects of any of the other independent variables and actually comparable to the effect of party identification, long considered the major factor in explaining vote choice in presidential elections. This is clearly evident from the coefficient values, since the continuous variables have been rescaled to range from 0 to 1. Yet to provide a more substantively meaningful interpretation, we computed the discrete change in the predicted probability of Trump support, given an increase in each variable from its minimum to maximum value. An increase of this magnitude in outgroup hostility is associated with an increase of .87 (ANES) and .79 (VOTER) in the probability of a vote for Trump compared to another candidate. This was comparable to the effect of party identification, for which an increase from strong Democrat to strong Republican is predicted to result in an increase of .81 (ANES) and .83 (VOTER) in the probability of a Trump vote. Clearly, outgroup hostility had an important effect on voter decisions in 2016.

In contrast to the strong effects of outgroup hostility on support for Trump, WRI had no direct effect on vote choice in 2016. This result is consistent across a variety of different indicators of WRI available in the 2016 ANES, including indicators of whites' perception of discrimination against whites used in the study of the 2016 election by Sides, Tesler, and Vavreck;[15] an index of racial attitudes employed by Jardina in her study of white identity;[16] and the feeling thermometer score measuring "warmth" toward "whites."[17] The major reason for the difference between our results and the findings of these other studies in the elections literature appears to be that these studies fail to control for hostility toward all three racial outgroups that comprise our outgroup hostility scale, as well as the failure of these studies to control for sexism and attitudes toward LGBT people—what we might term "social" outgroups. Nevertheless, it is still possible that even though WRI does not exert a direct effect on vote choice, it affects vote choice indirectly through its impact on outgroup hostility (as suggested by our theoretical framework, presented in Chapter 2). We return to this point later.

Additional Tests of the Effect of Outgroup Hostility in 2016

We subjected our analyses to two robustness tests. First, we might wonder if the results for outgroup hostility are weaker when the ethnocentrism scale developed by Kinder and Kam is included in the model.[18] Our general position is that it is not necessary or even appropriate to include both measures in the same model because both are designed to model the same theoretical process: the effects of ingroup and outgroup attitudes on vote choice. In Chapter 2, however, we argued that the Kinder and Kam ethnocentrism scale is now outdated because it includes Asians as an outgroup but not Muslims and therefore does not adequately represent the state of racial attitudes in contemporary American politics. Including this indicator in our analysis of vote choice in 2016 thus provides a direct test of this argument. As we report in our online appendix, the effect of the ethnocentrism scale is insignificant and its addition to the model makes no difference in our results for outgroup hostility.

Second, although outgroup hostility was shown to have a strong effect on Trump support, due to the composite nature of this measure one may legitimately question whether this effect is driven by hostility toward all three of the targeted outgroups or if attitudes toward one or two outgroups are driving the results. We tested this possibility by estimating a model that removes our measure of outgroup hostility and instead includes attitudes toward specific (single) outgroups. Specifically, we included the three components of our outgroup hostility scale (racial resentment, hostility toward immigrants, and hostility toward Muslims), the individual ethnocentrism scale items (feeling thermometer scores for Asians, blacks, and Hispanics, reverse-scaled to indicate coldness toward each group), a feeling thermometer score for Jews, and the WRI scale. The results of this model, which includes the same control variables as Models 1 and 2, are presented as Model 2 in Table 8.1. Consistent with the results for Model 2, none of the feeling thermometer items used in the ethnocentrism scale (for blacks, Hispanics, or Asians) had a significant effect on Trump support. The same is true for hostility toward Jews and the measure of white identity. Yet all three items that comprise the outgroup hostility scale had a positive and significant effect on support for Trump.

Trump and Outgroup Hostility Revisited: Candidate versus Party Effects

The results presented thus far are consistent with our argument that the effect of outgroup hostility in 2016 was attributable to the polarizing effect of Donald Trump. Yet it is not possible from these results to distinguish the unique effects of Trump the candidate from the effects of Trump the Republican nominee. In other words, is the effect of outgroup hostility on the 2016 vote choice due specifically to what Trump's candidacy represented and his targeting these outgroups, or is it more the result of Trump just being the nominee of a Republican Party that had spent eight years railing against the first nonwhite president, Barack Obama. It is possible that the racial polarization underlying voters' decisions in 2016 was simply another example of the "spillover of racialization" that began with the election of Obama in 2008. If this is the case, then the strong effect of outgroup hostility on support for Trump might simply have been a coincidence. That is, the same effect might have been seen for virtually any Republican running against a candidate like Clinton, who was effectively framed as Obama's handpicked successor. We can easily test this possibility by comparing the relationship between outgroup hostility and support for Trump to its effect on support for his primary challengers prior to the completion of the nomination process.

As we reviewed in Chapter 7, in January 2016 the ANES conducted a pilot study utilizing a national sample, similar to the ANES Time Series Studies. Nearly all of the same items exist in the 2016 pilot, allowing us to largely replicate our analyses presented in Table 8.1. Since the survey was conducted just prior to the primaries, we do not have a measure of vote choice to use as the dependent variable. Instead, we rely on feeling thermometer scores indicating how warmly or coldly respondents felt toward all of the major candidates in the primary. The items used to construct our measures of outgroup hostility and WRI are, however, identical to those used for our analyses of the general election. Finally, as there was no item included in the survey to measure pocketbook evaluations, we included an item measuring prospective evaluations of the economy (over the next twelve months) in addition to the standard retrospective evaluation item.[19] Both these prospective and retrospective economic items are scaled such that higher values indicate greater pessimism.

The results of our analyses are presented in Table 8.2 for the key explanatory variables. Similar to previous analyses, each independent variable has been rescaled to range from 0 to 1 so that the coefficients presented in the table represent the expected change in candidate warmth, given an increase from the minimum to maximum value of each independent variable. All models include a full set of control variables similar to those included in the analyses of the general election in Table 8.1. The results for outgroup hostility clearly indicate that the unusually strong effect of outgroup hostility in 2016 was due to Trump and not a preference for just any Republican candidate. Outgroup hostility had a statistically significant effect on support for just two Republican candidates, Trump and Ted Cruz. Yet the effect for Trump was four times stronger than the effect seen for Cruz and more than twice as large as the effect of party identification.

Table 8.2 Regression Results for the Effect of Selected Explanatory Variables on Candidate Warmth During the 2016 Primary Elections

Candidate	Outgroup Hostility	White Identity	Economic Evaluation (Past)	Economic Evaluation (Future)	Party ID
Trump	64.16**	3.106	6.116	2.566	29.15**
Cruz	16.50*	−4.659	0.747	3.347	29.01**
Bush	3.388	−1.003	−10.23	−1.095	31.48**
Rubio	10.18	−2.892	−2.180	3.456	33.75**
Carson	9.932	−10.76**	3.812	2.362	23.05**
Fiorina	13.64*	−6.150*	−3.626	1.242	24.10**

Note: The results are based on analyses of data from the 2016 ANES Pilot Study. The cell entries contain the effect of each column variable on the candidate-specific feeling thermometer score (0–100). Each independent variable has been rescaled to range from 0 to 1 so that the coefficient represents the expected change in candidate warmth given an increase from the minimum to the maximum value of the independent variable. The analysis was estimated using OLS regression, for white respondents only, controlling for respondent ideology, family income, age, gender, marital status, church attendance, and feeling thermometer items for "feminists" and LGBT people. Sample sizes ranged from 838 (Fiorina) to 857 (Trump). The full results are presented in our online Appendix.

* $p < 0.05$ ** $p < 0.01$.

The effect of WRI—measured using the standard indicator "How important is being white to your identity?"—was once again unrelated to support for Trump. This provides further support for our general results, suggesting that ingroup affect was far less important than outgroup hostility in 2016 in generating support for Trump. However, WRI did have a negative, statistically significant effect on warmth toward Carson and Fiorina, the only two Republican candidates who were not white males. Finally, the effects of economic pessimism were insignificant for all of the Republican candidates. This suggests that the effects of economic attitudes in our models of vote choice were likely being driven by evaluations of the incumbent (Democratic) party.

White Identity as a "Platform for Hate"

Despite the insignificance of WRI in our vote choice analyses, it would be premature to conclude that white identity played no role in 2016. Indeed, our theoretical framework suggests that white identity played an important role in the formation of white racial consciousness (WRC), which we argue is the catalyst for the production of outgroup hostility and the associated emotions that resulted in the political activation of white racial conservatives and extremists. As discussed in Chapter 2, we should expect that the effect of WRI is "psychologically primary," as Allport argued,[20] and that it has an indirect effect on voter behavior through its relationship with outgroup hostility. We can test this hypothesis directly by estimating a path model, which allows the estimation of the indirect effects of WRI on support for Trump, as mediated through outgroup hostility.

The primary dependent variable for our path model is the difference in the feeling thermometer scores for Trump and Clinton, scaled as a measure of net warmth for Trump.[21] Our path model includes four additional endogenous variables: party identification, outgroup hostility, the modern sexism scale, and the social issues scale (each of which we have reported as having an effect on supporting Trump over Clinton). As with any cross-sectional model, we had to make several assumptions about causal direction. First, we assume that party identification is endogenous to racial attitudes, sexism, and social issues.[22] Second, we assume that ideology is strictly exogenous and largely serves as a cause of racial attitudes, sexism, and social issue positions.[23] And third, we allow for the possibility that WRI affects sexism and social issue positions, in addition to outgroup hostility. This may be plausible if the boundaries of white identity are defined by a more restrictive white Anglo Protestant identity that prioritizes traditional Christian, patriarchal values. This is consistent with our analyses of white supremacist issue statements in Chapter 3 and may also be true for the broader population of white racial conservatives and extremists. As such, "white" identity may be a manifestation of a broader "dominant group" identity,[24] and as a result, strong white identifiers might respond negatively to threats to the dominant group status that originate from feminists and LGBT people, in addition to racial outgroups. There are good reasons to think this type of dominant group identity was relevant in making the vote choice between Trump and Clinton in 2016 but that its effects were exerted indirectly through greater hostility toward racial outgroups, feminists, and LGBT people.

The full results of our path analyses for both the ANES and VOTER samples are presented in our online Appendix. However, Figure 8.1 displays a path diagram reflecting the most important results, estimated using the ANES data.[25] Consistent with our initial analyses, which estimated only direct effects (Table 8.1), our path analyses confirmed the finding that WRI had no direct impact on net warmth toward Trump (nor did it have a direct effect

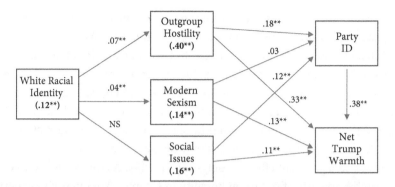

Figure 8.1 Path diagram of direct and indirect effects of white racial identity and outgroup hostility on net warmth for Trump (2016)

Note: The path model represented here was estimated by maximum likelihood, using the SEM procedure in Stata 15. Path coefficients are unstandardized regression coefficients. Total effects are reported (in bold) for each variable for which significant direct and indirect effects were estimated. In addition to the variables illustrated in the figure, the model also included the following exogenous variables: authoritarianism, ideology, national and personal economic evaluations, education level, family income, church attendance, marital status, age, and gender. In addition to the paths shown, the model also includes estimated paths for correlation among the error terms for outgroup hostility, modern sexism, and social issues scale. The sample consists of white respondents from the 2016 ANES Time Series Study. The full results are presented in the online Appendix. LR test of the estimated model vs. saturated: chi2(6) = 5.23, Prob > chi2 = 0.5152.

$^*p < .05, ^{**}p < .01, NS = p > .05$

on party identification). Therefore, these paths are omitted from the path diagram. Yet as reflected in Figure 8.1, WRI had a significant effect on outgroup hostility, sexism (but not social issue positions). Thus, while WRI may have not directly influenced the 2016 vote choice, it seems to have played an important role in the activation of outgroup hostility, as well as of attitudes that might be interpreted as representing other types of threats to white (male) supremacy.

Outgroup Hostility and Economic Anxiety

In our initial analyses presented in Table 8.1 we did not find strong evidence, as others have posited,[26] that economic anxiety was an important factor in predicting support for Trump, especially compared to the effect of outgroup hostility. Yet, much like white racial identity, it is possible that economic anxiety had important indirect effects on vote choice in 2016 via its effect on accentuating outgroup hostility. We again turn to path analysis to access the direct and indirect effects of economic anxiety (as measured by the personal and national economic evaluations of respondents in the ANES).

Detailed results for our path model to tease out the direct and indirect effects of economic anxiety are available in our online appendix. To summarize, we find that economic anxiety—as measured by both a voter's evaluation of their personal economic situation as well as their evaluation of the state of the national economy—did in fact have significant indirect effects on vote choice due to the fact that both measures of economic anxiety had a positive and significant effect on outgroup hostility. As we first noted in our descriptive analysis of outgroup hostility in Chapter 2, whites who experienced high levels of economic pessimism were significantly more likely to reflect higher than average levels of outgroup hostility, even after controlling for the standard demographic indicators, including education and income. This suggests that the debate concerning which was more important—economic or outgroup hostility—has been misguided to some extent. These two explanations, which have often been framed as alternative explanations, are simply telling a different part of the same story. Nevertheless, the combined direct and indirect effects of both personal and national economic evaluations on vote choice were still significantly weaker than the total effect of outgroup hostility. Further analysis indicates that these combined effects of economic anxiety were also no larger than their effects in prior presidential elections, 2004–2012. Therefore, even though we find that economic anxiety had some role in affecting the 2016 presidential vote choice, its effects cannot logically account for the distinctive, racially charged nature of the 2016 election.

Outgroup Hostility and the 2016 Election in Historical Perspective

Thus far we have found that outgroup hostility had a substantively significant, positive effect on support for Trump in 2016. And as we demonstrated in Chapter 5, Trump was unique in his use of inflammatory, racialized rhetoric during his campaign. Yet is this what caused outgroup hostility to have such a strong effect on vote choice in 2016? We have already provided some evidence to address this question by showing that outgroup hostility had a much stronger effect on support for Donald Trump than it did for any other Republican presidential candidate during the primaries. However, our theoretical arguments concerning Trump's role in the mainstreaming of racism would also predict that the effect of outgroup hostility on vote choice in 2016 was significantly greater than its effect on vote choice in the elections leading up to 2016.

Several studies have found that racial attitudes have come to play a more important role in vote choice in presidential elections since Obama's candidacy in 2008.[27] Yet with the absence of Obama on the ticket in 2016, one might expect racial attitudes to play less of a role, all else being equal. Certainly it would be difficult to explain why the effect of outgroup hostility would increase in 2016 if it were not for Trump's racialized campaign themes.

To provide this historical perspective we estimated a model of candidate preference for three recent presidential elections—2008, 2012, and 2016—using ANES data. We estimated models for vote choice as well as for candidate feeling thermometer difference scores (Republican candidate warmth minus Democratic candidate warmth). Unfortunately we cannot exactly replicate the model specification reported in Table 8.1 because the modern sexism scale was not available in 2008 and the transgender rights item for the social issues scale was not available in both 2008 and 2012. As a substitute for the social issues scale we include the feeling thermometer score for Christian fundamentalists. In place of the modern sexism scale we rely on the feeling thermometer score for feminists. Each of these substitutes is strongly correlated with the 2016 variable it is replacing ($r = .55$ and $.56$, respectively). The results of our analyses for 2008–2016 are presented in Table 8.3. As can be seen by comparing the coefficient for outgroup hostility in 2016 in this revised model to the coefficient reported in Table 8.1, this alteration to the model specification made no difference in the estimated effect of outgroup hostility.

For vote choice, we find that outgroup hostility had a positive and highly significant effect on support for the Republican candidate in all three elections. More important, consistent with the backlash narrative, the effect of outgroup hostility on vote choice was larger in 2016 than it was for either of the two elections won by Obama. We see a similar pattern of effects when the dependent variable is net Republican warmth. Indeed, for the net warmth models, the effect of outgroup hostility in 2016 was more than twice as large as the 2012 effect. For both dependent variables, the effect of outgroup hostility in 2008 was considerably larger than it was in 2012, but the 2008 effect still falls short of the 2016 value. It is likely that Obama's association with Hillary Clinton continued to influence the salience of racial attitudes in 2016;

Table 8.3 Regression Results for Effect of Outgroup Hostility on Republican Candidate Support in the General Election, 2008–2016

Independent Variables	DV = Vote for Republican (Logit)			DV = Net Republican Warmth (OLS)		
	2008	2012	2016	2008	2012	2016
Outgroup hostility	4.610**	3.538**	6.084**	0.306**	0.121**	0.352**
	(1.009)	(0.769)	(0.834)	(0.0359)	(0.0276)	(0.0296)
Christian fundamentalists FT	1.681**	2.422**	2.515**	0.110**	0.134**	0.114**
	(0.641)	(0.540)	(0.450)	(0.0253)	(0.0171)	(0.0159)
Feminists FT (hostility)	0.597	0.139	1.552**	0.0400	0.0789**	0.127**
	(0.712)	(0.565)	(0.568)	(0.0284)	(0.0203)	(0.0192)
Party identification						
Strong Repub vs. strong Dem	4.468**	6.131**	4.953**	0.319**	0.337**	0.332**
	(0.664)	(0.586)	(0.613)	(0.0243)	(0.0181)	(0.0194)
Ideological identification						
Ext Conservative vs. ext Liberal	2.127	0.773	2.421	0.133**	0.128**	0.0916**
	(1.630)	(1.191)	(1.507)	(0.0506)	(0.0308)	(0.0271)
Economic evaluation (national)						
Much better vs. much worse	1.570	4.242**	3.567**	-0.0993	0.139**	0.157**
	(1.052)	(0.864)	(0.836)	(0.0768)	(0.0271)	(0.0222)
Economic evaluation (personal)						
Much better vs. much worse	-0.590	-0.688	0.758	-0.00726	0.0226	0.0287
	(0.568)	(0.741)	(0.695)	(0.0193)	(0.0208)	(0.0213)

Education (baseline = H.S. or <)

College degree	-0.131	-0.113	-0.0322	0.00634	0.0151*	-0.00988
	(0.329)	(0.257)	(0.244)	(0.0132)	(0.00738)	(0.00820)
Graduate degree	0.109	-0.146	-0.396	0.00253	0.0239*	-0.0149
	(0.518)	(0.364)	(0.293)	(0.0155)	(0.0103)	(0.00899)
Observations	696	2,341	1,610	859	2,827	2,039

Note: Cell entries are logit coefficients (for vote choice) and OLS slope coefficients (for net Republican warmth), with standard errors in parentheses. In addition to the variables reported in the table, all models also included controls for ideology, church attendance, marital status, union status, family income, age, and gender. The sample for all models consists of white respondents only. The full results are presented in our online Appendix.

*p < .05, **p < .01

however, it is difficult to explain why the effect of outgroup hostility would be larger in 2016 if it were not at least partly due to the presence of Trump.

Understanding the Politicization of Outgroup Hostility in 2016

Thus far we have shown that outgroup hostility had an extremely strong effect on vote choice in 2016. Yet can we characterize this as a white backlash, and if so, how did this backlash occur? In Chapter 2 we presented evidence that helps us assess the validity of the most straightforward prediction of the backlash narrative: that Trump's rhetoric led to an increase in the level of outgroup hostility compared to previous years. We saw that between 2012 and 2016 the level of outgroup hostility actually decreased. Figure 8.2 provides further evidence of this decline in outgroup hostility by examining the trends for the three major partisan subgroups: Democrats, Independents, and Republicans. The figure indicates that outgroup hostility increased among Republicans and Independents between 2004 and 2012, while among Democrats outgroup hostility remained stable. But between 2012 and 2016 outgroup hostility decreased across all three partisan subgroups. The magnitude of the decrease was smallest among Republicans, and as we saw in Chapter 6, it appears that among some subgroups (male, Fox News viewers) outgroup hostility may have actually increased. Yet these trends do not support the conclusion that Trump's campaign led to an increase in outgroup hostility, broadly speaking, even among strong Republicans.

One limitation of examining the mean level of outgroup hostility is that the mean is only capable of capturing net change in the variable of interest. A more informative picture emerges when we examine *the distribution of outgroup hostility* across the three presidential elections. This is presented in Figure 8.3. We can now see that the increase in mean outgroup hostility in 2012 was largely driven by an increase in the number of racial conservatives in the right side of the distribution. The decrease in mean outgroup hostility seen in 2016 was mostly due to a significant increase in warmth toward racial outgroups among racial liberals in the left tail of the distribution. This clearly shows that recent trends in outgroup hostility among whites are more aptly characterized as polarization rather than backlash.

If outgroup hostility did not increase in 2016, then it seems that to the extent that a white backlash helped propel Trump to victory, it must have come

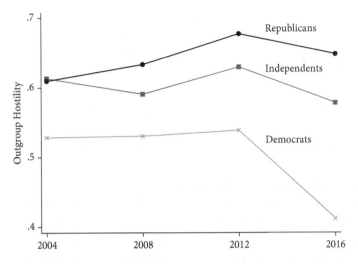

Figure 8.2 Trends in outgroup hostility 2004–2016, by party identification

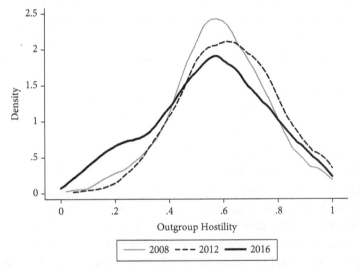

Figure 8.3 Polarization of outgroup hostility, 2008–2016

in the form of a greater degree of partisan sorting on outgroup hostility, compared to prior elections. Yet this sorting could take two different forms, and only one of these processes is consistent with a racially conservative backlash. First, the backlash narrative would suggest that more racial extremists and conservatives voted for the Republican candidate in 2016 than in previous years because of Trump's explicit racial messaging. Sorting, however, could also be achieved by a greater share of racial progressives casting their votes for the Democratic candidate, perhaps because of their rejection of Trump's racist rhetoric. This type of reaction would be consistent with the thesis by Tali Mendelberg[28] and others[29] that while dog-whistling might be tolerated, explicit race-baiting is rejected by many voters. Since either sorting process could lead to the observed increase in the effect of outgroup hostility in 2016, we must turn to a more nuanced analysis to help determine the relative importance of each form of sorting in 2016.

To accomplish this task we re-estimated the effect of outgroup hostility on net Republican candidate warmth for the 2008, 2012, and 2016 elections. Rather than assume linearity of the effect of outgroup hostility, we estimated these models using a semiparametric estimation method that places no restriction on the functional form of the relationship between outgroup hostility and candidate support (but assumes linearity for the effects of all other independent variables).[30] Importantly, the nonlinear specification allows us to determine whether the stronger effect of outgroup hostility in 2016 was due to an especially positive reaction to Trump among racial conservatives, a particularly positive reaction to Clinton (i.e., a rejection of Trump) among racial liberals, or both.

These results from the semiparametric regressions are graphically presented in Figure 8.4. Specifically, the figure presents the predicted effect of outgroup hostility on net Republican candidate warmth after controlling for the effects of all the other independent variables. By examining the left side of the graph, we can see that the level of net Republican warmth among racial progressives did not vary all that much across the three elections. Moving to the right side of the figure, we can see precisely how outgroup hostility became more politicized in 2016. Compared to their predicted level of net Republican warmth in 2008 and 2012, racially conservative voters were significantly more likely to prefer Trump. This provides clear evidence that the 2016 white backlash was real but more complicated than most observers appreciated at the time.

Table 8.4 presents additional evidence of the consequences of Trump's magnetic appeal among racial conservatives and extremists in 2016, this time based on a more straightforward analytical strategy. The first panel of Table 8.4 presents the percentage of racial extremists and conservatives who voted for the Republican presidential candidate in 2016, along with their rate

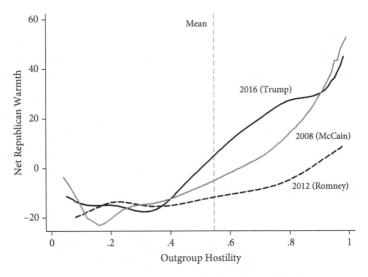

Figure 8.4 Semiparametric regression results for relationship between outgroup hostility and net warmth for Republican presidential candidates, 2008–2016

Table 8.4 Presidential Voting Behavior of Racial Extremists, 2004–2016

Percent of Racial Conservatives	Racial Extremists	Racial Conservatives
	Percent Voting for the Republican Nominee	
2004 (N = 678)	81.0	76.5
2008 (N = 1,154)	82.7	68.1
2012 (N = 3,817)	81.7	72.6
2016 (N = 2,524)	94.5	90.7
	Percent of Republican Voters	
2004 (N = 678)	13.4	11.1
2008 (N = 1,154)	19.2	13.1
2012 (N = 3,817)	23.2	16.5
2016 (N = 2,524)	21.9	15.8

of support for the Republican candidate in the three previous elections. We defined racial extremists and conservatives as we did in Chapter 2, based on their responses to the outgroup hostility scale items. Trump amazingly secured the support of more than nine out of ten racial extremists and approximately 84 percent of less extreme racial conservatives. As best as we can determine, this rate far exceeds the historical norm for any candidate getting support from racial conservatives. Thus, the evidence suggests that there is no question Trump benefited from his strategy to emphasize themes tapping outgroup hostility (even the number of voters with high levels of outgroup hostility was not increasing). The second panel of Table 8.4 adds to this picture by showing that Trump's success in attracting support from racial conservatives in 2016 occurred even though there was a decrease from 2012 in the percentage of Republican voters who were identified as racial extremists and racial conservatives.

Outgroup Hostility and the Importance of Emotion as a Mechanism for Action

One important consequence of the generation of outgroup hostility, we have argued, is that it can often lead to emotional responses that facilitate political action, especially when it becomes salient in a political campaign, as it did in 2016. We conclude this chapter with a brief examination of this hypothesis: Is there evidence that Trump's campaign generated an unusually strong emotional response associated with outgroup hostility? And if so, were these emotions disproportionately felt among racial conservatives and extremists? Although political behavior has been found to be affected by several emotions, the research suggests that one of the most politically potent emotions is anger.[31] Generally, anger is triggered when individuals encounter a situation in which they feel that their goals or objectives are blocked, when they perceive they have been insulted, or when they perceive an injustice or violation of standards has occurred.[32] To the extent that individuals identify with a specific social group, group-based injustices and grievances may also trigger "group-based anger," which can serve as an important motivational force to seek retribution through collective (political) action.[33] As a result, we expect that outgroup hostility should be strongly associated with anger and that candidates who successfully align themselves with policies that target anger-inducing outgroups—such as Trump—should become especially attractive to voters experiencing hostility and anger toward outgroups.

In addition to its direct effects on political behavior, anger may also indirectly affect voter behavior because of its effect on the positive emotion of enthusiasm. As a response to threat, anger is most likely to be experienced when the threat is attributable to a specific source, when people believe that they have control over the situation and that the threat can therefore be overcome.[34] Generally, enthusiasm is experienced when individuals perceive that their goals are being met.[35] When ingroup members experience outgroup-induced anger, a political candidates can elicit enthusiasm from angry voters by signaling to them that the candidate is both willing to and capable of implementing punitive policies targeting the outgroup, thus eliminating the source of their anger. Like anger, the generation of enthusiasm has also been found to have important effects on political decision-making and mobilization in recent elections.[36] For this reason, when the behavioral effects of voter anger and enthusiasm align in the same partisan direction in a political campaign, this can have a decisive effect on the outcome. As we demonstrate in the following discussion, this is precisely what happened in 2016.

To better understand the relationship between outgroup hostility, anger, and enthusiasm, we analyzed data from the ANES, which allowed us to create two measures of partisan-directed emotion. We first created a measure of "net anger" toward the Republican and Democratic presidential candidates. For each election we constructed this measure by subtracting the degree of anger felt toward the Republican candidate from the degree of anger felt toward the Democratic candidate. We also created a similarly constructed measure of net enthusiasm toward the presidential candidates based on items measuring enthusiasm toward the Democratic and Republican candidates. As each of the anger and enthusiasm items is measured using a five-point scale (1–5), the final scales for both measures range from -4 to 4, where values greater than 0 represent a more favorable emotional balance for the Republican candidate (i.e., greater anger toward the Democrat, greater enthusiasm toward the Republican). Based on literature connecting outgroup affect to political behavior,[37] we expect that the outgroup hostility scale should be positively correlated with these measures of partisan-directed emotion.

Our results, displayed in Table 8.5, strongly support this expectation. The table presents the simple bivariate correlation between outgroup hostility and both measures of partisan-directed emotion for the four presidential elections from 2004 to 2016. We also present the bivariate correlation between partisan-directed emotion and WRI for the years in this item is available in the ANES (2012 and 2016). In parentheses next to each simple correlation we also present a partial correlation between each indicator of racial attitudes (outgroup hostility, WRI) and partisan-directed anger and enthusiasm which is estimated after controlling for the effect of partisanship.

Table 8.5 The Relationship between Partisan Directed Emotion and Outgroup Hostility, 2004–2016

Election Year	Net Anger Toward Democratic Presidential Candidate		Net Enthusiasm Toward Republican Presidential Candidate	
	Outgroup Hostility	White Racial Identity	Outgroup Hostility	White Racial Identity
2004	.30* (.18*)	—	.28* (.14*)	—
2008	.33* (.23*)	—	.39* (.29*)	—
2012	.43* (.27*)	.06* (.01)	.44* (.28*)	.04* (−.01)
2016	.64* (.44*)	.13* (−.04)	.65* (.45*)	.13* (−.05*)

Note: The sample for this analysis includes white (non-Hispanic) voters and is taken from the American National Election Time Series Study, 2004–2016. Coefficients in parentheses are partial correlation coefficients, controlling for partisan identification for 2004 and 2008 and partisan identification and white racial identity (for outgroup hostility), and partisanship and outgroup hostility (for white racial identity) for 2012 and 2016.

For 2012 and 2016 the partial correlation also reflects additional controls for WRI (for outgroup hostility) and outgroup hostility (for WRI). The bivariate correlation is always stronger, of course, because partisan-directed emotion is driven to a significant extent by one's degree of party attachment. Yet even after controlling for strength of party identification, outgroup hostility remains significantly correlated with both anger and enthusiasm.

The same cannot be said for WRI. As we have previously noted, the item used to measure WRI is not available prior to 2012. Nevertheless, when we examine the simple bivariate correlations for WRI and partisan-directed emotion, we find that they are much smaller than the correlations estimated for outgroup hostility. Once we control for partisanship and outgroup hostility, the WRI correlations are reduced to insignificance or, as we see for 2016, the sign flips. This result suggests that WRI has no direct relationship at all with partisan-directed emotion, consistent with the null effects on candidate preference we first reported in Table 8.1.

One of the most striking features of these results is the growing strength of these correlations over time. This pattern is consistent with studies that find an increasing effect of racial resentment (variously measured) on vote choice and partisanship since the 2008 election, as well as our analysis of the historical effects of outgroup hostility reported in Table 8.3.[38] Yet the increase in the outgroup hostility-emotion correlation between 2012 and 2016 is far greater than the increase seen for either 2008 or 2012. This is consistent with

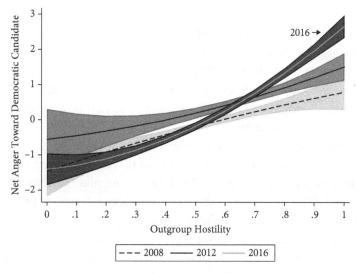

Figure 8.5 Net anger toward Democratic presidential candidate by outgroup hostility, 2008–2016

the timing of Trump's campaign and is entirely expected given his frequent use of racially charged rhetoric characterizing blacks, Latinx immigrants, and Muslims as threats to whites' status and security. If this were the case, we should expect that the generation of anger and enthusiasm was especially likely to be felt by racial extremists and conservatives. This is exactly what we see in Figure 8.5. In the figure we plot the expected level of partisan-directed anger across the outgroup hostility scale for three presidential elections (2008, 2012, and 2016), in each case controlling for respondent party identification (using the standard seven-point scale) and allowing for the possibility of a nonlinear relationship. As can be seen, 2016 was unique in that racial conservatives and extremists were significantly more likely to experience net anger toward Clinton.[39]

Outgroup Hostility and the Vote for Trump

Donald Trump shocked the world when he won the 2016 presidential election with a campaign that stoked white outgroup hostility. Economic concerns often were indicated as the reason Trump got as much support as he did. Yet, our research finds that economic pessimism was primarily an indirect factor through its role in accentuating the outgroup hostility that motivated support for Trump. Another argument often made was that Trump supporters were primarily motivated by concerns grounded in their ingroup solidarity as whites rather than their hostility toward outgroups. In this chapter, we show that the effect of outgroup hostility was more proximate and considerably larger in magnitude than either economic anxiety or white identity in affecting the 2016 vote choice.

While much of the research and commentary about the election suggests that whites became more racist in 2016 (and that is why Trump won), we show that the opposite occurred. The level of outgroup hostility actually peaked in 2012, during an election won by an African American Democrat. In 2016, when Trump won, he did so despite a significant backlash against his strategy of explicitly fanning the flames of outgroup hostility. Thus, what was unique about 2016 was not that outgroup hostility increased but that the distribution of outgroup hostility among whites was more polarized than it had been in recent elections. The increase in polarization, largely due to the surge in the number of racial progressives, should come as no surprise to political scientists. A firmly established finding in the literature is that the use of explicit racial cues by candidates will often backfire.[40] Trump's victory is therefore all the more surprising given that his candidacy led to an increase in polarization.

Finally, we show that as whites became more polarized on outgroup hostility, they also became more likely to sort politically on outgroup hostility. Yet they did so in a specific way that is consistent with the conventional wisdom of a white backlash in 2016. Racial progressives continued to feel negatively toward Trump in 2016, just as they had about Romney and McCain. What changed in 2016 was that racial conservatives were far more likely to support Trump than his Republican predecessors. This offers some clues to how Trump was able to win even though many more whites had moved to the left side of the outgroup hostility distribution in 2016. As we show in the next chapter, Trump was able to win because he mobilized racial conservatives and extremists more effectively than Mitt Romney or John McCain, especially in the states where it mattered the most. Although Trump did not persuade more voters to become hostile toward blacks, Latino immigrants, and Muslims, he was able to capitalize on the growth in outgroup hostility that occurred during Obama's presidency, channeling it from the political fringe to the mainstream and ultimately to the voting booth. Trump's victory in the 2016 presidential election was a monument to the mainstreaming of racism.

9

How Trump Used Outgroup Hostility to Win

Mobilizing Nonvoters and Mainstreaming Racists

Prior chapters have provided copious evidence that Donald Trump's 2016 presidential campaign persistently sought to stoke white outgroup hostility to increase his support among white voters. We also made note that Brad Parscale,
the director of the campaign's digital operations, explicitly stated that a primary goal of the campaign was to mobilize disaffected "low-propensity" voters
in swing states.[1] To be sure, Trump's campaign espoused a variety of incendiary
themes designed to appeal to the disaffected whites who were alienated from
mainstream politics. Some of Trump's most strident appeals targeted people's
anger at "globalists" who did not put "America First." With this sort of dog-
whistling,[2] Trump positioned himself as the champion of white Americans
who were feeling marginalized by the actions of a federal government that they
saw as promising inclusion to outgroups at the expense of white Americans.
Trump often blatantly smeared African Americans and the Latinx and Muslim
populations as threats to white America. African Americans were often associated with crime and welfare and Latinos with illegal immigration and the
drug trade, and Muslims were depicted as non-Christians who could also be
terrorists. In other words, Trump would often put down the dog-whistle in
favor of the bullhorn to explicitly demonize the three targeted outgroups.

This chapter provides evidence from our research that Trump's smears
directed at these three groups paid off, enabling him to do exactly what his
campaign tried to do, which was to flip swing states by mobilizing disaffected
white nonvoters who had high levels of outgroup hostility. As we have shown
in Chapter 8, this sort of campaign was off-putting to a large segment of the
voting public, whites included. Yet as offensive as this campaign was to some
voters, it still energized a specific base of disaffected whites in swing states,
and that proved enough for him to win the electoral college even while losing
the popular vote to Clinton by almost three million votes.

Hard White, Richard C. Fording and Sanford F. Schram. Oxford University Press (2020). © Oxford University Press.
DOI: 10.1093/oso/9780197500484.001.0001

We provide evidence that this voter mobilization campaign was more important than any attempt to get those who had previously voted for Barack Obama to cross party lines and vote for Trump. Parscale has suggested that trying to persuade voters with facts and reasoning to switch sides was not really something the Trump campaign emphasized.[3] Instead, the campaign focused on emotional appeals designed to mobilize an enlarged base of people already predisposed to support Trump. This strategy made appealing to disaffected white nonvoters all the more important. While we find that there were some Obama-Trump "switchers," the number of voters who flipped their votes from Democratic to Republican in the 2016 presidential election was actually about in line with historical norms.[4] In comparison to prior elections of recent years, the Trump campaign's success in mobilizing voters was much more distinctive than its rate of flipping voters to switch parties. Our findings are consistent with other research, in particular the studies published by the Democratic Fund Voter Study Group.[5] Yet our research is the first to rely on validated turnout data (rather than self-reported turnout), making our analysis of voter mobilization in 2016 all the more credible.

As we also show in this chapter, not only was the strategy of stoking outgroup hostility to mobilize disaffected whites decisive in Trump's victory, but his embrace of the white nationalist agenda also created a significant opening in the political opportunity structure for racial extremists to join the mobilization of other non-voters and become part of mainstream politics. Racial extremists came to believe that Trump spoke for them, which in turn incentivized their participation in the 2016 campaign. Since assuming office Trump has continued his strategy of racial appeals, thus leading to the co-optation of a significant faction of the white nationalist movement (WNM) by the Trump-led Republican Party. By the time Trump took office in 2017, racism had become effectively mainstreamed in American politics.

Did Trump Win, or Did Clinton Lose?

Our emphasis on the Trump campaign's racist voter mobilization strategy does not mean it was the only factor in determining his victory. One major factor related to race was the failure of Hillary Clinton's campaign to sustain the relatively high levels of African American turnout that had occurred when Obama was running in 2008 and 2012. In 2016 African American turnout in the presidential election declined for the first time in twenty years, with only 59.9 percent of blacks voting, whereas in 2012 their turnout rate had been a record-high 67.4 percent (which at the time exceeded the turnout rate for whites for the first time ever). This seven-percentage-point decline from the previous presidential election was the largest on record for African Americans. It was also the largest percentage-point decline among any racial or ethnic group stretching back to when white voter turnout dropped from 70.2 percent in 1992 to 60.7 percent in 1996.[6] The decline in the overall turnout rate for African Americans was notable because the overwhelming majority of African Americans voted Democratic in both 2012 and 2016, as they have for many years. Therefore, a decline in the overall black vote in any year is a problem for the Democratic candidate in particular.

There are a number of possible explanations for the decline in the black vote. Some have cited Republican attempts to make voting more difficult for African Americans and others who tend to identify with the Democratic Party.[7] Negative campaign advertising by the Trump campaign, and especially by its surrogates like Cambridge Analytica, was another possible culprit.[8] Russian meddling, in particular via its Internet Research Agency's "troll farm," included running numerous ads designed to mislead African Americans about Clinton.[9] Some reports suggest that the Trump campaign shared the Russians' interest in using the internet in particular to suppress the black vote.[10] Yet perhaps the most important factor was simply the fact that Hillary Clinton was not Barack Obama.[11]

Although Obama was popular among most Democrats, as the first African American president he was particularly beloved by many, if not all, African American voters. It is not that Hillary Clinton was unpopular among African Americans. Indeed, the African American vote was critical to her success in winning the nomination. It is simply that African American support for Obama was and continues to be unusually high,[12] and like most black candidates who run against white candidates, Obama benefited from a surge in African American turnout in both 2008 and 2012. Although the black turnout rate of 59.9 percent in 2016 may seem low compared to what we witnessed when Obama ran, it is actually in line with the black turnout rate (61.4) in 2004—the last time that a white candidate (John Kerry) was the Democratic nominee. Thus, there is no reason to think that Clinton should have or even could have generated more enthusiasm among black voters than any other white candidate, and for this reason it would seem unreasonable to cite the decline in black turnout in 2016 as evidence that Clinton caused her own defeat.

Nevertheless, the fact remains that if Clinton had simply matched Obama's vote totals in each state in 2016, she would have won the election. At the national level, Clinton nearly did this. Indeed, she received only 64,000 fewer votes than Obama had nationally, a number that comprised a mere .1 percent of the vote total. Yet, the picture changes dramatically when we examine the results for the six states that Trump flipped from blue to red in 2016: Florida, Iowa, Michigan, Ohio, Pennsylvania, and Wisconsin. As we can see in Table 9.1, Clinton underperformed compared to Obama in five of these six states by a margin that ranged from approximately 64,000 votes in Pennsylvania to about a quarter million votes in Michigan and Wisconsin. Across these six states, Clinton received about 900,000 fewer votes than Obama had. If Clinton had simply matched Obama's vote totals in these states and Trump's vote total had remained the same, Clinton would have gained another fifty-two electoral votes and would have won the election. Clinton's failure to match Obama's 2012 performance in these swing states was therefore significant.

We can also compare Trump's performance to that of the Republican nominee in 2012, Mitt Romney. At the national level, Trump improved upon Romney's vote total by approximately 2 million votes. The key to Trump's 2016 election victory, however, was his performance in the six states that he flipped. As we see in Table 9.1, Trump essentially matched Romney's total in Wisconsin and outperformed him in the other five states by a total of 1.1 million votes. If Trump had not received these additional votes and Clinton's vote total had remained the same as what she actually got in 2016, Clinton would have won three of the six swing states and gained sixty-five

Table 9.1 Turnout in Six Flipped States, 2016 vs. 2012

Flipped States	Clinton (2016)	Obama (2012)	Clinton Minus Obama	Trump (2016)	Romney (2012)	Trump Minus Romney
FL	4,504,975	4,237,756	267,219	4,617,886	4,163,447	454,439
IA	653,669	822,544	−168,875	800,983	730,617	70,366
MI	2,268,839	2,564,569	−295,730	2,279,543	2,115,256	164,287
OH	2,394,164	2,827,709	−433,545	2,841,005	2,661,437	179,568
PA	2,926,441	2,990,247	−63,833	2,970,773	2,680,434	290,299
WI	1,382,536	1,620,985	−238,449	1,405,284	1,407,996	−2,682
Total	14,130,624	15,063,810	−933,213	14,915,474	13,759,187	1,156,277

electoral votes, thereby easily winning the election. Those sixty-five electoral votes were more than the fifty-two that Clinton would have won if she had matched Obama's total. Therefore, while Clinton's failure to match Obama is noteworthy, Trump's outperforming Romney in the swing states was even more significant.

This exercise has its limitations, as we have already noted, in not accounting for forces beyond the Clinton campaign that may have contributed to depressing her vote, especially among African Americans in these swing states. The numbers presented in Table 9.1 do suggest, however, that at the very least Trump's victory was not entirely due to Clinton's failures (though those are not to be denied). In fact, the data make it clear that there is a strong likelihood that Trump would have lost the election had he not significantly improved upon his party's performance in 2012. In fact, in the analysis that follows we show that Trump's ability to mobilize disaffected whites, especially in swing states, was critical to his electoral success. And outgroup hostility proved to be the most significant factor driving that mobilization.

How Did Outgroup Hostility Enable Trump to Win?

In the previous chapter we provided evidence that outgroup hostility was an extremely important predictor of candidate support in 2016. Yet this analysis is somewhat unsatisfying if we are interested in the specific way that Trump won. The question of why people voted for Trump is different than the question of how he won. Nonetheless, as different as these questions are, they are in this case somewhat related: outgroup hostility figures in both answers. Outgroup hostility has already been shown to be the main predictor of whether someone chose to support Trump, and as we show in what follows, it was the main factor associated with whether nonvoters mobilized to vote for Trump in the swing states, which made all the difference in his winning the electoral college.

Understanding the role of white attitudes toward outgroups in explaining not just why Trump won but how he won begins with assessing in detail those attitudes' effects across the political spectrum. Implicit in many prior assessments of Trump's victory is the possibility that the number of racial conservatives and extremists grew in 2016, perhaps as a response to Trump's inflammatory rhetoric. As we noted in Chapter 2, this seems to be the implied understanding of political commentators, Van Jones in particular, who claim that 2016 represented a racially driven white backlash—aka, a "whitelash."[13] Yet as we have shown, this explanation falls short because the number of racial conservatives and extremists did not increase in 2016. Indeed, as we saw in the previous chapter, the data suggest just the opposite: there was a significant backlash against Trump in 2016, leading to an overall decrease in outgroup hostility among the population overall. Rather, Trump's white backlash resulted from his doing a far better job than his predecessors of persuading already existing racial conservatives and extremists to get out and vote for him.

In theory, there are two ways that Trump could have attracted "new" Republican voters, whom we define here as voters who did not vote for Mitt Romney in 2012. First, we argue that the critical factor in Trump's victory was the mobilization of inactive voters who did not vote in 2012 but were attracted to Trump by his rhetoric of outgroup hostility. Yet we must consider an alternative source of new Republican votes: voters who did vote in 2012 but cast their votes for Obama.

Since the 2016 election there has been much discussion about "Obama-Trump voters."[14] There was intense interest in the fact that 207 counties that had gone for Obama in either 2008 or 2012 went for Trump in 2016. Research indicates that these counties were disproportionately rural, concentrated in the upper Midwest and their residents were largely white and high school educated.[15] Counties that switched from supporting Obama to Trump tended to have had high rates of unemployment, drug overdoses, and suicides; that is, they were "landscapes of despair."[16] Yet as has been noted, "Counties do not vote. People do."[17] A further problem is that the initial analyses of vote-switching individuals were based on survey data that relied on self-reported turnout data. The picture changes when we use better data based on confirmation of self-reports about whether voters actually voted in the prior election.[18]

Specifically, we rely on voter-validated data in the 2016 American National Election Study (ANES). The 2016 ANES is especially useful for this test because for each respondent it provides validated turnout information for both 2012 and 2016. Based on these data, we find that Trump actually received more support from people who did not vote in 2012 than he did from people who switched from voting for Obama in 2012. We estimate that nationally 69 percent of Trump's support came from people who had voted for Romney in 2012, 10 percent came from people who had voted for Obama, and

21 percent came from people who had not voted in 2012.[19] In other words, Trump attracted twice as many mobilized 2012 nonvoters as Obama-Trump switchers. This statistical disparity between nonvoters mobilized to vote for Trump and Obama-Trump switchers highlights just how important mobilization was as the critical factor in Trump's victory. Mobilization was twice as important as switching in getting new votes for Trump beyond the existing pool of Republican voters who had voted in 2012.

Outgroup Hostility and the Mobilization of Trump Supporters

The key to Trump's victory, it seems, was mobilization. And as we show in the remainder of this chapter, this mobilization represents the final stage of the political mainstreaming of white racism, because it is whites with high levels of outgroup hostility who were most significantly mobilized to turn out and vote for Trump. Further, this was most noticeable in the swing states the Trump campaign had targeted for mobilization. We provide evidence of this targeted mobilization argument in three analyses of survey data. We begin with an analysis of political participation over the course of the 2012 and 2016 campaigns using data from the ANES 2012 and 2016 Time Series Studies. We utilized an index of political participation as the dependent variable, constructed by summing affirmative responses to a series of items recording respondent participation in four types of campaign involvement: (1) attendance at political meetings, rallies or speeches, (2) wore a campaign button, or posted a yard sign or bumper sticker, (3) worked for a political party or candidate, and (4) contributed money to a specific candidate.

We estimated the effect of outgroup hostility on political participation in the 2012 and 2016 elections, controlling for the full range of variables utilized in our vote choice models (partisanship, ideology, and other demographic controls). We modeled the effect of outgroup hostility (as well as the other control variables measuring political attitudes) using a nonlinear (polynomial) specification to allow for the possibility that participation may be highest at the extremes, where voters have the strongest attitudes (either positive or negative). Figure 9.1 presents the predicted participation level across the range of outgroup hostility values (from low to high) for 2012 and 2016, holding all other variables constant at their mean value. In 2012, participation steadily decreased with outgroup hostility and as a

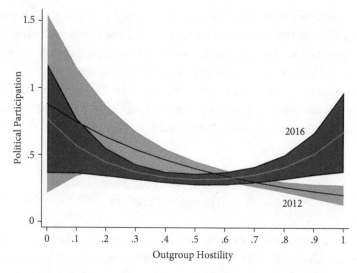

Figure 9.1 Relationship between outgroup hostility and political participation, 2012 and 2016

Source: ANES 2012 and 2016 Time Series Study

result, racially conservative and extremist voters displayed the lowest level of participation. This finding is consistent with our analyses in previous chapters which show that historically racial extremists are more likely to display low levels of political efficacy and therefore are less likely to participate in politics. In 2016, the relationship largely followed the same pattern for racial progressives and racial moderates as it did in 2012. Yet for racial conservatives and extremists we see a very different picture for 2016: the relationship between outgroup hostility and participation reverses and becomes positive. Thus, it appears that the greater level of enthusiasm for Trump in 2016 among people with high levels of outgroup hostility, as reflected in Table 8.2 (in Chapter 8), also translated to active participation in the 2016 campaign. Almost all whites with high levels of outgroup hostility supported Trump, and this is the group that underwent the most dramatic increases in participation. This mobilization advantage that Trump experienced with racially conservative and extremist voters may in fact very well have been enough to secure his victory in those critical swing states that enabled him to win the election.

We examine this question more closely by zeroing in on the behavior of newly mobilized voters in 2016 and how their rate of mobilization may have differed in swing states in contrast to the mobilization of 2012 nonvoters in non-swing states. As we have noted, according to Brad Parscale, swing state nonvoters were prioritized for mobilization by the Trump campaign. We now examine whether the campaign's effort to mobilize them in fact materialized.

For this analysis we turned to the 2016 Cooperative Congressional Election Study (CCES), which is much better suited to analyze the behavior of regional subgroups because it takes samples from all fifty states. Like the ANES, the CCES also provides validated voter data based on actual government voter files from across the country. The validated voter turnout data available in the 2016 CCES allow us to verify turnout for each respondent for the 2012 and 2016 elections, thus allowing us to focus on the sample of voters who did not vote in 2012 but did in 2016. There is one important disadvantage to this dataset: the 2016 CCES does not include an item measuring hostility toward Muslims. Therefore, we constructed an outgroup hostility scale based on three items measuring hostility toward African Americans and four items measuring hostility toward Latinx immigrants (details are provided in our online Appendix).

Utilizing the sample of 2012 nonvoters, we estimated the relationship between outgroup hostility and two measures of their mobilization in 2016. First, we constructed a measure of political participation in the 2016 campaign, measured as a 0-1 indicator of participation in at least one of four campaign activities beyond voting: (1) attended a political meeting, rally, or speech; (2) wore a campaign button or posted a yard sign or bumper sticker; (3) worked for a political party or candidate; and (4) contributed money to a specific candidate. Our second measure of mobilization was voter turnout in the general election, verified based on state voter files. For each measure of mobilization, we estimated its relationship with outgroup hostility, first for swing states and then for non-swing states, to see if there are differences that can be attributed to the Trump campaign's targeting of nonvoters in swing states. We limited our definition of swing states to the six states that Trump flipped from blue to red in 2016. Finally, we modeled the effect of outgroup hostility as we did in Figure 9.1, using a nonlinear (polynomial) specification for the effects of outgroup hostility (as well as measures of political attitudes used as controls). Our main hypothesis is that if the Trump campaign was successful in achieving its stated goal of mobilizing nonvoters in swing states by relying on Trump's incendiary emotional appeals, the mobilizing effects of outgroup hostility should have been greatest in those critical swing states compared to the non-swing states that were a much lower priority for the Trump campaign.

Figure 9.2 presents the results from our regression analyses of campaign participation and turnout, which control for many other variables that may affect political participation and turnout (see the online Appendix for details). The top panel shows the results for the measure of political participation and the bottom panel displays results for voter turnout. Looking at the left end of the top panel, we see that white 2012 nonvoters with low levels of outgroup hostility actively participated in the campaign at a similar rate in 2016 in both swing and non-swing states. The predicted participation rates for voters in each group of states are basically indistinguishable and overlap at the left end of the graph. Yet when we focus on the right end of the top panel, we can see that a statistically significant gap emerges in the participation rate of new voters in swing states and nonswing states. Specifically, there is a noticeably larger (and statistically significant) rate of participation of nonvoters in the swing states compared to the non-swing states. This suggests that the outgroup hostility the Trump campaign was so focused on intensifying in swing states may very well have had a decisive effect on the 2016 election. The increased mobilization of whites with high levels of outgroup hostility was substantially greater in swing states and in all likelihood helped to flip several of these key swing states in Trump's favor (just as the Trump campaign had hoped).

The bottom panel of Figure 9.2 presents the results of a similar analysis, which substitutes voter turnout for political participation as the dependent variable. The predicted relationship for non-swing states is largely linear and negative, similar to what we have witnessed in other analyses of the relationship between outgroup hostility and participation. Yet this statistically significant negative relationship disappears when we look at swing states. Among white 2012 nonvoters in swing states, those with high levels of outgroup hostility were just as likely to vote in 2016 as other white 2012 nonvoters. As a result, their voter turnout rate significantly exceeded that of white 2012 nonvoters in the non-swing states. In swing states, whites with high levels of outgroup hostility who had not voted in 2012 were in fact mobilized, while those in non-swing states were not. Something happened in those swing states to make that difference. Since the Trump campaign was explicit about trying to make a difference in those swing states with emotional appeals to nonvoters, it is distinctly possible that the campaign's stoking of outgroup hostility was the critical factor.

Together, the two analyses presented in Figure 9.2 provide evidence that Trump's strategy of fanning the flames of outgroup hostility in the key swing

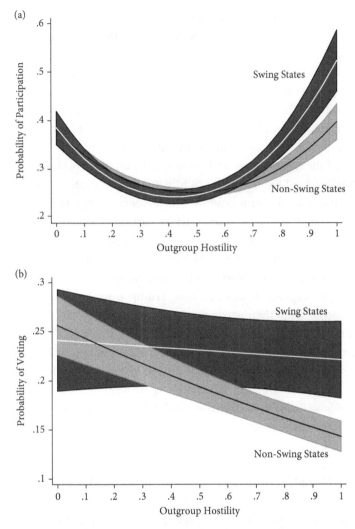

Figure 9.2 Relationship between outgroup hostility, campaign participation, and turnout among 2012 nonvoters, 2016 swing states vs. non-swing states: (A) campaign participation and (B) voter turnout

states may have paid big dividends in increasing turnout among disaffected voters who had not voted in 2012. These data offer strong evidence that the emotional appeals of the Trump campaign targeted at white nonvoters in swing states may in fact have had the desired effect, especially among whites with high levels of outgroup hostility.

Trump's Candidacy and the Co-optation
of White Nationalists

The preceding analysis shows that Trump was able to mobilize whites with racially conservative and extremist attitudes in 2016 who had sat out the 2012 election. This mobilization was undoubtedly an important factor in his close victory over Clinton. The research we present in this section also suggests that a significant part of that broader mobilization included the hardest of the extremists actively associated with the WNM, who in Trump had finally found a presidential candidate who motivated them to participate actively in electoral politics. Our evidence suggests that soon after Trump announced his candidacy, white nationalists increasingly came to believe that Trump shared their values more than any other candidate in recent history. Further, once white nationalists came to see Trump as their leader, this led to two related trends in WNM activity. First, WNM groups increasingly aligned themselves with Trump through movement propaganda and through their active participation in Trump events. Second, the "Trump movement" in the Republican Party became so attractive to racial extremists that it effectively became a substitute for WNM participation, contributing to a significant decline in WNM activity. In other words, Trump's candidacy not only attracted hard white extremists to support him for president; it also mobilized them to focus their energies on active participation in mainstream electoral politics.

Donald Trump as the White Nationalist Candidate

Donald Trump's appeal to white nationalists began in 2015, almost immediately after he announced his candidacy in what has to be the most racially inflammatory announcement speech by a major candidate in modern presidential election history. The first major WNM figure to endorse Trump was Andrew Anglin, the founder of the well-known neo-Nazi website The Daily Stormer. Almost immediately after Trump's announcement, Anglin wrote: "I urge all readers of this site to do whatever they can to make Donald Trump President." As Trump's poll numbers rose in the months after his entry into the race, Anglin became even more enthusiastic, declaring: "If The Donald gets the nomination, he will almost certainly beat Hillary, as White men such as you and I go out and vote for the first time in our lives for the one man who actually represents our interests."[20]

Although Trump's incendiary rhetoric was undoubtedly a critical factor in his appeal to white nationalists, their allegiance to him was just as much due to what many WNM activists chose to interpret as a series of subtle acknowledgments of their cause. The first of these incidents was the "accidental" use of Nazi SS soldiers in the promotional image tweeted by the Trump campaign in July 2015. Encouraged by this, white nationalists from all over the country began a campaign to direct messages to Trump via Twitter. Trump responded on two occasions by retweeting messages from a known online white nationalist whose Twitter handle contained the WNM's rallying cry "white genocide" (@WhiteGenocideTM). White nationalists took notice, and by all accounts Trump's popularity within the WNM skyrocketed. As one online WNM activist posted on the website Stormfront: "This is the best thing ever! If this gets any play in the media, it gives us an opening to discuss the issue of white genocide with friends and family that we may have been too uncomfortable to discuss with before. This could be an opportunity to wake a whole lot of people up, which frankly is far more important than any presidential candidacy anyway."[21]

More endorsements were to follow from such well-known WNM leaders as Jared Taylor (American Renaissance) and Bob Whitaker (American Freedom Party presidential candidate), who lent their voices to robocalls to encourage primary voters in New Hampshire to support Trump. The day after his victory in New Hampshire, Trump was endorsed by Richard Spencer, the leading voice of the alt-right movement. Trump also received endorsements from Don Black, a former KKK grand dragon and the founder of the Stormfront organization; Kevin Macdonald, the former psychology professor dubbed "the Neo-Nazi's favorite academic" by the Southern Poverty Law Center (SPLC); James Edwards, host of the hate-mongering radio show *The Political Cesspool*; Rocky J. Suhayda, the head of the American Nazi Party; Rachel Pendergraft, national organizer for the KKK-affiliated Knights Party; and many other visible activists in the WNM community. Yet the biggest endorsement of them all came on the day of the Nevada primary when David Duke, the most recognizable figure within the WNM, finally endorsed Trump during his online radio show. As Duke passionately implored his listeners: "You have an absolute obligation to vote for Donald Trump, and to vote against Cruz and Rubio. . . . If you vote for Ted Cruz, you are acting in a traitorous way to our people. You are betraying our people. Period."[22]

From Political Endorsements to Political Action

Trump's success in garnering the endorsement of white nationalist leaders was representative of a broader mobilization of the white nationalist community behind his campaign. As we have argued, Trump played a significant role in this mobilization through his strategy of racialized rhetoric. Yet Trump also benefited from the fact that his campaign was perfectly timed to maximize the support of a restless WNM community desperate to make a real impact in American politics. As we discussed in Chapter 4, the election of Obama was a turning point for the WNM. Movement leaders increasingly turned toward strategies to maximize numbers to overcome the majority that had elected him. Increasingly it was recognized that to accomplish this goal white nationalists needed to come together as more unified movement and that they needed to draw more followers to their cause. This meant that the movement's tactics had to change. This debate played out on Stormfront in a thread titled "Strategy and Tactics." As one WNM activist argued in June 2009:

> As I've said numerous times, what we Whites need to do (regardless of whether we're National Socialist, White Nationalist, Socialist, Communist, Anarchist) we agree that immigration and multiculturalism cannot continue. What we need to do:
>
> - Ditch the braces, boots, and bomber jackets
> - Be pillars of the community, involved in sports clubs and committees
> - Slowly open peoples eyes. Run for election on non-racial issues
> - Form or infiltrate legitimate organisations. Such as nationalists political groups, immigration control groups, etc. and use these as a platform to espouse MODERATE views before going ALL OUT against immigration/mutlcultism
>
> ALL POLITICS IS LOCAL, BELIEVE ME, I'VE BEEN INVOLVED IN IT FOR YEARS AND THAT'S WHERE MINDS ARE CHANGED.[23]

Years later, of course, this call for unification and a mainstream appearance culminated in the Charlottesville "Unite the Right" rally. But even with greater unity and mainstream tactics, WNM activists recognized the need for a strong national leader to energize the WNM community and lead them to victory. This was the problem with the Tea Party. While it provided the ve-hicle for moving the WNM into the mainstream, it lacked an effective leader as its national voice. In the same Stormfront thread, a WNM activist made this point abundantly clear:

> A true leader that can unite us all has yet to be found. He may rise through the ranks of an org and lead us from there. Or he may show himself some other way. I understand the need to have a clear leader. Right now we have leaders but we lack a clear cut leader that can unite us all. . . . Who knows what fate will bring. I think that if we get active and begin to make the cause more of a community that we will have a real leader emerge and a new person will be discovered. One who can unite us and who can be turned to for true leadership and direction.[24]

In the years following this post, that leader never emerged. That is, not until Donald Trump rode down that escalator in 2015 and declared that Mexican immigrants were rapists. Following Trump's entry into the race, momentum for his candidacy quickly built within the WNM activist base. On Stormfront, in the "Events" thread one could now find details of Trump rallies in Cedar Rapids, Akron, Jackson, and Austin alongside announcements of more ex-clusive WNM gatherings such as a meeting of the Loyal White Knights of the KKK in Georgia featuring "free food and a cross lighting at dark" and a "meet and greet" hosted by the National Socialist Movement in Tupelo, Mississippi. Most white nationalists who attend Trump rallies go under the radar because they intentionally dress and behave in a way that does not attract attention. Yet at a Trump rally in Louisville in March 2016, white nationalist attendance at Trump's events received national attention when Matthew Heimbach, leader of the Traditionalist Youth Network, was arrested for assaulting an African American protester during Trump's speech. More recently, some white na-tionalist groups—like the Proud Boys—have been participating more openly because of what they claim is the need to defend other far-right Trump supporters from being attacked by Antifa and other far-left protestors.

For those who cannot attend Trump's rallies, there have been many other opportunities to get involved in the Trump movement. As we noted in Chapter 1, they could follow the action by listening to James Edwards's live broadcasts through his radio show, *The Political Cesspool*. Or they could follow Trump's every move on a daily basis through the popular website The Daily Trump, which "blends white supremacist messages with news about Trump's candidacy."[25] And in the social media age, WNM Trump followers were (and continue to be) able to congregate on Twitter and other platforms (like Stormfront) to build a sense of community around their support for Trump. The importance of this white nationalist networking around Trump was documented in a report by the George Washington University Program on Extremism, based on Twitter data collected during 2016: "Followers of white nationalists on Twitter were heavily invested in Donald Trump's presidential campaign. White nationalist users referenced Trump more than almost any other topic, and Trump-related hashtags outperformed every white nationalist hashtag except for #whitegenocide within the sets of users examined."[26]

Trump and the Mainstreaming of White Nationalists

Trump's popularity within the WNM has had two important consequences for that movement. First, many white nationalists have become increasingly involved in mainstream electoral politics. Much of this activity has been related to Trump's campaign and since the election, his ongoing re-election campaign, which essentially started the day he assumed office. White nationalist activists continue to attend Trump rallies but also attend related conservative gatherings, such as the March for Life and various free speech and gun rights protests. In addition to their participating in campaigns and rallies, Trump's victory has inspired white nationalists to run for office.[27] Many have run for congressional seats, such as the following slate of candidates endorsed by the largest neo-Nazi group in the country, the National Socialist Movement, in 2016:

Art Jones (Illinois, District 3)—former American Nazi Party leader
Rick Tyler (Tennessee, District 3)—A white supremacist whose campaign slogan was "Make America White Again"
Karl Hand (New York, U.S. Senate)—A white nationalist activist and former organizer of a "White Lives Matter" rally in Buffalo
David Duke (Louisiana, U.S. Senate)—The most well-known white supremacist in the world

Although self-avowed white nationalist candidates almost always lose, some have had enough success to receive significant visibility for their cause.[28] For example, in June 2018 YouTube celebrity and American Identity

Movement activist James Allsup was elected to be the precinct committee officer (PCO) for Precinct 129 of the Washington State Republican Party.[29] The office does wield significant power, but Allsup was never seated by the state party; yet it was a symbolic victory and resulted in a significant amount of national attention. Allsup has been one of the WNM's leading advocates of an electoral strategy targeted at the local level.

A number of other candidates have run who do not openly describe themselves as "white nationalists" but have clear white nationalist ties. Candidates in this category often fare much better. One of the most well-known recent examples was Corey Stewart, who won the Republican primary for Tim Kaine's U.S. Senate seat in Virginia in 2018.[30] Stewart has been described as "pro-confederate" with "white nationalist ties" because he actively fought to preserve Confederate monuments in Virginia and made several appearances with Jason Kessler, the organizer of the "Unite the Right" rally in Charlottesville. Stewart lost the general election but received a respectable 41 percent of the vote as well as significant media attention.

While these candidates may not be successful in winning their races, the goal is not necessarily to win, at least in the short term. Rather, the immediate goal is to have their views become part of mainstream public discourse. When articulating this strategy, WNM leaders often cite the so-called Overton window, named for political scientist Joseph P. Overton.[31] Overton argued that at any given time there is a finite set of ideas that are acceptable and therefore viable as policy. Ideas that lie outside of this "window" are considered too extreme and therefore unacceptable. Yet the window can shift, expand, or contract as ideas that were once extreme become more mainstream. The hope of WNM strategists is that as their ideas are repeatedly disseminated through political candidates who appear to be mainstream, they can shift the Overton window to the right, causing their ideas to become mainstream. Only time will tell if this strategy is successful.

The Decline of the White Nationalist Movement

In addition to bringing established white nationalist groups into the mainstream, it appears that Trump has also had a less visible effect on the WNM, one that is equally significant. Since Trump has so regularly articulated white nationalist values, many white racial extremists undoubtedly view participation in his campaign as a substitute for participation in established white

nationalist groups. In other words, the Trump campaign has effectively become a new, more moderate version of a white nationalist group, and in the
process this influx of racial extremists into his base has led to fewer racial
extremists populating established white nationalist groups. Just as the Tea
Party movement (TPM) led to a decline in WNM activity, this has continued
with Trump.

We have already provided some evidence that is consistent with this argument. As we saw in Chapter 3, the number of WNM groups has continued to
decline in recent years, even after Trump's emergence as a presidential candidate. And in Chapter 4 we saw that this decline in WNM activity coincided
with a significant increase in external political efficacy among white racial
extremists. This is exactly what we would expect to see if racial extremists
have increasingly come to feel that the federal government—through
Trump—represents their interests and that participation in fringe, protest
politics is therefore unnecessary. Yet we can provide a stronger test of this argument by examining the relationship between Trump support and trends in
WNM activity at the county level. We provide such a test here.

For this analysis, we first collected data on the number of white nationalist
groups by county for the years 2008, 2012, and 2016, using data provided
by the SPLC. We then examined the relationship between the rate of WNM
group activity and the percentage of the vote received by Trump in each
county for 2016, 2012, and 2008. The logic of this test is simple. We would expect that WNM groups would be more likely to form in Republican-leaning
counties because they will have a higher percentage of racial extremists. Yet
if Trump's campaign had the effect of absorbing or diverting racial extremists
from white nationalist groups, then we would expect that the county-level
Republicn vote in 2016 would be less strongly predictive of white nationalist group activity compared to 2012 and 2008. Indeed, this is exactly
what we find. This result is presented in Figure 9.3. In 2008, Republican
counties had a significantly higher rate of white nationalist group activity
than Democratic counties. This is consistent with national trends that we
observed in Chapter 3. Recall that WNM activity surged with Obama's emergence as a presidential candidate and continued to increase through his first
year as president. The relationship weakened some by 2012 as the rate of
WNM activity declined in the most Republican-leaning counties, likely due
to the emergence of the Tea Party (as we argued in Chapter 4). By 2016 this
relationship had weakened even further and, most important, this was entirely due to the decrease in predicted WNM activity in heavily Republican

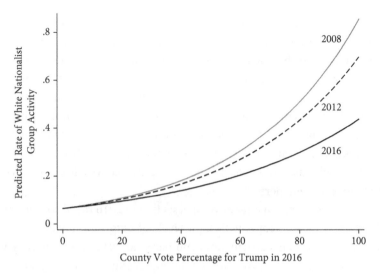

Figure 9.3 The relationship between county Republican vote and rate of white nationalist group activity, 2008 and 2016

Note: The figure presents the predicted rate of white nationalist group activity in a county by the percentage of the county vote percentage for Trump in 2016. The model was estimated using negative binomial regression and controls for percent black, percent Hispanic, family poverty rate, rate of college degrees, median age, and per capita income (all measured at the county level). We control for county population size as the exposure variable (which converts the dependent variable to the rate of white nationalist group activity).

counties.[32] In combination with the anecdotal evidence of white nationalist activists' attraction to the Trump campaign already provided, this evidence provides further support for the co-optation of the WNM into the Republican Party through Trump's politics of outgroup hostility. In 2008 and 2012, the Republican Party did not appeal enough to white nationalists for them to put aside their organizing; however, in 2016 with Trump running, white nationalists felt it was worthwhile to put aside their extremist group activity and be involved in supporting Trump in conventional electoral politics.

Stoking Outgroup Hostility among Disaffected Whites Wins Elections and Results in the Mainstreaming of Racism

The data presented in this chapter suggest that Trump's mobilizing of nonvoters with appeals to whites' outgroup hostility was a critical factor in how he won the 2016 presidential election. That is how Trump increased his base among racial conservatives enough to win, even as he alienated racial liberals with his racialized rhetoric. Our data suggest he gained support among racial conservatives at an unprecedented rate even as a growing number of racial liberals reacted negatively to what he said. This mobilizing of nonvoters with emotional appeals ended up being much more important than persuading voters to cross party lines. Mobilizing bested switching. Emotions beat facts and reason. In the end, the result was that Trump ended up getting twice as many votes by mobilizing people who had not voted in 2012 than from switchers.

The analysis in this chapter also suggests that in 2016 racial conservatives and extremists (i.e., people with high levels of outgroup hostility) significantly increased their participation, compared to 2012 when Romney was the Republican nominee. We find that the energizing effect of outgroup hostility in 2016 was especially critical for the mobilization of voters in the swing states that were decisive in Trump's victory. What was it that was so different in 2016 in these competitive, swing states that led racial conservatives and extremists to increase their voting so dramatically? One thing we know for sure is that Parscale explicitly stated that the primary goal of that campaign was to mobilize "low-propensity voters" who were already sympathetic to Trump, and that the campaign was most focused on doing that in swing states. Parscale also has explicitly discussed that the Trump campaign sought to achieve this goal by making emotional appeals tailored to a receptive audience whom the campaign had profiled as having an affinity for Trump. This was the primary strategy: to mobilize sympathetic Trump nonvoters by way of emotional appeals rather than trying to use facts and reason to persuade Obama voters to switch sides. There is no doubt that Parscale was keenly interested in expanding the base of Trump supporters by making emotional appeals to people already predisposed to vote for him rather than by persuading Obama voters to change sides. It is nothing less than ironic that Parscale called his target group "persuadables."[33] While Parscale does not say explicitly that this strategy was implemented by making incendiary statements designed to agitate people with high levels of outgroup hostility, there is good reason to suspect that is exactly what they sought to do, and our data analysis suggests that it worked.

In the process of appealing to the broader group of voters with high levels of outgroup hostility, Trump's rhetoric naturally resonated with white nationalist activists, including those who identified among the alt-right. As we documented in Chapter 4, the election of Obama in 2008 led to a tactical shift within the WNM as movement leaders increasingly sought ways to have more of a voice in mainstream politics. This began with efforts to infiltrate the Republican Party through the TPM, yet this strategy had a limited impact due to the absence of a national leader who was willing to give voice to white nationalist priorities. For many within the WNM, Trump proved to be that leader. Most WNM leaders endorsed Trump in 2016 and have continued to support him during his presidency as Trump continues to hammer away at agitating white people's outgroup hostility.

The WNM has become increasingly intertwined with the Trump campaign, as many WNM groups now include attendance at Trump rallies in their repertoire of movement activities. This also has led to an increasing number of candidates with white nationalist ties following Trump's lead and running for office themselves. While they have yet to match Trump's success, they have partly succeeded in the sense that WNM rhetoric is increasingly becoming part of mainstream political discourse. Somewhat ironically, Trump's success in appealing to the WNM has led to a partial demobilization of the movement, at least as measured by the number of active WNM groups. Yet this provides little comfort. White nationalists have not gone away; they have simply become less recognizable as they have redirected their activism from overtly racist organizations to the Republican Party. Where that leaves our politics is an important question. Our final chapter examines the implications of the mainstreaming of racism for U.S. politics going forward and the question of how to best respond to minimize its impact.

10

Outgroup Hostility and the Mainstreaming of Racism

A Strategic Response

In the foregoing chapters we have demonstrated that the resurgence of white racism is a critical factor influencing contemporary U.S. politics. The white supremacy that haunted America's past remains an enduring feature of U.S. politics. While it never left, its return to the mainstream in recent years awaited a prominent demagogue who would effectively champion the cause of aggrieved whites. That champion arrived with Donald Trump's ascendancy to the presidency.

Yet the modern mainstreaming of white racism does not have a simple trajectory. It is the result of the cyclical nature of racial politics and politics more generally.[1] The dynamics of political contention regarding issues such as race are most significantly characterized by reform movements being opposed by countermovements in a push and pull fashion.[2] White reluctance to embrace the implications of the civil rights movement intensified with resistance to the presidency of Barack Obama, the first nonwhite president in the history of the United States. Yet that white resistance has evolved into something broader.

Today many whites have become self-conscious about their racial identity.[3] White identity today takes the form of a politicized white consciousness that is activated by what we have called racialized political narratives focused on outgroups as threats to whites' position in the socioeconomic order.[4] Nonetheless, even this countermovement has come to face its own opposition. Just as an Obama effect, as Michael Telser called it,[5] led to a significant segment of the white population becoming activated to resist the threat they saw coming from racialized outgroups, what we can now call a Trump effect is leading racial liberals to become more active in resisting the resurgence of racism in the form of a new white ethnocentrism that today racializes Muslims, African Americans, and the Latinx population as threatening

Hard White, Richard C. Fording and Sanford F. Schram. Oxford University Press (2020). © Oxford University Press. DOI: 10.1093/oso/9780197500484.001.0001

outgroups.[6] It is in this dynamic that we learn how to best counter the current upsurge in white racism.

In what follows, we argue that our research leads us to conclude that given today's extremely tribalistic political environment,[7] the most effective strategy to combat the mainstreaming of white racism is to mobilize its opponents, white and nonwhite alike, rather than to try to persuade people to become more tolerant.[8] Relatedly, we think that the popular counterstrategy of stressing economic appeals to the white working class will on its own not prove enough for repudiating white racism compared to directly mobilizing a broader multiracial coalition to defeat that racism at the ballot box.[9] How this dynamic will play out in years to come and what an effective response to counter resurgent white racism looks like is the focus of this concluding chapter.

The Trump Effect: Structure and Agency

There is a somber lesson in the empirical research we presented in the foregoing chapters. The path forward to social justice is never straight and smooth but two steps forward, one step back, at best.[10] There is a cyclical tendency to political change, as movements are inevitably responded to by countermovements.[11] And the success of movements and countermovements is due in no small part to their ability to broaden their appeal to a wider audience, as leaders embolden those beyond their core followers to give voice to their suppressed views and others join in as the message becomes mainstreamed.[12] Furthermore, and no less critically, a successful movement understands both the structural conditions that enable it and the role of effective leaders in consummating it. These lessons need to be constantly relearned, especially by the people interested in countering the current mainstreaming of racism.

In the decades of the post–civil rights era, white racism was delegitimated and pushed largely to the margins of U.S. politics, thanks in no small part to the success of the civil rights movement (CRM), led by African American grassroots activists, including not just prominent leaders such as Martin Luther King Jr. and Rosa Parks, but many others as well.[13] Critical to the success of the CRM was its ability to widen its appeal to the white population, especially outside the South, to support federal government intervention in what had previously been seen as matters left largely to the states.[14] That success was measured in good part by the passage of critical civil rights legislation by a mostly white Congress that created real opportunities for racial inclusion regarding voting, education, employment, housing, and treatment by the government.

Yet these policies never received overwhelming support from America's white population, suggesting the potential for a countermovement to rise up and roll back federal reforms. A white countermovement grew over time, in part by submerging its most explicit calls for white supremacy and emphasizing a white identity politics that stood up for white people against a federal government that was demonized as denying whites basic freedoms. In recent years the claim has been that new white identity groups, most prominently the alt-right, were standing up for white identity rather than seeking to attack nonwhites. The alt-right built on a long-term movement among white supremacists, white nationalists, and other racial conservatives such that in recent years the emphasis on standing up for whites to counter government policies against racial discrimination became more acceptable to the broader white population.

This racist countermovement was, however, most dramatically catalyzed by the election of Barack Obama as the first nonwhite president in the nation's history. Now the federal government was not just coded black in whispered dog-whistles but was explicitly personified by a black president, who nonetheless often spoke in carefully measured and muted terms about issues of race. The Tea Party movement (TPM) proved to be the main vehicle for this installment of the white resistance.[15] Its success served to create a change in the political opportunity structure[16] that led to the incorporation of white extremists, both rabid supremacists and less ideologically explicit nationalists, with the broader population of white racial conservatives whose focus was primarily opposition to policies supporting racial diversity. The coalition jelled sufficiently to accelerate the transformation of the Republican Party into a party of white people, led by the wealthy, but attracting others in focusing on protecting the rights of white people against the federal government and its support for racially inclusive public policies.

Yet change in the political opportunity structure was not enough on its own; also necessary was the agency of a charismatic leader. Donald Trump supplied that missing ingredient. As he furtively, if cravenly, searched for anything that could serve as a political base for his quest for the presidency, Trump first worked with people like Steve Bannon and others associated with the alt-right and aligned groups to make this coalition a critical part of his base support as he contemplated running for the Republican nomination. This alliance started emerging as far back as 2012, when he became a leading voice of the birther movement focused on repudiating Obama as an illegitimate president who allegedly was not born in the United States.

It was Trump's leadership in the championing of a resurgent racism in the new form of white outgroup hostility that proved to be the key missing ingredient in legitimating the re-mainstreaming of racism that the United States has experienced in recent years. Trump's targeting of groups whom he called out as threatening to white America went beyond traditional white racism focused on demonizing people who identified as African Americans, like Obama. He joined with others in also targeting the Latinx and Muslim populations. In Trump's lexicon, the Latinx population personified illegal immigrants and Muslim terrorists, and both these demonized groups were joined with African Americans who were marked in this discourse of outgroup hostility as a denigrated population whose deficiencies prominently included criminality and living off federal assistance. Reflective of the evolution of white resentment in a changing society, Trump's triumvirate of key prejudicial stereotypes became standard stump speech moments in his vaunted rallies, at which he ginned up white hate and anger toward these groups. In the process, Trump both exploited and championed white outgroup hostility toward these groups. In this way he accelerated the racialization of the Latinx and Muslim populations to join with the already thoroughly racialized African American populations in the white American consciousness. He helped remake racism while intensifying it and mainstreaming it. Trump's success in exploiting white outgroup hostility proved to be more important than his more coded dog-whistles for "nationalism" (coded white). It was his appeals to white outgroup hostility more than white identity that were important to Trump's electoral success. The result was that racism could ensconce itself in mainstream politics, now hidden in the plain sight of Trump's plaintive appeals on behalf of white identity politics to "Make America Great Again" (as a white country).

From Research to Action

Our research creates the basis for making recommendations on how best to respond to this situation. Our findings are consistent with other studies of the 2016 election that show outgroup hostility proved to be more important than economic concerns in mobilizing critical support for Trump, even as he claimed to be running on behalf of the "forgotten people."[17] We do find that economic concerns were important, but primarily as context for people's anger directed at outgroups who could be blamed for their anxieties about a changing society more generally.[18] While Trump was able to mobilize disaffected whites by exacerbating their outgroup hostility, his opponent, Hillary Clinton, was unable to re-create the Obama coalition in full and suffered from declines in Democratic turnout, especially among African Americans. Trump was able to best Clinton by mobilizing disaffected whites on the basis of ginning up their outgroup hostility. Further, we find that Trump's mobilization on the basis of race was more important than flipping voters on any grounds from one party to the other.

As our research shows, Trump was able to activate whites in part by exploiting information deficits among the public. In this way, he was able to strengthen coalition building on the basis of appeals to emotions rather than reasoned thought and analysis based on facts. In this effort, Trump greatly benefited from Fox News and other right-wing media outlets, which amplified his emotional appeals and helped spread Trump's incessant lies regarding just about everything. The misinformed who believed Trump's lies joined with the willfully ignorant resentful whites who chose to support him as *their* liar, who was lying on their behalf. Fox News catered to them all, including both racial conservatives and racial extremists, sometimes citing the avowed the white nationalists and white supremacists among them as examples of prominent political leaders who had been maligned by the mainstream media and blocked by social media platforms.[19] The normalization of proponents of racism and bigotry as people who had legitimate political positions that were above condemnation has undoubtedly furthered the mainstreaming of racism. That Trump often retweeted Fox News resentments on this issue only accelerated the process of mainstreaming.[20]

Some of our strongest evidence shows that many Trump supporters were indeed misinformed because they remained siloed in the right-wing media bubble that served as Trump's echo chamber. In this sort of highly tribalistic media environment, where people only listened to political views that reinforced their preexisting biases, white Trump supporters were increasingly becoming disenchanted, not just with the government but with democracy itself, as something that worked more on behalf of the interests of threatening outgroups than the concerns of the white population.[21] Trumpism was founded on such tribalism. It further accelerated preexisting polarization of political attitudes, making compromise impossible and threatening political stability itself. In other words, as we have shown in the preceding chapters, Trump's agency exploited and built on a burgeoning, if changing, political opportunity structure.

Accelerating tribalism to Trumpian levels, especially when centered on hate and anger toward racialized others, makes partisan politics itself racial. This trend also was already established prior to Trump but has now intensified. Outgroup hostility preexisted Trump, but he explicitly and aggressively exploited it. He stuck with this focus as president, further accelerating the mainstreaming of racism in a revised form of outgroup hostility directed at Latinos and Muslims as well as African Americans as racialized populations who personified threats to white America.

This new ethnocentrism now has a significant partisan dimension, in that it has proven crucial to the remaking of the Republican Party. Those leaders of the party who opposed Trump have been pushed out, and his angry white base threatens the electoral survivability of those who remain. Former "Never-Trump" Republicans like Senators Ted Cruz (R-TX) and Lindsey Graham (R-SC) have become his acolytes in profoundly disturbing and very public ways. With Trump as the leader of the party, his white base could insist on loyalty from all other Republican elected officials. Trump's litmus tests for loyalty are grounded in his insistence on ginning up outgroup hostility to the three groups on which he has chosen to focus. Republicans are loathe to cross him on issues for fear of retaliation by his base of supporters, whether it is bans on immigration from selected Muslim countries; a wall to keep out illegal immigrants; cuts in social welfare programs; the rollback of antidiscrimination policies in employment, housing, and education; or other retrograde policies. Most recently, Trump's persistent demonization of outgroups has come to include remaking Asian Americans as an outgroup as when he blamed the "Chinese virus" for the Covid-19 pandemic. Although he eventually backed away from this tactic, right-wing pundits continue to do so and as we write this final chapter, a new hostility toward Asians appears to be spreading throughout the country. The result is that Trump's actions and words as president have helped sustain outgroup hostility as a building block of a remade Republican Party.

Given the changes in the political environment we have documented in this book, we need to consider that ever after Trump is gone, white outgroup hostility in whatever form it takes is likely to remain a potent partisan force in U.S. politics for some time. In fact, the dynamics of contention in racial politics manifests itself now as central to current era of increased political polarization.[22] We live under increased polarization, especially regarding outgroup hostility (thanks in no small part to Trump), and our party politics are centered around this division. Trump and his supporters have made the most of this division, vilifying their opponents for making white America vulnerable to increased threats by outgroups. Given our research findings, we are forced to conclude that they are not about to be dissuaded, whether Trump continues to lead them or not. Their success was found in strategic mobilization by stoking white outgroup hostility. The appropriate response is to be found in finding a corresponding political leadership that is dedicated to mobilizing all people who oppose resurgent white racism in its new form and to defeat it at the ballot box (which, for now, means voting Democratic).

Legitimating White Racial Extremism

Defeating white nationalism today involves not just repudiating it as an irrational emotional response to a changing society in an age of increased globalization, immigration, and demographic diversification. It now also requires confronting the supposedly reasoned arguments being made on its behalf. As difficult as it is to believe, today white outgroup hostility is being given intellectual legitimacy. We have reached the point where white resistance to demographic, cultural, and political change is no longer just a product of agitating the fears of the ignorant or stoking the anger of the resentful who base their political choices on irrational emotional reactions to the current political scene. Instead, the willfully ignorant and others are finding that intellectuals are now giving white outgroup hostility its own ideological premises. White nationalism today, for instance, has its intellectual counterpart in what is being called "national conservatism" or sometimes "conservative nationalism," which is championed by intellectuals on the right as an argument for standing up for the alleged white cultural roots of America as a country founded on Anglo Western values.[23]

For instance, Amy Wax argues that it is important to pursue "cultural-distance nationalism" that resists demographic diversification and cultural pluralism. Only then, Wax asserts, will we be able to protect the Anglo values that have made America strong.[24] Wax insists her position is not racist because it emphasizes cultural, not biological, differences. For conservative nationalists and others like Wax, the cultural threat is best confronted by limiting immigration of nonwhites from countries where a different set of values tend to inculcated.

Other intellectuals, not necessarily identifying as conservative nationalists, such as Lawrence Mead, agree:

> Fear of racism has long suppressed discussion of these differences. Our establishment insists that all Americans of whatever background are *the same*. But ever since his election campaign in 2016, President Trump has flouted that taboo. He often disparages minorities and immigrants in flagrant terms, inciting charges of racism. The defenders of sameness call him racist. But whether he is or not, he has made it clear that group and national differences in culture must be faced rather than denied....
>
> We must consider the fact that American society derives mostly from Europe, where individualism arose, whereas most of our long-term poor derive from the non-West, where most people have a more passive and less competitive temperament. The collision between this cautious worldview and mainstream individualism has come to dominate American politics. It causes advocates for disadvantaged groups to claim that they are oppressed even in a free country—something that most Americans who stem from Europe cannot understand. Heavy immigration has recently deepened those divisions, both in the United States and in Europe....
>
> Against all its rivals, only the United States possesses both the will and the capacity to lead. That potential, however, depends on the maintenance of an individualist way of life at home.[25]

Evidently, according to his own words, Mead casts his lot with Trump regardless of whether it turns out he is a racist or not. This kind of thinking lends intellectual credence to a white nationalism that insists it is a nonracist movement to stand up for a threatened white culture, regardless of the guilt by association with white nationalist ideology. Proclamations like Mead's embolden white nationalists to resist claims that they are denigrating nonwhites on racist grounds. This type of thinking makes white nationalists less ashamed to push their white identity agenda. It leads to today's equivalent of what once was heralded as "American exceptionalism."[26] With such intellectual cover, resurgent white racism, as expressed in today's outgroup hostility, becomes all the more difficult to challenge and its place in a remade Republican Party all the more secure.

Mobilization over Persuasion

Regardless of these intellectual rationalizations, there is good reason to think that vanquishing resurgent racism in the current political climate will not be achieved by convincing white nationalists or proponents of white identity politics to reconsider their suspect arguments on behalf of preserving white culture and resisting diversification. Under these conditions, persuasion is not likely to come from listening and then responding to whites who feel they are the new victims of identity politics. Instead, beating back the scourge of white nationalism is most likely best achieved by out-mobilizing the other side.

The research we presented in the preceding chapters demonstrates that Trump won the presidency less by getting Democrats to switch and more by mobilizing nonvoters on the basis of emotional appeals that agitated and legitimated their outgroup hostility toward Muslims, African Americans, and Latinxs. Mobilization in opposition to resurgent racism is therefore likely to prove to be the most effective response, given the contemporary contours of electoral politics. Democrats will likely be most effective politically if they also focus on mobilizing a broader base of groups likely to be sympathetic to resisting resurgent racism. Perhaps most disconcerting, we need to consider the sad situation that alternative strategies of trying to flip the white working class to return to the Democratic Party are likely to be at best an uphill struggle with less than the needed electoral impact in the current era of resurgent racism and the new contours of partisan politics.

There are multiple reasons for this situation. First, the two major parties are increasingly sorted by race and racial attitudes in a highly polarized and tribalistic environment.[27] Economic appeals are still relevant, especially since most nonwhites are working class or below. Yet our research shows that the economic anxiety that laid the basis for resurgent racism is a problem that reaches far beyond the white working class. Furthermore, many people with such concerns, regardless of class standing, now have deeply entrenched views toward outgroups. As a result, the key is instead to mobilize racial liberals more generally rather than trying to convert racial conservatives in the working class or elsewhere to vote for a progressive economic agenda. Second, the white working class is itself fractured. Not all of the white working class is predisposed to express high levels of outgroup hostility and accede to resurgent racism as championed in the White House. Increasing turnout among racial liberals in the white working class can help counter resurgent racism by responding to anti-racist appeals. Third, true Independents are actually a small group, and economic appeals to them might be attractive but not necessarily significant.[28] Fourth, many young people are more racially liberal than older cohorts and more racially diverse than older cohorts.[29] Nonetheless, while the young have significant economic concerns in the increasingly inequitable economy, they have consistently low voting turnout rates. Mobilizing the young on either racial or economic grounds is important but not likely to be a silver bullet.

Last, it is very important to recognize the gender gap in support for Trump. A slight majority of white women voted for Trump even though they tended to have lower levels of outgroup hostility than white men. Many of these women supported Trump for policy reasons regarding the economy, abortion, the power of the federal government, and related issues.[30] Yet female support for Trump, including among those in the working class and especially the middle class, has waivered as his racist agenda has intensified as president, as witnessed by the 2018 midterm elections that flipped the House back to the Democrats.[31] Women's mobilization to join with others in getting out the vote and voting themselves could further improve the chances of beating back the mainstreaming of racism today, starting with defeating its main legitimator, Trump. In fact, in the resistance to Trump women have been at the forefront of rebuilding the Democratic Party from the ground up via grassroots organizations.[32] Trump may have put resurgent racism into the White House, but his growing unpopularity with women can begin the process of pushing it back to the fringe.

All told, a winning coalition to defeat resurgent racism will be more likely to materialize if it goes beyond what turns out to be the narrower economic appeals. The winning strategy is to confront the issue head on with a broad coalition of racial liberals among women, the young, and nonwhites who can coalesce to defeat their racist opposition at the ballot box.[33]

The Rise of the Resistance

There is already evidence that resisting outgroup hostility at the ballot box is an effective strategy. In the 2018 midterm elections, a Blue Wave of voters rose up, resulting in the Democrats picking up forty seats in the House of Representatives. The Democrats took back the House, becoming the majority party by a thirty-four-seat margin. Healthcare was widely reported to be a major issue in many House races, more so than the economy, which was improving. President Trump and his hateful politics were widely challenged. The 2018 election seemed very much to be a referendum on Trump and his stoking the flames of outgroup hostility. In fact, what came to be called the Resistance actually started to form among voters as soon as Trump was elected in 2016, mobilized on a district-by-district basis.[34] Repudiating Trump was at the top of their agenda even though he was not on the ballot. The question for us is whether the coalition that the Resistance and others created by 2018 was one in which racial liberals were significant.

One way to test this proposition is to examine the relationship between outgroup hostility and (1) support for Trump and (2) voter mobilization during the 2016 and 2018 campaigns. We begin with an examination of support for Trump using the feeling thermometer items for Trump from the 2016 American National Election Studies (ANES) Time Series Study and the 2018 ANES Pilot Study (administered soon after the 2018 midterm election). Specifically, we estimate the relationship between our outgroup hostility scale and the feeling thermometer for Trump for both 2016 and 2018, controlling for party identification, ideology, and other standard demographic factors. As with our analyses presented in Chapters 8 and 9, we allow for nonlinearity in the effect of outgroup hostility due to our specific interest in voters located at the extreme ends of the outgroup hostility scale. Finally, unlike most of our analyses in previous chapters, our sample consists of voters from all racial backgrounds, not solely whites. The results for this analysis are presented in panel A of Figure 10.1 and generally confirm our finding from earlier chapters: outgroup hostility has a strong, positive effect on support for Trump. Our interest in this case, however, is whether the pattern of support for Trump has changed, especially among racial liberals. The results suggest that has not happened. Racial liberals opposed Trump in 2018 just as strongly as they did in 2016. In many ways, this is not surprising. Trump's racism was well-known during the 2016 campaign, and there is probably not much he could have done to worsen his reputation among racial liberals after being elected.

Interestingly, there appears to have been a small yet statistically significant decrease in support for Trump among those at the far right of the outgroup hostility scale—those whom we might consider racial extremists. Although racial extremists still supported Trump far more than racial liberals and moderates in 2018, we find that they have become a bit more lukewarm about him than in 2016. Trump set high expectations with his racially

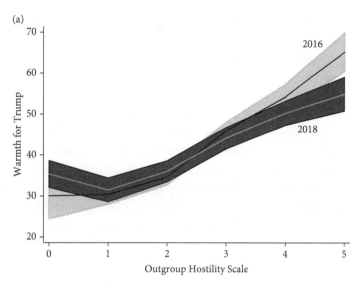

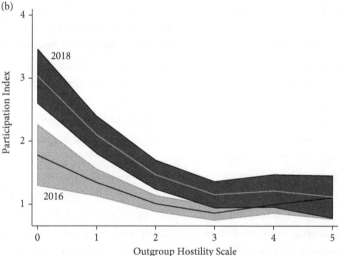

Figure 10.1 Effect of outgroup hostility on warmth toward Donald Trump and political mobilization, 2016–2018: (A) support for Trump and (B) political participation

Note: The figure displays the predicted level of (A) warmth toward Trump and (B) political participation by outgroup hostility. Outgroup hostility is collapsed to a 6-point ordinal scale to allow for nonlinearity. Predicted Trump warmth and participation index values are computed based on a regression model that controls for party identification, ideology, economic evaluations, education, income, age, gender, church attendance, and support for Trump (in the participation model). Data sources include the 2016 ANES Time Series Study and the 2018 ANES Pilot Study. See the online Appendix for estimation and measurement details.

inflammatory rhetoric during the 2016 campaign, but like most presidents, he has been unable to fully deliver on his promises. This includes one of his most popular promises among racial conservatives: to build a wall along the Mexican border. Perhaps the most public criticism of Trump among the far right is from "alt-lite" commentator Ann Coulter. In response to what she saw as Trump's lack of progress on immigration policy, she stated in early 2019 that "the only national emergency is that our president is an idiot."[35] Even Richard Spencer, the most widely known figure within the alt-right, eventually expressed dissatisfaction with Trump over his foreign policy, tweeting in early 2020: "I deeply regret voting for and promoting Donald Trump in 2016."[36] Nevertheless, the decrease in support for Trump from 2016 to 2018 is small, and there is no doubt that white racial conservatives and extremists continue to support Trump, even if they have been disappointed to some degree.

Our next analysis however shows that while opposition to Trump among racial liberals had not changed by 2018, political mobilization has indeed intensified in opposition to Trump's racism, contributing to the 2018 Blue Wave. We provide two sources of evidence to support this conclusion. First, we return to the 2016 and 2018 ANES surveys to examine the relationship between outgroup hostility and an index of political participation that we were able to construct for both 2016 and 2018. Specifically, the index was constructed by summing the number of political activities reported by the respondent over the previous twelve months, where the activities included (1) posting a political comment on social media, (2) giving money to a political candidate or organization, (3) attending a political meeting, (4) attending a political protest, (5) displaying or wearing campaign materials, and (6) trying to persuade others to vote one way or another. We then estimated the relationship between outgroup hostility and the political participation index, once again controlling for party identification, ideology, the feeling thermometer for Trump, and other demographic factors. The results are presented in panel B of Figure 10.1. Ordinarily we would expect that the level of mobilization in 2018 would be lower than it was in 2016 because participation usually drops off during midterm elections. Remarkably, this did not happen. The level of participation remained the same on the extreme right, despite the fact that enthusiasm for Trump may have dampened a bit among racial extremists. Most important, however, is that there was a significant increase in participation on the racial left, with the magnitude of the increase growing with the level of racial liberalism. Given that this increase in mobilization is found after controlling for party identification, ideology, and general opposition to Trump, this result is especially compelling and suggests that racial liberalism is indeed an important mechanism underlying the Resistance that led to the Blue Wave.

We supplement this analysis using validated turnout data from the most recent version of the VOTER panel survey for 2016–2018. With this survey we can track the same voters over time to see if attitudes toward racial outgroups affected turnout in the 2018 midterm. For this analysis we focus on two processes that affected the composition of the midterm electorate: the mobilization of new voters (defined as those who voted in 2018 but did not vote in 2016) and the demobilization of 2016 voters (defined as those who voted in 2016 but did not vote in 2018). If racial liberals were mobilized more than racial conservatives in 2018, outgroup hostility should be negatively associated with the turnout of 2016 nonvoters in 2018 (racial liberal mobilization). Conversely, we would expect to see a positive relationship between outgroup hostility and turnout among those who voted in 2016 but did not vote in 2018 (racial conservative demobilization). In other words, racial liberals who were keen to participate in the Blue Wave to repudiate Trump are hypothesized to both be more likely to be mobilized and less likely to be demobilized in 2018. Finally, our analysis adds one last wrinkle. Unlike the previous analysis of political participation as reported in Figure 10.1, we focus exclusively on white voters for our turnout analysis to determine if the effects of racial liberalism could be seen solely among white voters.

The results of our analyses of 2018 turnout are presented in Figure 10.2. The figure displays the predicted relationship between outgroup hostility and voter mobilization and demobilization in 2018, based on logistic regression analyses that control for the same political and demographic variables utilized in our models of vote choice in Chapter 8. Generally, the results are entirely consistent with our analysis of political participation and provide strong support for our specific hypotheses regarding the importance of outgroup hostility in the process of mobilization and demobilization in 2018. Specifically, we find that outgroup hostility had a statistically important effect in both the mobilization and demobilization analyses, and in both cases it was the primary factor predicting turnout (see our online Appendix for detailed results). The only other variables that significantly predicted mobilization were ideology and gender, while only age, education, and gender had a significant effect on demobilization. Of note is that economic evaluations (sociotropic and pocketbook) were found to be insignificant, suggesting that

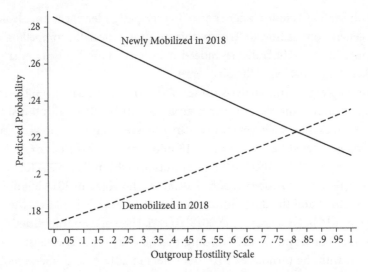

Figure 10.2 Effect of outgroup hostility on changes in voter turnout, 2016–2018

Note: The figure displays the probability of voting in the 2018 general election among 2016 nonvoters (newly mobilized) and the probability of not voting in 2018 among 2016 voters (demobilized). Predicted probabilities were generated based on logistic regression models of newly mobilized and demobilized using validated turnout data for 2016 and 2018 from the 2018–2019 VOTER survey. The logistic regression models control for party identification, ideology, social issues scale, modern sexism scale, support for universal healthcare, importance of healthcare as an issue, evaluation of the economy, importance of the economy as an issue, education level, age, and gender.

white turnout that helped create the Blue Wave was more about standing up against Trump's racism than about expressing economic anxiety in light of his policies. Overall, these findings offer strong evidence that the success of the Blue Wave was in part driven by the participation of racial liberals and that mobilizing racial liberals, even white liberals, may indeed be an effective electoral strategy to combat the mainstreaming of racism.

Race and Class Reconsidered

These findings suggest that the strategy of multiracial coalition building to resist the mainstreaming of racism needs to be taken seriously. This strategy of drawing whites into a multiracial coalition takes into consideration that whites, in particular the white working class, have been leaving the Democratic Party for years, predating the rise of Trump in a trend that started as far back as the early 1990s. While the Democratic Party in some of the best estimates is said to have received 50 percent of the white working class vote in 1992 and 51 percent in 1996, that percentage declined sharply to 41 percent in 2000 and has never risen above that since, ultimately falling precipitously to 20 percent in 2016.[37] There is good reason to think that the white working class feels betrayed by the Democratic Party. Trump once again built on a preexisting trend and made the most of it. Yet the big question regarding this trend is whether the betrayal white working class voters feel is about their being white or about their being working class. Our research suggests that racial animosity in the form of outgroup hostility is a big part of white working-class persistent desertion of the Democratic Party in the post–civil rights era. The strategic focus inevitably, it therefore seems, should be on the many working-class whites who are not racial conservatives or extremists and can still be recruited into a multiracial, multiclass coalition to counter the resurgent racism that has come to be centered in the Republican Party.

Given our research, we are skeptical of the prominent argument that disaffected whites could possibly become less resentful of outgroups if they were to be seen as less threatening, especially on issues of economic opportunity.[38] Our empirical analyses have demonstrated that economic anxiety was secondary in producing today's polarization and was not critical in producing the Blue Wave of 2018. Economic anxiety operated more as an important pretext, along with other factors including especially demographic change, to be exploited by hate mongers who targeted outgroups to blame for people's disaffection with the current political regime. As a result, we believe that there will continue to be political entrepreneurs who will promote narratives of white economic decline caused by minorities that will resonate with whites, regardless of what is really happening economically. In addition, as long as minorities continue to occupy powerful political positions, these narratives will resonate. White outgroup hostility is likely to persist under these conditions, especially given that it is driven in good part by demographic changes that are most likely to continue and in fact will only intensify in an age of globalization and increased immigration. Based on our research, we conclude that while many whites are open to supporting candidates who speak to their economic concerns, appeals to whites on economic grounds will not be enough on their own to defeat resurgent racism. Instead, they may sadly actually help sustain white hostility toward outgroups who are seen as threatening to whites' economic standing.

Whites in the working class have indeed been feeling left behind as the Democratic Party has sought to incorporate nonwhites not just as a critical voting bloc but also as candidates and leaders of the party. If nonwhites assume more power in the party, will that change suggest greater attention to white economic concerns? An important electoral consideration is how the changing complexion of Democratic Party leadership will play in rural areas and economically declining areas where swing states predominate. For many whites, the changing racial composition of the party signals that their specific economic concerns may be ignored.

That said, emphasizing confronting racism directly does not mean class is irrelevant. Instead it is important to recognize the imbrication of race and class.[39] Most working-class voters still vote Democratic, but that is because the nonwhite working class is overwhelmingly Democratic, whereas the white working class is increasingly not. Yet none of this is to suggest that the legitimate economic grievances of ordinary people, white or nonwhite, should be ignored. That would be unjust as well as wrong. In fact, addressing economic grievances of whites as well as nonwhites can be part of a strategy to defeat racism. At a minimum, policies that exacerbate the underlying economic concerns that give rise to racialized scapegoating can make that scapegoating less effective. The failed policies of the fear mongers will be revealed to be the real threat, and the scapegoating is likely to be seen as the thinly veiled diversion strategy that it always has been. The interrelationship of race and class is at work in both the success but also the failure of race-baiting. We need to learn that lesson and act on it.

A Stepwise Approach to Countering Racism Directly in the Face of Extreme Polarization

Our research shows that U.S. politics today is highly polarized around racial issues and especially attitudes toward the major outgroups: African Americans and the Latinx and Muslim populations. With globalization, immigration, and demographic diversification becoming more prominent, issues of race are increasingly not a simple white-black antagonism. White outgroup hostility in the United States has become more multicultural as Latinx and Muslim populations have become targets of white hostility along with African Americans. In this, the United States joins with other countries in reacting to issues of globalization, immigration, and

demographic diversification as sources of white anxiety.[40] The white population in the United States, as elsewhere, is not uniform but is increasingly
polarized, due in part to the cycles of contention leading one movement to
counter the other.

While our research has shown that overall outgroup hostility has not
increased in recent years, whites' attitudes toward outgroups have become
more polarized, with those whites with high levels of outgroup hostility
expressing increased anxiety. This polarization is but part of a broader polarization that has now become highly partisan (as our research has shown).[41]
The political parties increasingly seem to be existing in alternative universes
with their own sets of facts and understandings of what is happening, helped
along by a transformed media landscape that sows division and reduces consideration of competing points of view. The possibilities for civil discourse
are minimal when there is this type of affective partisanship in a tribalistic
environment. Today's extreme polarization is arguably about more than
ideology; it is tribalistic in the sense that the parties are warring factions
grounded in deep emotional divisions that transcend policy differences.
Rather than ideology driving partisanship, there is a case to be made that
partisan loyalty drives ideology.[42] Today's polarization takes place more on
an emotional plane beyond rational dispute about fundamental beliefs. It
is an intensification of the long-standing group-based nature of American
electoral politics, an us-versus-them mentality that now sees adversaries as
enemies.[43]

One reason for this bleak assessment is that our research has shown that
the roots of racist mainstreaming run much deeper than Trump's success in
getting people to respond to the racialized threat narratives that stoke white
outgroup hostility.[44] Given the established trajectory of this type of resentful
politics, it is likely to continue to be significant even after Trump leaves
the political scene. Any recommendations we offer must be grounded in a
strong sense of realism. While ideally the goal should be to rid U.S. politics
of white hostility toward outgroups, realistically it is best to approach this
goal incrementally. The first step is containment: manage white outgroup
hostility as a virulent force in contemporary politics by not reducing its isolation but increasing it. One major way to begin this process is to challenge
the Republican Party to disavow the white racial extremists in its coalition
so as to marginalize them and put them back on the fringe of mainstream
politics as discredited. For this to happen, it is essential to drive a wedge
between white moderates and white racial extremists. It will not be easy

because white moderates in the Republican Party have been benefiting electorally by forming alliances with white racial conservatives and white racial extremists. Therefore, the most direct way to achieve this goal is make white moderates pay a price for this allegiance, especially at the ballot box, so that they will be forced to reconsider. This is not persuasion as much as it is adamant resistance.

The best way to drive a wedge between white racial moderates and white racial conservatives and extremists is by mobilizing racial liberals. Given the tribalism and polarization, persuading people on the other side is becoming less of a viable option; out-mobilizing them to defeat them at the ballot box is the better alternative. This is where the energy for defeating white outgroup hostility must be directed. The success of the Democratic Party in the 2018 midterm elections in out-mobilizing the Republicans suggests that this is not just wishful thinking.

Ultimately, in the current political climate the issue is ineliminably partisan. A defeated Republican Party is the best thing that could happen in the struggle to beat back rising white nationalism in U.S. politics. And that is best done by directly mobilizing both white and nonwhite opponents of outgroup hostility to vote Democratic.

Saving Democracy by Defeating Racism

While the racial battlelines today are indeed partisan, the urgency to reduce racial polarization transcends partisanship. The stakes include the viability of liberal democracy itself. People are more likely to see their opposition not as mere adversaries but as full-blown enemies to the extent that puts democracy in crisis. The divide is so wide that partisans hardly ever talk to each other except under the most constrained conditions. The extreme polarization around race and other issues leads to persistent policy gridlock at all levels of government. In the face of inaction in confronting pressing issues, hopes for an inclusive democracy are at risk of being derailed for dictatorship.[45] In fact, whites increasingly today offer declining support for democracy, given that to a growing number it means nothing more than a stronger government that supports outgroups.[46] This means that whites with high levels of outgroup hostility are less likely to be interested in maintaining the rule of law and more likely to turn to a strong leader to break the gridlock in their favor and impose order at the expense of democracy. This possibility constantly haunts our politics as Trump and his supporters, and the Republican Party more generally, have worked overtime to undermine the system of elections. This is undoubtedly polarization at its limits, where the differences are no longer liberal versus conservative but between those who support or oppose democratic governance.

Even the Coronavirus pandemic in mid-2020 became an opportunity for Trump and his base to politicize the crisis in ways that suggested they were willing to allow it to get worse so they could blame Democratic governors.[47] A critical response to such anti-democratic politicization of the public health crisis was the call by political scientists for election reforms that would allow safe voting via mail-in ballots and other changes.[48] The battlelines over the crisis by then had become between those for protecting democracy and those willing to undermine it.

Trump has mainstreamed racism in a new form by stoking outgroup hostility among disenchanted whites, turning them into a solid base of support that increasingly expresses antidemocratic tendencies and a willingness to undermine the federal government in order to resist the enforcement of laws that are designed to make American society more inclusive. Trump's racially divisive politics has created a base of supporters that could lead to an American fascism, less toxic than the European kind but still nativistic, exclusionary, and antidemocratic.

This fraught situation calls for a countermovement consistent with the dynamics of contention. While some on the left today would like this countermovement to be one for socialism over capitalism, that is not what electoral politics is about today. Instead, the critical countermovement should be a movement to out-mobilize the racists. Our research has shown that this strikes at the core of reactionary politics today and it is what best activates the Resistance. Racial liberals are best primed to form a broad-based coalition that shows up at the polls and defeats the racial conservatives, nationalists, and supremacists. That is the fulcrum of contemporary electoral politics. Given that racial division has become so politicized along partisan lines, that means racially liberal Democrats in alliance with others must mobilize to defeat the racially conservative Republican Party, across the ballot, in all elections, at least until the Republican Party accepts that there is a price to pay for affiliating with racists and campaigning for votes by stoking white outgroup hostility. Once Republicans lose consistently because racial liberals succeed in defeating them at the ballot box, then perhaps the Republican Party will begin to disaffiliate, and white racism even in its new form of outgroup hostility will begin to be pushed back to the margins of U.S. politics. Should that happen, however, we should not become complacent, for if anything our research has shown that in U.S. politics racism is ever present, if sometimes not ascendant, and able to be reawakened and brought back to the center of mainstream politics. If we have learned anything from our research, it is that ridding U.S. politics of racism requires eternal vigilance.

Notes

Chapter 1

1. See, for instance, Karen E. Fields and Barbara Fields, *Racecraft: The Soul of Inequality in American Life* (London: Verso, 2012); Nell Irvin Painter, *Creating Black Americans: African-American History and Its Meanings, 1619 to the Present* (New York: Oxford University Press, 2006) and *The History of White People* (New York: W. W. Norton, 2010); Nikole Hannah-Jones, "American Wasn't a Democracy, Until Black Americans Made It One," *New York Times*, August 14, 2019, https://www.nytimes.com/interactive/2019/08/14/magazine/black-history-american-democracy.html ; and Eric Foner, *The Second Founding: How the Civil War and Reconstruction Remade the Constitution* (New York: W. W. Norton, 2019).
2. Michael Tesler, "The Return of Old-Fashioned Racism to White Americans' Partisan Preferences in the Early Obama Era," *Journal of Politics* 75, 1 (2013): 110–23.
3. Donald R. Kinder and David O. Sears, "Prejudice and Politics: Symbolic Racism versus Racial Threats to the Good Life," *Journal of Personality and Social Psychology* 40, 3 (1981): 414–31; and Michael Tesler and David Sears, *Obama's Race: The 2008 Election and the Dream of a Post-Racial America* (Chicago: University of Chicago Press, 2010).
4. Donald R. Kinder and Cindy D. Kam, *Us Against Them: Ethnocentric Foundations of American Opinion* (Chicago: University of Chicago Press, 2009).
5. Ashley Jardina, *White Identity Politics* (New York: Cambridge University Press, 2019).
6. Doug McAdam, Sidney G. Tarrow, and Charles Tilly, *Dynamics of Contention* (New York: Cambridge University Press, 2001). Also see Sanford F. Schram, *The Return of Ordinary Capitalism: Neoliberalism, Precarity, Occupy* (New York: Oxford University Press, 2015), chapter 1.
7. John Sides, Michael Tesler, and Lynn Vavreck, *Identity Crisis: The 2016 Presidential Campaign and the Battle for the Meaning of America* (Princeton, NJ: Princeton University Press, 2018); Rory McVeigh and Kevin Estep, *The Politics of Losing—Trump, the Klan, and the Mainstreaming of Resentment* (New York: Columbia University Press, 2019).
8. Robert D. Benford and David A. Snow, "Framing Processes and Social Movements: An Overview and Assessment," *Annual Review of Sociology* 26 (2000): 611–39.
9. McAdam, Tarrow, and Tilly, *Dynamics of Contention*.
10. Rick Perlstein, *Nixonland: The Rise of a President and the Fracturing of America* (New York: Simon and Schuster, 2010).
11. Ronald Brownstein, "Bill Clinton: Witness for the Defense," *The Atlantic*, September 6, 2012, https://www.theatlantic.com/politics/archive/2012/09/bill-clinton-witness-for-the-defense/262036/.

12. Ian Haney Lopez, *Dog Whistle Politics: Strategic Racism, Fake Populism, and the Dividing of America* (New York: Oxford University Press, 2013).

13. Nicholas Kristof, "Trump Is Racist to the Bone," *New York Times*, July 17, 2019, https://www.nytimes.com/2019/07/17/opinion/donald-trump-racist.html .

14. Joshua Green, *Devil's Bargain: Steve Bannon, Donald Trump, and the Nationalist Uprising* (New York: Penguin Books, 2017).

15. Pippa Norris and Ronald Inglehart, *Cultural Backlash: Trump, Brexit, and Authoritarian Populism* (New York: Cambridge University Press, 2019).

16. Vanessa Williamson and Isabella Gelfand, "Trump and Racism: What Do the Data Say?," *Brookings* (blog), August 14, 2019, https://www.brookings.edu/blog/fixgov/2019/08/14/trump-and-racism-what-do-the-data-say/.

17. David Leonhardt and Ian Prasad Philbrick, "Donald Trump's Racism: The Definitive List, Updated," *New York Times*, January 15, 2018, https://www.nytimes.com/interactive/2018/01/15/opinion/leonhardt-trump-racist.html.

18. German Lopez, "Donald Trump's Long History of Racism, from the 1970s to 2019," *Vox*, July 25, 2016, https://www.vox.com/2016/7/25/12270880/donald-trump-racist-racism-history.

19. Tim McDonnell, "The Insane Story behind Trump's Deleted Nazi Tweet," *Mother Jones*, July 14, 2015, https://www.motherjones.com/politics/2015/07/insane-story-behind-trumps-nazi-tweet/.

20. Ira Katznelson, *Fear Itself: The New Deal and the Origins of Our Time* (New York: Liveright, 2014).

21. Josh Dawsey, "Trump Derides Protections for Immigrants from 'Shithole' Countries," *Washington Post*, January 12, 2018, https://www.washingtonpost.com/politics/trump-attacks-protections-for-immigrants-from-shithole-countries-in-oval-office-meeting/2018/01/11/bfc0725c-f711–11e7–91af-31ac729add94_story.html.

22. Matthew Yglesias, "Trump's Racist Tirades against 'the Squad,' Explained," *Vox*, July 15, 2019, https://www.vox.com/2019/7/15/20694616/donald-trump-racist-tweets-omar-aoc-tlaib-pressley.

23. Adam Edelman and Alex Moe, "'Too Bad!': Trump Reacts to Break-in at Cummings' Baltimore Home," *NBC News*, August 2, 2019, https://www.nbcnews.com/politics/donald-trump/too-bad-trump-reacts-break-cummings-baltimore-home-n1038586.

24. Chauncey Devaga, "He Sounded the Alarm on 'Hateland': Daryl Johnson Warned Us about Right-Wing Terror in 2009," *Salon*, August 12, 2019, https://www.salon.com/2019/08/12/he-sounded-the-alarm-on-hateland-daryl-johnson-warned-us-about-right-wing-terror-in-2009/.

25. McAdam, Tarrow, and Tilly, *Dynamics of Contention*.

26. Alan Rappeport, "In Robocall, White Nationalist Accuses Utah's Evan McMullin of Secretly Being Gay," *New York Times*, November 1, 2016, https://www.nytimes.com/2016/11/02/us/politics/william-johnson-evan-mcmullin-robocalls-utah.html.

27. Eliza Collins, "David Duke: Comparing Trump to Hitler Is Great for Hitler," *Politico*, March 17, 2016, https://www.politico.com/blogs/2016-gop-primary-live-updates-and-results/2016/03/david-duke-donald-trump-hitler-220934

28. Christina Wilkle, "White Supremacists Are Broadcasting from Inside Trump Rallies," *HuffPost*, March 2, 2016, https://www.huffpost.com/entry/white-supremacists-donald-trump-rallies_n_56d663cfe4b03260bf789a09

29. Shaun King, "A History of Donald Trump Inciting Violence against Protesters at His Rallies and Campaign Events," *New York Daily News*, March 11, 2016, https://www.nydailynews.com/news/politics/king-donald-trump-history-violence-protesters-article-1.2561656.

30. Adam Serwer, "After Charlottesville, White Nationalists Are Winning," *The Atlantic*, August 10, 2018, https://www.theatlantic.com/ideas/archive/2018/08/the-battle-that-erupted-in-charlottesville-is-far-from-over/567167/.

31. Ray Sanchez and Melissa Gray, "Three Suspects, Three Crimes: A Hate-Filled Week in America," *CNN*, October 29, 2018, https://www.cnn.com/2018/10/28/us/72-hours-of-hate-in-america/index.html.

32. Ashley Parker and Philip Rucker, "'I Could Really Tone It Up': Trump Shows Little Interest in Uniting the Nation during Crises," *Washington Post*, October 26, 2018, https://www.washingtonpost.com/politics/i-could-really-tone-it-up-trump-shows-little-interest-in-uniting-the-nation-during-crises/2018/10/26/6a859c38-d891-11e8-a10f-b51546b10756_story.html.

33. Tara Isabella Burton, "The Pittsburgh Synagogue Shooting Comes amid a Years-Long Rise in Anti-Semitism," *Vox*, October 27, 2018, https://www.vox.com/2018/10/27/18032250/pittsburgh-synagogue-tree-of-life-shooting-antisemitism-soros

34. Saeed Ahmed and Paul Murphy, "Robert Bowers: What We Know So Far about the Pittsburgh Synagogue Shooting Suspect," *CNN*, October 27, 2018, https://www.cnn.com/2018/10/27/us/synagogue-attack-suspect-robert-bowers-profile/index.html

35. John Fritze, "Trump Used Words Like 'Invasion' and 'Killer' to Discuss Immigrants at Rallies 500 Times," *USA Today*, August 8, 2019, https://www.usatoday.com/story/news/politics/elections/2019/08/08/trump-immigrants-rhetoric-criticized-el-paso-dayton-shootings/1936742001/

36. See, for instance, McAdam, Tarrow, and Tilly, *Dynamics of Contention*.

37. Benford and Snow, "Framing Processes and Social Movements."

38. McAdam, Tarrow, and Tilly, *Dynamics of Contention*.

39. See, for instance, Stephen L. Morgan and Jiwon Lee, "Economic Populism and Bandwagon Bigotry: Obama-to-Trump Voters and the Cross Pressures of the 2016 Election," *Socius: Sociological Research for a Dynamic World* 5 (August 26, 2019), https://journals.sagepub.com/doi/10.1177/2378023119871119.

40. On Obama-Trump voters, see Tyler T. Reny, Loren Collingwood, and Ali A. Valenzuela, "Vote Switching in the 2016 Election: How Racial and Immigration Attitudes, Not Economics, Explain Shifts in White Voting," *Public Opinion Quarterly* 83, 1 (2019): 91–113.

41. Sides, Tesler, and Vavreck, *Identity Crisis*; and Jardina, *White Identity Politics*.

42. Liliana Mason, *Uncivil Agreement: How Politics Became Our Identity* (Chicago: University of Chicago Press, 2018).

43. Steven Levitsky and Daniel Ziblatt, *How Democracies Die* (New York: Crown/Archetype, 2018).

44. Steven Miller and Nicholas Davis, "White Outgroup Intolerance and Declining Support for American Democracy," 2018, http://svmiller.com/research/white-outgroup-intolerance-democratic-support/

45. Katherine Cramer, "Listening to Strengthen Democracy," The Gerald R. Ford School of Public Policy at the University of Michigan, October 23, 2019, http://fordschool. umich.edu/video/2019/katherine-cramer-listening-strengthen-democracy.

46. Larry Womack, "Opinion: I Grew up in Rural, Small-Town America—and I Can Tell You the Real Reason Why People Love Donald Trump," The Independent, November 22, 2019, https://www.independent.co.uk/voices/trump-supporters-california-clinton-fake-news-vote-2020-a9214131.html

Chapter 2

1. Alan I. Abramowitz, "Issue Evolution Reconsidered: Racial Attitudes and Partisanship in the U.S. Electorate," American Journal of Political Science 38, 1 (1994): 1–24; Edward G. Carmines and James A. Stimson, Issue Evolution: Race and the Transformation of American Politics (Princeton, NJ: Princeton University Press, 1989); and Nicholas A. Valentino and David O. Sears, "Old Times There Are Not Forgotten: Race and Partisan Realignment in the Contemporary South," American Journal of Political Science 49, 3 (2005): 672–88.

2. Nayda Terkildsen, "When White Voters Evaluate Black Candidates: The Processing Implications of Candidate Skin Color, Prejudice, and Self-Monitoring," American Journal of Political Science 37, 4 (1993): 1032–53; Tasha S. Philpot and Hanes Walton, "One of Our Own: Black Female Candidates and the Voters Who Support Them," American Journal of Political Science 51, 1 (2007): 49–62; Adam J. Berinsky, "The Two Faces of Public Opinion," American Journal of Political Science 43, 4 (1999): 1209–30; Donald R. Kinder and David O. Sears, "Prejudice and Politics: Symbolic Racism versus Racial Threats to the Good Life," Journal of Personality and Social Psychology 40, 3 (1981): 414–31; and Jonathan Knuckey and Byron D'Andra Orey, "Symbolic Racism in the 1995 Louisiana Gubernatorial Election," Social Science Quarterly 81, 4 (2000): 1027–35.

3. Josh Pasek et al., "Attitudes Toward Blacks in the Obama Era: Changing Distributions and Impacts on Job Approval and Electoral Choice, 2008–2012," Public Opinion Quarterly 78, S1 (2014): 276–302; B. Keith Payne et al., "Implicit and Explicit Prejudice in the 2008 American Presidential Election," Journal of Experimental Social Psychology 46, 2 (2010): 367–74; Brian F. Schaffner, "Racial Salience and the Obama Vote," Political Psychology 32, 6 (2011): 963–88; Michael Tesler and David Sears, Obama's Race: The 2008 Election and the Dream of a Post-Racial America (Chicago: University of Chicago Press, 2010); and Michael Tesler, Post-Racial or Most-Racial? Race and Politics in the Obama Era (Chicago: University of Chicago Press, 2016).

4. Marisa Abrajano and Zoltan L. Hajnal, White Backlash: Immigration, Race, and American Politics (Princeton, NJ: Princeton University Press, 2015).

5. Abrajano and Hajnal, *White Backlash*; and Zoltan Hajnal and Michael U. Rivera, "Immigration, Latinos, and White Partisan Politics: The New Democratic Defection," *American Journal of Political Science* 58, 4 (2014): 773–89.

6. Richard C. Fording and Sanford F. Schram, "The Cognitive and Emotional Sources of Trump Support: The Case of Low-Information Voters," *New Political Science* 39, 4 (2017): 670–86; Schaffner, "Racial Salience and the Obama Vote"; John Sides, Michael Tesler, and Lynn Vavreck, *Identity Crisis: The 2016 Presidential Campaign and the Battle for the Meaning of America* (Princeton, NJ: Princeton University Press, 2018); Nazita Lajevardi and Kassra A. R. Oskooii, "Old-Fashioned Racism, Contemporary Islamophobia, and the Isolation of Muslim Americans in the Age of Trump," *Journal of Race, Ethnicity and Politics* 3, 1 (2018): 112–52; and Brian F. Schaffner, Matthew McWilliams, and Tatishe Nteta, "Understanding White Polarization in the 2016 Vote for President: The Sobering Role of Racism and Sexism," *Political Science Quarterly* 133, 1 (2018): 9–34.

7. Ashley Jardina, *White Identity Politics* (New York: Cambridge University Press, 2019).

8. Justin A. Berry, David Ebner, and Michelle Cornelius, "White Identity Politics: Linked Fate and Political Participation," *Politics, Groups, and Identities* (2019): 1–19; and Gregory A. Petrow, John E. Transue, and Timothy Vercellotti, "Do White In-group Processes Matter, Too? White Racial Identity and Support for Black Political Candidates," *Political Behavior* 40, 1 (2017): 197–222.

9. See Sides, Tesler, and Vavreck, *Identity Crisis*.

10. Donald R. Kinder and Cindy D. Kam, *Us Against Them: Ethnocentric Foundations of American Opinion* (Chicago: University of Chicago Press, 2009). Also see Marilynn B. Brewer, "The Psychology of Prejudice: Ingroup Love and Outgroup Hate?," *Journal of Social Issues* 55, 3 (1999): 429–44.

11. Kinder and Kam, *Us Against Them*; Cindy D. Kam and Donald R. Kinder, "Ethnocentrism as a Short-Term Force in the 2008 American Presidential Election," *American Journal of Political Science* 56, 2 (2012): 326–40; and Donald R. Kinder and Nathan P. Kalmoe, *Neither Liberal nor Conservative: Ideological Innocence in the American Public* (Chicago: University of Chicago Press, 2017).

12. Kinder and Kam, *Us Against Them*.

13. In particular, see Antoine J. Banks, *Anger and Racial Politics: The Emotional Foundation of Racial Attitudes in America* (New York: Cambridge University Press, 2014); and Antoine J. Banks and Heather M. Hicks, "Fear and Implicit Racism: Whites' Support for Voter ID Laws," *Political Psychology* 37, 5 (2016): 641–58. Also see Abrajano and Hajnal, *White Backlash*; Zoltan Hajnal and Michael U. Rivera, "Immigration, Latinos, and White Partisan Politics: The New Democratic Defection," *American Journal of Political Science* 58, 4 (2014): 773–89; and Nicholas A. Valentino, Ted Brader, and Ashley E. Jardina, "Immigration Opposition Among U.S. Whites: General Ethnocentrism or Media Priming of Attitudes About Latinos? Immigration Opinion and Media Group Priming," *Political Psychology* 34, 2 (2013): 149–66.

14. See Marilynn B. Brewer, "In-Group Bias in the Minimal Intergroup Situation: A Cognitive-Motivational Analysis," *Psychological Bulletin* 86, 2 (1979): 307–24; and B Steve Hinkle and R. J. Brown, "Intergroup Comparisons and Social Identity: Some

Links and Lacunae," in *Social Identity Theory: Constructive and Critical Advances*, Dominic Abrams and Michael A. Hogg, eds. (New York: Harvester Wheatsheaf, 1990), pp. 48–70; Rick Kosterman and Seymour Feshbach, "Toward a Measure of Patriotic and Nationalistic Attitudes," *Political Psychology* 10, 2 (1989): 257–74; and Jardina, *White Identity Politics*.

15. Thomas F. Pettigrew, James S. Jackson, Jeanne Ben Brika, Gerard Lemaine, Roel W. Meertens, Ulrich Wagner, and Andreas Zick, "Outgroup Prejudice in Western Europe," *European Review of Social Psychology* 8, 1 (1997): 241–73.

16. Diana Mutz, "Status Threat, Not Economic Hardship, Explains the 2016 Presidential Vote," PNAS, May 8, 2018, https://www.pnas.org/content/115/19/E4330.

17. Donald R. Kinder and Lynn M. Sanders, *Divided by Color: Racial Politics and Democratic Ideals* (Chicago: University of Chicago Press, 1997).

18. Tesler, *Post-Racial or Most-Racial?*; Tesler and Sears, *Obama's Race*; and Nicholas A. Valentino and David O. Sears, "Old Times There Are Not Forgotten: Race and Partisan Realignment in the Contemporary South," *American Journal of Political Science* 49, 3 (2005): 672–88.

19. David P. Redlawsk, Caroline J. Tolbert, and Natasha Altema McNeely, "Symbolic Racism and Emotional Responses to the 2012 Presidential Candidates," *Political Research Quarterly* 67, 3 (2014): 680–94.

20. Ted Brader, Nicholas A. Valentino, and Elizabeth Suhay, "What Triggers Public Opposition to Immigration? Anxiety, Group Cues, and Immigration Threat," *American Journal of Political Science* 52, 4 (2008): 959–78; and Todd K. Hartman, Benjamin J. Newman, and C. Scott Bell, "Decoding Prejudice Toward Hispanics: Group Cues and Public Reactions to Threatening Immigrant Behavior," *Political Behavior* 36, 1 (2014): 143–66.

21. Abrajano and Hajnal, *White Backlash*.

22. Abrajano and Hajnal, *White Backlash*.

23. Abrajano and Hajnal, *White Backlash*.

24. Louis A. Cainkar, *Homeland Insecurity: The Arab American and Muslim American Experience After 9/11* (New York: Russell Sage Foundation, 2009).

25. Kerem Ozan Kalkan, Geoffrey C. Layman, and Eric M. Uslaner, "'Bands of Others'? Attitudes toward Muslims in Contemporary American Society," *The Journal of Politics* 71, 3 (2009): 847–62; and Vilna Bashi Treitler, "Social Agency and White Supremacy in Immigration Studies," *Sociology of Race and Ethnicity* 1, 1 (2015): 153–65.

26. John Sides and Kimberly Gross, "Stereotypes of Muslims and Support for the War on Terror," *The Journal of Politics* 75, 3 (2013): 583–98.

27. Erik C. Nisbet, Ronald Ostman, and James Shanahan, "Public Opinion toward Muslim Americans: Civil Liberties and the Role of Religiosity, Ideology, and Media Use," in *Muslims in Western Politics*, Abdulkader H. Sinno, ed. (Bloomington: Indiana University Press, 2009); and Muniba Saleem et al., "Exposure to Muslims in Media and Support for Public Policies Harming Muslims," *Communication Research* 44, 6 (2017): 841–69.

28. Tesler and Sears, *Obama's Race*; and Tesler, *Post-Racial or Most-Racial?*

29. Kalkan, Layman, and Uslaner, "'Bands of Others'?" Also see Nazita Lajevardi and Marisa Abrajano "How Negative Sentiment toward Muslim Americans Predicts Support for Trump in the 2016 Presidential Election," *Journal of Politics* 81, 1 (2020), https://www.journals.uchicago.edu/doi/abs/10.1086/700001?mobileUi=0.

30. Kinder and Kam, *Us Against Them*.

31. See Banks, *Anger and Racial Politics*; Banks and Hicks, "Fear and Implicit Racism"; Abrajano and Hajnal, *White Backlash*; Hajnal and Rivera, "Immigration, Latinos, and White Partisan Politics"; and Kinder and Kam, *Us Against Them*.

32. Theodor Adorno, Else Frenkel-Brunswik, Daniel J. Levinson, and Sanford R. Nevitt, *The Authoritarian Personality* (London: Verso Books, [1950] 2019); Brian Laythe, Deborah Finkel, and Lee A. Kirkpatrick, "Predicting Prejudice from Religious Fundamentalism and Right-Wing Authoritarianism: A Multiple-Regression Approach," *Journal for the Scientific Study of Religion* 40, 1 (2001): 1–10; and Marinus H. Van IJzendoorn, "Moral Judgment, Authoritarianism, and Ethnocentrism," *The Journal of Social Psychology* 129 (1989): 37–45.

33. Jim Sidanius and Felicia Pratto, *Social Dominance: An Intergroup Theory of Social Hierarchy and Oppression* (New York: Cambridge University Press, 1999).

34. Bo Ekehammar, Nazar Akrami, Magnus Gylje, and Ingrid Zakrisson, "What Matters Most to Prejudice: Big Five Personality, Social Dominance Orientation, or Right-Wing Authoritarianism?," *European Journal of Personality* 18, 6 (2004): 463–82; Bernard E. Whitley Jr., "Right-Wing Authoritarianism, Social Dominance Orientation, and Prejudice," *Journal of Personality and Social Psychology* 77, 1 (1999): 126–34; and Sidanius and Pratto, *Social Dominance*.

35. Kinder and Kam, *Us Against Them* also constructed an ethnocentrism scale based on items measuring stereotypes toward whites, blacks, Hispanics, and Asians. In our online Appendix we replicate the analyses presented in Table 2.1 with this version of the ethnocentrism scale. The pattern of results is the same. The outgroup hostility scale is more strongly correlated with both RWA and SDO.

36. We also considered defining a racial extremist as someone who displays the highest possible value for all three of the scales included in our outgroup hostility measure. Based on our analysis of ANES data, the population of extremists identified by this definition is so small—approximately 1 percent of all whites—that it is not useful for our analyses. Of the 2,555 whites who responded to all of the outgroup hostility items, only 29 respondents chose the most extreme

37. Josiah Ryan "'This Was a Whitelash': Van Jones' Take on the Election Results," *CNNPolitics*, November 6, 2016.

38. Sides, Tesler, and Vavreck, *Identity Crisis*.

39. Boris Bizumic and John Duckitt, "What Is and Is Not Ethnocentrism? A Conceptual Analysis and Political Implications," *Political Psychology* 33, 6 (2012): 887–909; and David Raden, "Ingroup Bias, Classic Ethnocentrism, and Non-Ethnocentrism Among American Whites," *Political Psychology* 24, 4 (2003): 803–28.

40. William Graham Sumner, *Folkways: A Study of the Sociological Importance of Usages, Manners, Customs, Mores, and Morals* (New York: Ginn, 1906).

41. Raden, "Ingroup Bias, Classic Ethnocentrism, and Non-Ethnocentrism Among American Whites."

42. Brewer, "The Psychology of Prejudice," pp. 429–44; Brewer, "In-Group Bias in the Minimal Intergroup Situation," pp. 307–24; Hinkle and Brown, "Intergroup Comparisons and Social Identity," pp. 48–70; and Kosterman and Feshbach, "Toward a Measure of Patriotic and Nationalistic Attitudes," pp. 257–74.

43. Pettigrew et al., "Outgroup Prejudice in Western Europe," pp. 241–73.

44. Jardina, *White Identity Politics*; and Sides, *Identity Crisis*. Also see Gregory A. Petrow, John E. Transue, and Timothy Vercellotti, "Do White In-Group Processes Matter, Too? White Racial Identity and Support for Black Political Candidates," *Political Behavior* 40, 1 (2018): 197–222.

45. Jardina, *White Identity Politics*; Eric D. Knowles and Kaiping Peng, "White Selves: Conceptualizing and Measuring a Dominant-Group Identity," *Journal of Personality and Social Psychology* 89, 2 (2005): 223–41; Cara J. Wong and Grace E. Cho, "Two-Headed Coins or Kandinskys: White Racial Identification," *Political Psychology* 26, 5 (1995): 699–72; and Jean S. Phinney, "Understanding Ethnic Diversity: The Role of Ethnic Identity," *American Behavioral Scientist* 40, 2 (1996): 143–52.

46. Henri Tajfel, *Human Groups and Social Categories: Studies in Social Psychology* (New York: Cambridge University Press, 1981).

47. Gordon W. Allport, *The Nature of Prejudice* (Oxford: Addison-Wesley, 1954).

48. Brewer, "The Psychology of Prejudice," p. 430.

49. William A. Gamson, *Power and Discontent* (Homewood, IL: Richard D. Irwin, 1968); Doug McAdam, *Political Process and the Development of Black Insurgency, 1930–1970* (Chicago: University of Chicago Press, 1982); Arthur H. Miller, Patricia Gurin, Gerald Gurin, and Oksana Malanchuk, "Group Consciousness and Political Participation," *American Journal of Political Science* 25 (1981): 494–511; and Richard D. Shingles, "Black Consciousness and Political Participation: The Missing Link," *American Political Science Review* 75, 1 (March 1981): 76–91.

50. Miller, Gurin, Gurin, and Malanchuk, "Group Consciousness and Political Participation," pp. 494–511; and McAdam, *Political Process and the Development of Black Insurgency*.

51. Patricia Gurin, Arthur H. Miller, and Gerald Gurin, "Stratum Identification and Consciousness," *Social Psychology Quarterly* 43, 1 (1980): 30–47.

52. For instance, see Gamson, *Power and Discontent*; Stephen C. Craig, "Efficacy, Trust, and Political Behavior: An Attempt to Resolve a Lingering Conceptual Dilemma," *American Politics Quarterly* 7, 2 (1979): 225–39; and Shingles, "Black Consciousness and Political Participation."

53. See Dennis Chong and Reuel Rogers, "Racial Solidarity and Political Participation," *Political Behavior* 27, 4 (2005): 347–74; Craig, "Efficacy, Trust, and Political Behavior"; Miller, Gurin, Gurin, and Malanchuk, "Group Consciousness and Political Participation"; and Shingles, "Black Consciousness and Political Participation."

54. Susan Milligan, "Trump Plays to His Base with His Escalating Rhetoric," *US News*, July 19, 2019, https://www.usnews.com/news/the-report/articles/2019-07-19/trump-plays-to-his-base-with-his-escalating-rhetoric.

55. Rachel Wetts and Robb Willer, "Privilege on the Precipice: Perceived Racial Status Threats Lead White Americans to Oppose Welfare Programs," *Social Forces* 97, 2 (2018): 793–822.

56. Dennis Chong, "Creating Common Frames of Reference on Political Issues," in *Political Persuasion and Attitude Change*, Diana Mutz, Paul M. Sniderman and Richard A. Brody, eds. (Ann Arbor: University of Michigan Press, 1996), pp. 195–224; and Robert D. Benford and David A. Snow, "Framing Processes and Social Movements: An Overview and Assessment," *Annual Review of Sociology* 26 (2000): 611–39.

57. Ian Haney Lopez, *Dog Whistle Politics: Strategic Racism, Fake Populism, and the Dividing of America* (New York: Oxford University Press, 2013).

58. Jim Sidanius Felicia Pratto, Colette van Laar, and Shana Levin, "Social Dominance Theory: Its Agenda and Method," *Political Psychology* 25, 6 (2004): 845–80.

59. Herbert Blumer, "Race Prejudice as a Sense of Group Position," *The Pacific Sociological Review* 1, 1 (1958): 3–7; and Brewer, "In-Group Bias in the Minimal Intergroup Situation," p. 307.

60. Blumer, "Race Prejudice as a Sense of Group Position."

61. Jardina, *White Identity Politics*; and Herbert Blumer, "Reflections on Theory of Race Relations," in *Race Relations in World Perspective*, Andrew W. Lind, ed. (Honolulu: University of Hawaii Press, 1955), pp. 3–21.

62. Banks, *Anger and Racial Politics*.

63. Banks, *Anger and Racial Politics*.

64. Jennifer S. Lerner, Ye Li, Piercarlo Valdesolo, and Karim S. Kassam, "Emotion and Decision Making," *Annual Review of Psychology* 66, 1 (2015): 799–823.

65. Nico H. Frijda, Peter Kuipers, and Elisabeth ter Schure, "Relations among Emotion, Appraisal and Emotional Action Readiness," *Journal of Personality and Social Psychology* 57, 2 (1989): 212–28.

66. Martijn van Zomeren, Russell Spears, Agneta H. Fischer, and Colin W, Leach, "Put Your Money Where Your Mouth Is! Explaining Collective Action Tendencies through Group-Based Anger and Group Efficacy," *Journal of Personality and Social Psychology* 87, 5 (2004): 649–64.

67. Brian E. Weeks, "Emotions, Partisanship, and Misperceptions: How Anger and Anxiety Moderate the Effect of Partisan Bias on Susceptibility to Political Misinformation: Emotions and Misperceptions," *Journal of Communication* 65, 4 (2015): 699–719; and Nicholas A. Valentino et al., "Is a Worried Citizen a Good Citizen? Emotions, Political Information Seeking, and Learning via the Internet," *Political Psychology* 29, 2 (2008): 247–73.

68. Lerner et al., "Emotion and Decision Making."

69. McAdam, *Political Process and the Development of Black Insurgency*; and Suzanne Staggenborg, "Social Movement Communities and Cycles of Protest: The Emergence and Maintenance of a Local Women's Movement," *Social Problems* 45, 2 (1998): 180–204.

70. Herbert P. Kitschelt, "Political Opportunity Structures and Political Protest: Anti-Nuclear Movements in Four Democracies," *British Journal of Political Science* 16,

1 (1986): 57–85; and Doug McAdam, John D. McCarthy, and Mayer N. Zald, eds., *Comparative Perspectives on Social Movements: Political Opportunities, Mobilizing Structures, and Cultural Framings* (New York: Cambridge University Press, 1996).

71. David S. Meyer, *A Winter of Discontent: The Nuclear Freeze and American Politics* (New York: Praeger, 1990); and David S. Meyer, "Peace Protest and Policy," *Policy Studies Journal* 21, 1 (1993): 35–51.

72. J. Craig Jenkins, *The Politics of Insurgency: The Farm Worker Movement in the 1960s* (New York: Columbia University Press, 1985).

73. Donald R. Kinder and Tali Mendelberg, "Cracks in American Apartheid: The Political Impact of Prejudice among Desegregated Whites," *Journal of Politics* 57, 2 (1995): 402–24.

74. Doug McAdam, Sidney G. Tarrow, and Charles Tilly, *Dynamics of Contention* (New York: Cambridge University Press, 2001).

Chapter 3

1. Adam Serwer, "After Charlottesville, White Nationalists Are Winning," *The Atlantic*, August 10, 2018; and Rory McVeigh and Kevin Estep, *The Politics of Losing—Trump, the Klan, and the Mainstreaming of Resentment* (New York: Columbia University Press, 2019).

2. Doug McAdam, Sidney G. Tarrow, and Charles Tilly, *Dynamics of Contention* (New York: Cambridge University Press, 2001).

3. Tahi L. Mottl, "The Analysis of Countermovements," *Social Problems* 27, 5 (1980): 620–35.

4. *2009 Annual Report* (Washington, DC: Joint Center for Political and Economic Studies, 2009), https://jointcenter.org/about/annual-reports/.

5. *Statistical Abstract of the United States: 2006* (Washington, DC: U.S. Bureau of the Census, 2006), 59.

6. Lincoln Quillian, "New Approaches to Understanding Racial Prejudice and Discrimination," *Annual Review of Sociology* 32, 1 (2006): 299–328.

7. Tali Mendelberg, *The Race Card: Campaign Strategy, Implicit Messages, and the Norm of Equality* (Princeton, NJ: Princeton University Press, 2001).

8. Marianne Worthington, "The Campaign Rhetoric of George Wallace in the 1968 Presidential Election," *The Upsilonian* 4, 1 (1992): 1–5, https://Inside.Ucumberlands.Edu/Downloads/Academics/History/Vol4/Marianneworthington92.html.

9. Dan T. Carter, *The Politics of Rage: George Wallace, the Origins of the New Conservatism* (New York: Simon and Shuster, 1995), p. 296.

10. Carter, *The Politics of Rage*, p. 320.

11. National Alliance, "What Is the National Alliance?," 2011, https://natall.com/about/what-is-the-national-alliance/.

12. Betty A. Dobratz and Stephanie L. Shanks-Meile, *The White Separatist Movement in the United States: "White Power, White Pride!"* (Baltimore, MD: Johns Hopkins University Press, 2000).

13. Only about one-quarter of all militia and patriot groups are connected with the white nationalist movement. See Southern Poverty Law Center: https://www. splcenter.org/hate-map/by-ideology; and Michael Barkun, "Religion, Militias and Oklahoma City: The Mind of Conspiratorialists," *Terrorism and Political Violence* 8, 1 (1996): 50–64,

14. Linda Gordon, *The Second Coming of the KKK: The Ku Klux Klan of the 1920s and the American Political Tradition* (New York: Liveright, 2017).

15. Stuart Wexler, "When White Supremacist Terror Hit U.S. Jews Before, the President Stepped in to End It. This Is How," *Haaretz*, May 3, 2019, https://www.haaretz.com/opinion/.premium-deadliest-year-ever-to-be-jewish-in-america-what-trump-must-do-to-end-the-terror-1.7188156.

16. The SPLC actually counts Aryan Nations in the "neo-Nazi" category, despite its connection with seed-line doctrine, since it borrows heavily from Nazi ideology and symbolism. On the Christian identity movement, see James A. Aho, *The Politics of Righteousness: Idaho Christian Patriotism* (Seattle: University of Washington Press, [1990] 1995); Michael Barkun, "Religion, Militias and Oklahoma City," pp. 50–64; Michael Barkun, *Religion and the Racist Right: The Origins of the Christian Identity Movement*, rev. ed. (Chapel Hill: University of North Carolina Press, 1997); David W. Brannan, "The Evolution of the Church of Israel," *Terrorism and Political Violence* 11, 3 (1999): 106–18; Jeffrey Kaplan, *Radical Religion in America: Millenarian Movements from the Far Right to the Children of Noah* (Syracuse, NY: Syracuse University Press, 1997); Jeffrey Kaplan, "The Context of American Millenarian Theology," *Terrorism and Political Violence* 5, 1 (1993): 30–82; and Kerry Noble, *Tabernacle of Hate: Why They Bombed Oklahoma City* (Prescott, ON: Voyageur Publishing, 1998).

17. Prior to 1997, when the SPLC collected data on the number of hate group organizations, it counted each organization only once even if it had multiple chapters. For this reason, data collected prior to 1997 are not comparable to our data.

18. Kathleen Belew, *Bring the War Home: The White Power Movement and Paramilitary America* (Cambridge, MA: Harvard University Press, 2018); Leonard Zeskind, *Blood and Politics: The History of the White Nationalist Movement from the Margins to the Mainstream* (New York: Farrar, Straus and Giroux, 2009); and Dobratz and Shanks-Meile, *The White Separatist Movement in the United States*.

19. Laura Smith, "In the Early 1980s, White Supremacist Groups Were Early Adopters (and Masters) of the Internet," Timeline, October 11, 2017, https://timeline.com/white-supremacist-early-internet-5e91676eb847.

20. George Hawley, *Right-Wing Critics of American Conservatism* (Lawrence: University Press of Kansas, 2016).

21. The Traditionalist American Knights of the Ku Klux Klan, 2017: https://kkk028.webnode.com/about-us/

22. Robert D. Benford and David A. Snow, "Framing Processes and Social Movements: An Overview and Assessment," *Annual Review of Sociology* 26 (2000): 611–39.

23. The sample was based on a list of hate group websites published by the SPLC in 2011 and largely consists of Klan and neo-Nazi organizations.

24. Gilbert Achcar, *Arabs and the Holocaust* (London: Al Saqi, 2009).

25. Southern Poverty Law Center, "Billy Roper," https://www.splcenter.org/fighting-hate/extremist-files/individual/billy-roper.

26. Bernard Grofman, Lisa Handley, and Richard G. Niemi, *Minority Representation and the Quest for Voting Equality* (Cambridge, UK: Cambridge University Press, 1994); and Frank R. Parker, *Black Votes Count: Political Empowerment in Mississippi after 1965* (Chapel Hill: University of North Carolina Press, 1990).

27. Richard Fording and John Cotter, "The Political Origins of Extremism: Minority Descriptive Representation and the Mobilization of American Hate Groups," SSRN Scholarly Paper (Rochester, NY: Social Science Research Network, August 26, 2014), https://papers.ssrn.com/abstract=2487603; Nella Van Dyke and Sarah A. Soule, "Structural Social Change and the Mobilizing Effect of Threat: Explaining Levels of Patriot and Militia Organizing in the United States," *Social Problems* 49, 4 (2002): 497–520; and Sarah A. Soule and Braydon G. King, "Competition and Resource Partitioning in Three Social Movement Industries," *American Journal of Sociology* 113, 6 (2008):1568–1610.

28. Jason Hanna, "Hate Groups Riled Up, Researchers Say," CNN.com, June 11, 2009, http://www.cnn.com/2009/US/06/11/hate.groups/.

29. Diana Temple-Raston, "Obama's Candidacy Angers, Excites Hate Groups," NPR Interview, October 28, 2018. https://www.npr.org/templates/transcript/transcript.php?storyId=96227586.

30. Stephanie Chen, "Growing Hate Groups Blame Obama, Economy," CNN.com, February 26, 2009. http://www.cnn.com/2009/US/02/26/hate.groups.report/index.html?eref=ib_us.

31. Josh Pasek et al., "Attitudes Toward Blacks in the Obama Era: Changing Distributions and Impacts on Job Approval and Electoral Choice, 2008–2012," *Public Opinion Quarterly* 78, S1 (2014): 276–302; B. Keith Payne et al., "Implicit and Explicit Prejudice in the 2008 American Presidential Election," *Journal of Experimental Social Psychology* 46, 2 (2010): 367–74; Brian F. Schaffner, "Racial Salience and the Obama Vote," *Political Psychology* 32, 6 (2011): 963–88; Michael Tesler, "The Return of Old-Fashioned Racism to White Americans' Partisan Preferences in the Early Obama Era," *The Journal of Politics* 75,1 (2013): 110–23; and Michael Tesler and David Sears, *Obama's Race: The 2008 Election and the Dream of a Post-Racial America* (Chicago: University of Chicago Press, 2010).

32. Ashley Jardina, *White Identity Politics* (New York: Cambridge University Press, 2019).

33. As reported in our data files for the Knights of the Southern Cross Soldiers of the Ku Klux Klan 2011.

34. McAdam, Tarrow, and Tilly, *Dynamics of Contention*.

35. Stephen C. Craig and Michael A. Maggiotto, "Measuring Political Efficacy," *Political Methodology* 8, 3 (1982): 85–109; Arthur Miller, Patricia Gurin, Gerald Gurin, and Oksana Malanchuk, "Group Consciousness and Political Participation," *American Journal of Political Science* 25 (1981): 494–511; and Richard D. Shingles, "Black Consciousness and Political Participation: The Missing Link," *American Political Science Review* 75, 1 (1981): 76–91.

36. A "racial extremist" was defined for the purpose of this analysis as a white respondent who reported a score less than 30 for the feeling thermometer items for both blacks and Hispanics. Since 1992, 7.4 percent of ANES white respondents have been classified as "racial extremists" based on this definition.
37. Philippe Naughton, "President Bush: America Should Be Proud of Barack Obama," *The Times*, November 5, 2008, https://www.thetimes.co.uk/article/president-bush-america-should-be-proud-of-barack-obama-59lgmtrdt78.

Chapter 4

1. Callum Borchers, "Is Richard Spencer a White Nationalist or a White Supremacist? It Depends on the News Source," *Washington Post*, October 19, 2017, https://www.washingtonpost.com/news/the-fix/wp/2017/10/19/is-richard-spencer-a-white-nationalist-or-a-white-supremacist-it-depends-on-the-news-source/.
2. Ashley Jardina, *White Identity Politics* (New York: Cambridge University Press, 2019).
3. Tom Mertes, ed., *A Movement of Movements: Is Another World Really Possible?* (London: Verso, 2004).
4. John D. McCarthy and Mayer N. Zald, "Resource Mobilization and Social Movements: A Partial Theory," *American Journal of Sociology* 82, 6 (1977): 1212–41.
5. Sarah A. Soule and Brayden G. King, "Competition and Resource Partitioning in Three Social Movement Industries," *American Journal of Sociology* 113, 6 (2008): 1568–1610.
6. Debra C. Minkoff, "The Sequencing of Social Movements," *American Sociological Review* 62, 5 (1997): 779–99; Susan Olzak and Emily Ryo, "Organizational Diversity, Vitality and Outcomes in the Civil Rights Movement," Social Forces 85, 4 (2007): 1561–91; and Sidney Tarrow, *Power in Movement: Social Movements and Contentious Politics* (Cambridge University Press, 1998).
7. Barry J. Balleck, *Modern American Extremism and Domestic Terrorism: An Encyclopedia of Extremists and Extremist Groups* (Santa Barbara, CA: ABC-CLIO, 2018), p. 352.
8. Bruce Hoffman, *Inside Terrorism*, rev. and expanded ed. (New York: Columbia University Press, 2006), pp. 104–5.
9. Rory McVeigh, Kraig Beyerlein, Burrel Vann Jr., and Priyamvada Trivedic, "Educational Segregation, Tea Party Organizations, and Battles over Distributive Justice," *American Sociological Review* 79, 4 (2014): 630–52.
10. Ronald B. Rapoport and Walter J. Stone, "Republican Factionalism and Tea Party Activists," http://citeseerx.ist.psu.edu/viewdoc/summary;jsessionid=DBA9EA4B363EF9E9FCFF9DF52165FAED?doi=10.1.1.673.3378.
11. Alan I. Abramowitz, "Grand Old Tea Party: Partisan Polarization and the Rise of the Tea Party Movement," in *Steep: The Precipitous Rise of the Tea Party*, Lawrence Rosenthal and Christine Trost, eds. (Berkeley: University of California Press, 2012), pp. 195–211.
12. Christopher S. Parker and Matt A. Barreto, *Change They Can't Believe In: The Tea Party and Reactionary Politics in America* (Princeton, NJ: Princeton University Press, 2013).

13. According to the *Huffington Post* (June 14, 2012), which posted audio of the speech by Inge Marler, she used the joke as an icebreaker. She eventually resigned her board position with the Ozark Tea Party as a result of the public criticism that followed. Marler reportedly said: "A black kid asks his mom, 'Mama, what's a democracy?' 'Well, son, that be when white folks work every day so us po' folks can get all our benefits.' 'But mama, don't the white folk get mad about that?' 'They sho do, son. They sho do. And that's called racism.'"

14. The speaker at the event was Ken Crow, former president of Tea Party of America. According to audio from the event, Crow said: "From those incredible blood lines of Thomas Jefferson and George Washington and John Smith. And all these great Americans, Martin Luther King. These great Americans who built this country. You came from them. And the unique thing about being from that part of the world, when you learn about breeding, you learn that you cannot breed Secretariat to a donkey and expect to win the Kentucky Derby. You guys have incredible DNA and don't forget it." See George Zornick, "Ugly Opposition to Immigration Reform Comes Back to Capitol Hill," *The Nation*, July 15, 2013, https://www.thenation.com/article/ugly-opposition-immigration-reform-comes-back-capitol-hill/.

15. Patrik Jonsson, "Reporters Grapple with the 'Right' Way to Cover the Far Right," *Christian Science Monitor*, December 28, 2017, https://www.csmonitor.com/USA/Society/2017/1228/Reporters-grapple-with-the-right-way-to-cover-the-far-right.

16. Earl Ofarl Hutchinson, "Method to Racist Madness in Fresh Racial Attacks on President Obama," *HuffPost*, October 13, 2013, https://www.huffpost.com/entry/method-to-racist-madness-_b_3749451.

17. See Abramowitz, "Grand Old Tea Party," pp. 195–211; Matt A. Barreto, Betsy L. Cooper, Benjamin Gonzalez, Christopher S. Parker, and Christopher Towler, "The Tea Party in the Age of Obama: Mainstream Conservatism or Out-Group Anxiety?," in *Political Power and Social Theory*, Julian Go, ed. (Bingley, UK: Emerald Group Publishing Limited, 2011), pp. 105–37; Leigh A. Bradberry and Gary C. Jacobson, "The Tea Party and the 2012 Presidential Election," *Electoral Studies* 40 (2015): 500–508; Angie Eaton Maxwell and T. Wayne Parent, "A 'Subterranean Agenda'? Racial Attitudes, Presidential Evaluations, and Tea Party Membership," *Race and Social Problems* 5 (2013): 226–37; Parker and Barreto, *Change They Can't Believe In*; and Daniel Tope, Justin T. Pickett, and Ted Chiricos, "Anti-Minority Attitudes and Tea Party Movement Membership," *Social Science Research* 51 (2015): 322–37.

18. Tope, Pickett, and Chiricos, "Anti-Minority Attitudes and Tea Party Movement Membership," p. 12.

19. Barreto et al., "The Tea Party in the Age of Obama," p. 1.

20. See Kerem Ozan Kalkan, Geoffrey C. Layman, and Eric M. Uslaner, "'Bands of Others'? Attitudes toward Muslims in Contemporary American Society," *The Journal of Politics* 71, 3 (2009): 847–62.

21. This figure was computed by the authors based on data from the 2016 ANES. See our online Appendix for details.

22. Andrea Elliott, "The Man Behind the Anti-Sharia Movement," *New York Times*, July 30, 2011, https://www.nytimes.com/2011/07/31/us/31shariah.html

23. See our online Appendix for details.

24. Kalkan, Layman, and Uslaner, " 'Bands of Others'?"

25. Theda Skocpol and Vanessa Williamson, *The Tea Party and the Remaking of Republican Conservatism*, updated ed. (New York: Oxford University Press, 2016).

26. Parker and Barreto, *Change They Can't Believe In*, Table 1.2.

27. Warren Kinsella, *Fight the Right: A Manual for Surviving the Coming Conservative Apocalypse* (New York: Random House, 2012), p. 75

28. To test the hypothesis concerning the effect of Tea Party organization on KKK death, we estimate a Cox proportional hazards model of KKK death over the period 2008–2017. We include the number of active Tea Party organizations in a county as our primary independent variable, along with that measure of active Tea Party organizations and its interaction with a dummy variable for the period when the Tea Party was active in 2010 to 2014. The logic of this test is that the number of Tea Party organizations should have a positive effect on KKK death, but only during the period when these organizations were active.

29. See Jeffrey Berry, "Tea Party Decline" (paper presented at the annual meeting of the American Political Science Association, San Francisco, August, 2017). In his analysis of trends in Tea Party organization lifespan, Berry found that no new Tea Party organizations formed after 2013 and that by 2017 nearly 40 percent of Tea Party chapters in his sample no longer existed. Although many Tea Party organizations officially launched in 2009, we do not include this year in the period we define as the TPM's years because 2009 was Obama's first year in office, and as we document in Chapter 3, white supremacist movements were in the midst of a brief period of resurgence. It was only when the TPM began to be recognized as a potent political force in 2010 that we would expect its presence to attract white supremacist group members.

Chapter 5

1. Christopher S. Parker and Matt A. Barreto, *Change They Can't Believe In: The Tea Party and Reactionary Politics in America* (Princeton, NJ: Princeton University Press, 2013); and Theda Skocpol and Vanessa Williamson, *The Tea Party and the Remaking of Republican Conservatism*, updated ed. (New York: Oxford University Press, 2016).

2. Hong Min Park, Joseph Smith, and Richard C. Fording, "When Elephants Drink Tea: Examining the Distinctiveness of Tea Party Republicans in the U.S. Congress, 2009–2014."

3. See Jeffrey Berry, "Tea Party Decline" (paper presented at the annual meeting of the American Political Science Association, San Francisco, August, 2017).

4. Rory McVeigh and Kevin Estep, *The Politics of Losing—Trump, the Klan, and the Mainstreaming of Resentment* (New York: Columbia University Press, 2019).

5. Michael D'Antonio, *Never Enough: Donald Trump and the Pursuit of Success*, 1st ed. (New York: Thomas Dunne Books, 2015).

6. George Hawley, *Right-Wing Critics of American Conservatism* (Lawrence: University Press of Kansas, 2016).

7. Joshua Green, *Devil's Bargain: Steve Bannon, Donald Trump, and the Nationalist Uprising*, reprint ed. (New York: Penguin Books, 2017).

8. David Farenthold and Frances Stead Sellars, "How Bannon Flattered and Coaxed Trump on Policies Key to the Alt-Right," *Washington Post*, November 15, 2016, https://www.washingtonpost.com/politics/how-bannon-flattered-and-coaxed-trump-on-policies-key-to-the-alt-right/2016/11/15/53c66362-ab69-11e6-a31b-4b6397e625d0_story.html.

9. Mike Pearl, "All the Evidence We Could Find about Fred Trump's Alleged Involvement with the KKK," *Vice*, March 1, 2016, https://www.vice.com/en_us/article/mvke38/all-the-evidence-we-could-find-about-fred-trumps-alleged-involvement-with-the-kkk.

10. Daryl Johnson, quoted in Greg Sargent, "Trump's Hate and Lies Are Inciting Extremists: Just Ask the Analyst Who Warned Us," *Washington Post*, October 29, 2018, https://www.washingtonpost.com/blogs/plum-line/wp/2018/10/29/trumps-hate-and-lies-are-emboldening-extremists-just-ask-the-analyst-who-warned-us/.

11. Steven Rosenfeld, "Leading Civil Rights Lawyer Shows 20 Ways Trump Is Copying Hitler's Early Rhetoric and Policies," Common Dreams, August 9, 2019, https://www.commondreams.org/views/2019/08/09/leading-civil-rights-lawyer-shows-20-ways-trump-copying-hitlers-early-rhetoric-and.

12. Cas Mudde, "Stephen Miller Is No Outlier: White Supremacy Rules the Republican Party," *The Guardian*, November 16, 2019, https://www.theguardian.com/commentisfree/2019/nov/16/stephen-miller-white-supremacy-republican-party.

13. Skocpol and Williamson, *The Tea Party and the Remaking of Republican Conservatism*.

14. Michael A. Bailey, Jonathan Mummolo, and Hans Noel, "Tea Party Influence: A Story of Activists and Elites," *American Politics Research* 40, 5 (2012): 769–804; Ian Gallagher and Brian Rock, "Reading the Tea Leaves: An Analysis of Tea Party Behavior Inside and Outside of the House," *Journal of Legal Metrics* 2, 1 (2012): 87–112; and Park, Smith, and Fording, "When Elephants Drink Tea." For an alternative view see Jordan M. Ragusa and Anthony Gaspar, "Where's the Tea Party? An Examination of the Tea Party's Voting Behavior in the House of Representatives," *Political Research Quarterly* 69, 2 (2016): 361–72.

15. Bryan T. Gervais and Irwin L. Morris, *Reactionary Republicanism: How the Tea Party in the House Paved the Way for Trump's Victory* (New York: Oxford University Press, 2018).

16. See the online Appendix for details on sources and methodology used to conduct the content analysis.

17. See Ho Chung Wu et al., "Interpreting TF-IDF Term Weights as Making Relevance Decisions," *ACM Transactions on Information Systems (TOIS)* 26, 3 (2008): 13. The TD-IDF is based on the rate at which the words in the dictionary of terms are used in each document Yet, it essentially adjusts the rate of usage to give less weight to words that are more commonly used in the total set of documents being analyzed. For this reason, the TD-IDF is considered to be a superior measure of rhetorical emphasis compared to a simple measure of term frequency.

18. It is certainly plausible that this relationship could be reversed—that in districts where Tea Party support was relatively high, TP candidates were more likely to use

negative rhetoric targeting racial outgroups. This possibility is mitigated by several features of our analysis. First, this interaction is statistically significant even after controlling for the number of TPOs in the respondent's county. Second, the results are robust to the inclusion of state fixed effects. We provide details of this analysis and our robustness checks in our online Appendix.

19. Philip Bump, "Even the Firm That Hired Actors to Cheer Trump's Campaign Launch Had to Wait to Be Paid," *Washington Post*, January 20, 2017, https://www.washingtonpost.com/news/the-fix/wp/2017/01/20/even-the-firm-that-hired-actors-to-cheer-trumps-campaign-launch-had-to-wait-to-be-paid/.

20. Jeremy Stahl, "Trump to Black Voters: You're Poor, So Why the Hell Don't You Vote for Me," *Slate Magazine*, August 19, 2016, https://slate.com/news-and-politics/2016/08/trump-to-black-voters-youre-poor-so-vote-for-me.html.

21. "Transcript of Donald Trump's Immigration Speech," *New York Times*, September 1, 2016, https://www.nytimes.com/2016/09/02/us/politics/transcript-trump-immigration-speech.html.

22. Tara Golshan, "Read Donald Trump's Most Inflammatory Speech Yet on Muslims and Immigration," *Vox*, June 13, 2016, https://www.vox.com/2016/6/13/11925122/trump-orlando-foreign-policy-transcript.

23. These other candidates included Bernie Sanders, Martin O'Malley, Jim Webb, Marco Rubio, Ted Cruz, John Kasich, Rick Perry, Ben Carson, Carly Fiorina, Chris Christie, Rand Paul, Scott Walker, Mike Huckabee, Rick Santorum, George Pataki, and Bobby Jindal.

24. Thomas F. Pettigrew, "Social Psychological Perspectives on Trump Supporters," *Journal of Social and Political Psychology* 5, 1 (2017): 107–16.

25. Daryl Johnson, "I Warned of Right-Wing Violence in 2009: Republicans Objected; I Was Right," *Washington Post*, August 21, 2017, https://www.washingtonpost.com/news/posteverything/wp/2017/08/21/i-warned-of-right-wing-violence-in-2009-it-caused-an-uproar-i-was-right/.

26. Lois Beckett, "'Blood on Their Hands': The Intelligence Officer Whose Warning over White Supremacy Was Ignored," *The Guardian*, August 8, 2019, https://www.theguardian.com/us-news/2019/aug/07/white-supremacist-terrorism-intelligence-analyst.

27. Igor Derysh, "Trump's DOJ Hid Shocking Report on Growing Terror Threat from White Supremacists," *Salon*, August 9, 2019, https://www.salon.com/2019/08/09/trumps-doj-hid-shocking-report-on-growing-terror-threat-from-white-supremacists/.

Chapter 6

1. Tali Mendelberg, *The Race Card: Campaign Strategy, Implicit Messages, and the Norm of Equality* (Princeton, NJ: Princeton University Press, 2001); and Gregory A. Huber and John S. Lapinski, "The 'Race Card' Revisited: Assessing Racial Priming in Policy Contests," *American Journal of Political Science* 50, 2 (2006): 421–40, https://isps.yale.edu/research/publications/isps06-005.

2. On the differential effects on whites of racial priming regarding different groups, see Tyler T. Reny, Ali A. Valenzuela, and Loren Collingwood, "'No, You're Playing the Race Card': Testing the Effects of Anti-Black, Anti-Latino, and Anti-Immigrant Appeals in the Post-Obama Era," *Political Psychology*, July 18, 2019, https://doi.org/10.1111/pops.12614.

3. Carole Cadwalladr, "My TED Talk: How I Took on the Tech Titans in Their Lair," *The Observer*, April 21, 2019, https://www.theguardian.com/uk-news/2019/apr/21/carole-cadwalladr-ted-tech-google-facebook-zuckerberg-silicon-valley.

4. Matthew Yglesias, "Trump's Racist Tirades against 'the Squad,' Explained," *Vox*, July 15, 2019, https://www.vox.com/2019/7/15/20694616/donald-trump-racist-tweets-omar-aoc-tlaib-pressley.

5. *The Great Hack*, Netflix, 2019, https://www.thegreathack.com/.

6. Gabriel Sherman, *The Loudest Voice in the Room: How the Brilliant, Bombastic Roger Ailes Built Fox News—and Divided a Country*, 1st ed. (New York: Random House, 2014).

7. Jane Mayer, "The Making of the Fox News White House," *The New Yorker*, March 4, 2019, https://www.newyorker.com/magazine/2019/03/11/the-making-of-the-fox-news-white-house.

8. Whether the trend toward polarization in media consumption will continue is an open question. See Indira A. R. Lakshmanan, "Finally Some Good News: Trust in News Is up, Especially for Local Media," Poynter, August 22, 2018, https://www.poynter.org/ethics-trust/2018/finally-some-good-news-trust-in-news-is-up-especially-for-local-media/.

9. Mayer, "The Making of the Fox News White House."

10. Yochai Benkler, Robert Faris, Hal Roberts, and Ethan Zuckerman, "Breitbart-Led Right-Wing Media Ecosystem Altered Broader Media Agenda," *Columbia Journalism Review*, March 3, 2017, https://www.cjr.org/analysis/breitbart-media-trump-harvard-study.php; and David Zurawik, "Nothing Funny about the Propaganda Machine Team Trump Is Building," *Baltimore Sun*, August 8, 2018, https://www.baltimoresun.com/opinion/columnists/zurawik/bs-fe-zontv-trump-sinclair-propaganda-20170808-story.html.

11. Dara Lind, "Donald Trump Lies. All the Time," *Vox*, September 26, 2016, https://www.vox.com/policy-and-politics/2016/9/26/13016146/donald-trump-liar-media.

12. Jamelle Bouie, "The Joy of Hatred," *New York Times*, July 19, 2019, https://www.nytimes.com/2019/07/19/opinion/trump-rally.html.

13. Mallory Simon and Sara Sidner, "White Supremacists Cheer Trump Racist Tweets," CNN, July 16, 2019, https://www.cnn.com/2019/07/16/politics/white-supremacists-cheer-trump-racist-tweets-soh/index.html.

14. "The Frontline Interview: Brad Parscale," *Frontline*, August 18, 2018, https://www.pbs.org/wgbh/frontline/interview/brad-parscale/.

15. *The Great Hack*.

16. Issie Lapowsky, "The Real Trouble with Trump's 'Dark Post' Facebook Ads," *Wired*, September 20, 2019, https://www.wired.com/story/trump-dark-post-facebook-ads/.

17. Michael Barajas, "'Project Alamo': Lessons from Inside Trump's SA-Based Digital Nerve Center." *San Antonio Current*, October 27 2016.

18. David A. Graham, "Trump's 'Voter Suppression Operation' Targets Black Voters," *The Atlantic*, October 27, 2016, https://www.theatlantic.com/politics/archive/2016/10/trumps-black-voter-dilemma/505586/.

19. See Brittany Kaiser, *Targeted: The Cambridge Analytica Whistleblower's Inside Story of How Big Data, Trump, and Facebook Broke Democracy and How It Can Happen Again* (New York: Harper, 2019), p. 229; and Lauren Etter and Michael Riley, "Inside the Pro-Trump Effort to Keep Black Voters from the Polls," *Bloomberg Businessweek*, May 29, 2018.

20. *The Great Hack.*

21. "The Frontline Interview: Brad Parscale."

22. Alex Hern, "Cambridge Analytica: How Did It Turn Clicks into Votes?," *The Guardian*, May 6, 2018, https://www.theguardian.com/news/2018/may/06/cambridge-analytica-how-turn-clicks-into-votes-christopher-wylie.

23. UK Parliament, "Evidence from Christopher Wylie, Cambridge Analytica Whistle-Blower, Published—News from Parliament," March 28, 2018, https://www.parliament.uk/business/committees/committees-a-z/commons-select/digital-culture-media-and-sport-committee/news/fake-news-evidence-wylie-correspondence-17-19/.

24. Mobashra Tazamal and Aamina Shaikh, "The Trump Campaign Weaponized Data to Exploit Prejudice and Islamophobia," Bridge Initiative, November 29, 2018, https://bridge.georgetown.edu/research/the-trump-campaign-weaponized-data-to-exploit-prejudice-and-islamophobia/.

25. Tazamal and Shaikh, "The Trump Campaign Weaponized Data to Exploit Prejudice and Islamophobia."

26. Cadwalladr, "My TED Talk."

27. David Colon, "Propaganda Is the Foundation of Liberal Democracy," Sciences Po, https://www.sciencespo.fr/en/news/news/%E2%80%9Cpropaganda-is-the-foundation-of-liberal-democracy%E2%80%9D/3992.

28. Sasha Issenberg, *The Victory Lab: The Secret Science of Winning Campaigns*, reprint ed. (New York: Broadway Books, 2013).

29. Lulu Garcia-Navarro, "How Does Cambridge Analytica Flap Compare with Obama's Campaign Tactics?" *NPR*, March 25, 2018.

30. George Packer, "A New Report Offers Insights into Tribalism in the Age of Trump," *The New Yorker*, October 13, 2018, https://www.newyorker.com/news/daily-comment/a-new-report-offers-insights-into-tribalism-in-the-age-of-trump.

31. Sylvia Taschka, "Trump-Hitler Comparisons Too Easy and Ignore the Murderous History," The Conversation, May 12, 2018, http://theconversation.com/trump-hitler-comparisons-too-easy-and-ignore-the-murderous-history-92394.

32. Ariel Leve, "Trump Is Gaslighting America—Here's How to Survive," *Business Insider*, March 18, 2017, https://www.businessinsider.com/trump-is-gaslighting-america-heres-how-to-survive-2017-3.

33. Leonard W. Doob, "Goebbels' Principles of Propaganda," *Public Opinion Quarterly* 14, 3 (1950): 419–42.

34. Amy Chua and Jed Rubenfeld, "The Threat of Tribalism," *The Atlantic*, October 2018, https://www.theatlantic.com/magazine/archive/2018/10/the-threat-of-tribalism/568342/.

35. Lapowsky, "The Real Trouble with Trump's 'Dark Post' Facebook Ads."

36. Hunt Allcott and Matthew Gentzkow, "Social Media and Fake News in the 2016 Election" (working paper, National Bureau of Economic Research, January 2017), https://doi.org/10.3386/w23089.

37. Aaron Blake, "A New Study Suggests Fake News Might Have Won Donald Trump the 2016 Election," *Washington Post*, April 3, 2018, https://www.washingtonpost.com/news/the-fix/wp/2018/04/03/a-new-study-suggests-fake-news-might-have-won-donald-trump-the-2016-election/.

38. Elizabeth Kolbert, "Why Facts Don't Change Our Minds," *The New Yorker*, February 20, 2017, https://www.newyorker.com/magazine/2017/02/27/why-facts-dont-change-our-minds.

39. Felix Simon, "Network Propaganda: How a Right-Wing Media Ecosystem Helped to Radicalise America," *European Journalism Observatory*, January 15, 2019, https://en.ejo.ch/research/network-propaganda-how-a-right-wing-media-ecosystem-helped-to-radicalise-america.

40. Sean Illing, "How Propaganda Works in the Digital Age," *Vox*, October 18, 2019, https://www.vox.com/policy-and-politics/2019/10/18/20898584/fox-news-trump-propaganda-jason-stanley.

41. Mayer, "The Making of the Fox News White House."

42. Mark K. McBeth and Donna L. Lybecker, "The Narrative Policy Framework, Agendas, and Sanctuary Cities: The Construction of a Public Problem," *Policy Studies Journal* 46, 4 (2018): 868–93, https://doi.org/10.1111/psj.12274.

43. Colleen E. Mills, "Framing Ferguson: Fox News and the Construction of US Racism," *Race & Class* 58, 4 (2017): 39–56, https://doi.org/10.1177/0306396816685030.

44. Courtney Hagle, "Fox Silent after Rep. Omar Says Death Threats Have Increased since Trump Claimed She Downplayed 9/11," Media Matters for America, April 4, 2019, https://www.mediamatters.org/donald-trump/fox-silent-after-rep-omar-says-death-threats-have-increased-trump-claimed-she.

45. Homero Gil de Zúñiga, Teresa Correa, and Sebastian Valenzuela, "Selective Exposure to Cable News and Immigration in the U.S.: The Relationship Between FOX News, CNN, and Attitudes Toward Mexican Immigrants," *Journal of Broadcasting & Electronic Media* 56, 4 (2012): 597–615, https://doi.org/10.1080/08838151.2012.732138.

46. René D. Flores, "Can Elites Shape Public Attitudes Toward Immigrants? Evidence from the 2016 US Presidential Election," *Social Forces* 96, 4 (2018): 1649–90, https://doi.org/10.1093/sf/soy001.

47. Tyler Monroe, "Fox News Has Aired over 20 Hours of Trump's Campaign Rallies Live in 2019," Media Matters for America, November 7, 2019, https://www.mediamatters.org/fox-news/fox-news-has-aired-over-20-hours-trumps-campaign-rallies-live-2019.

48. For instance, see R. Lance Holbert, R. Kelly Garrett, and Laurel S. Gleason, "A New Era of Minimal Effects? A Response to Bennett and Iyengar," *Journal of Communication*

60, 1 (2010): 15–34; and Natalie Jomini Stroud, "Polarization and Partisan Selective Exposure," *Journal of Communication* 60, 3 (2010): 556–76.

49. These results also hold up when controlling for ideological orientation, but the effect of Fox News consumption is a bit reduced.

50. Connie Hwong, "Tracking the News: Reader Demographics," *Advertising and Monetization*, March 7, 2018: https://vertoanalytics.com/chart-week-tracking-news-reader-demographics/.

51. Chauncey Devaga, "He Sounded the Alarm on 'Hateland': Daryl Johnson Warned Us about Right-Wing Terror in 2009," *Salon*, August 12, 2019, https://www.salon.com/2019/08/12/he-sounded-the-alarm-on-hateland-daryl-johnson-warned-us-about-right-wing-terror-in-2009/.

Chapter 7

1. Sue Halpern, "Hacking the Vote: Who Helped Whom?," *The New York Review of Books*, July19, 2017, https://www.nybooks.com/daily/2017/07/19/hacking-the-vote-trump-russia-who-helped-whom/.

2. Thomas B. Edsall, "The Great Democratic Inversion," *New York Times*, October 27, 2016, https://www.nytimes.com/2016/10/27/opinion/campaign-stops/the-great-democratic-inversion.html.

3. Angie Drobnic Holan, "In Context: Hillary Clinton and the 'Basket of Deplorables,'" Politifact, September 11 2016, http://www.politifact.com/truth-o-meter/article/2016/sep/11/context- hillary-clinton-basket-deplorables/.

4. For instance, see Philip Klinkner, "The Easiest Way to Guess if Someone Supports Trump? Ask if Obama Is a Muslim," *Vox*, June 2, 2016, http://www.vox.com/2016/6/2/11833548/donald-trump-support-race- religion-economy.

5. Holan, "In Context."

6. Yoav Ganzach, Yaniv Hanoch, and Becky L. Choma, "Attitudes Toward Presidential Candidates in the 2012 and 2016 American Elections: Cognitive Ability and Support for Trump," *Social Psychological and Personality Science*, September 27, 2018, https://journals.sagepub.com/doi/10.1177/1948550618800494.

7. For prior research, see David Norman Smith and Eric Hanley, "The Anger Games: Who Voted for Donald Trump in the 2016 Election, and Why?," *Critical Sociology*, February 9, 2018, https://journals.sagepub.com/doi/10.1177/0896920517740615.

8. Matthew McWilliams, "The Best Predictor of Trump Support Isn't Income, Education, or Age: It's Authoritarianism," *Vox*, February, 23, 2016, http://www.vox.com/2016/2/23/11099644/trump-support-authoritarianism; and Amanda Taub, "The Rise of American Authoritarianism: A Niche Group of Political Scientists May Have Uncovered What's Driving Donald Trump's Ascent; What They Found Has Implications That Go Well Beyond 2016," *Vox*, March, 1, 2016, http://www.vox.com/2016/3/1/11127424/trump-authoritarianism.

9. Carly Wayne, Nicholas Valentino, and Marzia Oceno, "How Sexism Drives Support for Donald Trump," *The Monkey Cage* (blog), *Washington Post*, October 23, 2016,

https://www.washingtonpost.com/news/monkey-cage/wp/2016/10/23/how-sexism-drives- support-for-donald-trump/.

10. John Sides, "Race, Religion, and Immigration in 2016: How the Debate over American Identity Shaped the Election and What It Means for a Trump Presidency," Democratic Fund: Voter Study Group, June 2017, https://www.voterstudygroup.org/reports/2016-elections/race-religion-immigration-2016. Also see Stephen L. Morgan and Jiwon Lee, "Economic Populism and Bandwagon Bigotry: Obama-to-Trump Voters and the Cross Pressures of the 2016 Election," *Socius: Sociological Research for a Dynamic World*, August 26, 2019, https://journals.sagepub.com/doi/10.1177/2378023119871119.

11. Edsall, "The Great Democratic Inversion."

12. See Dana Millbank, "There's No Such Thing as a Trump Democrat," *Washington Post*, August 5, 2017, https://www.washingtonpost.com/opinions/theres-no-such-thing-as-a-trump-democrat/2017/08/04/0d5d06bc-7920-11e7-8f39-eeb7d3a2d304_story.html?utm_term=.800b79e67895.

13. Zack Beauchamp, "White Riot: How Racism and Immigration Gave Us Trump, Brexit, and a Whole New Kind of Politics," *Vox*, September 19, 2016, http://www.vox.com/2016/9/19/12933072/far-right-white-riot-trump-brexit. Also see Diana C. Mutz, "Status Threat, Not Economic Hardship, Explains the 2016 Presidential Vote," PNAS, May 8, 2018, https://www.pnas.org/content/115/19/E4330.

14. Nate Silver, "The Mythology of Trump's Working-Class Support," FiveThirtyEight, May 3, 2016, http://fivethirtyeight.com/features/the-mythology-of-trumps-working-class-support/.

15. Beauchamp, "White Riot"; and Klinkner, "The Easiest Way to Guess If Someone Supports Trump?"

16. Pippa Norris and Ronald Inglehart, *Cultural Backlash: Trump, Brexit, and Authoritarian Populism* (Cambridge University Press, 2019).; and "Trump, Brexit, and the Rise of Populism: Economic Have-Nots and Cultural Backlash," Working Paper #RWP16-026 (Cambridge, MA: Harvard University Kennedy School of Government, August, 2016), https://research.hks.harvard.edu/publications/getFile.aspx?Id=1401.

17. Norris and Inglehart, "Trump, Brexit, and the Rise of Populism," p. 30.

18. Samuel Popkin, *The Reasoning Voter: Communication and Persuasion in Presidential Campaigns* (Chicago: University of Chicago Press, 1991).

19. Rush Limbaugh, "Colbert King's Low-Information Definition of the Term 'Low-Information Voter,'" *The Rush Limbaugh Show*, March 25, 2013, http://www.rushlimbaugh.com/daily/2013/03/25/colbert_king_s_low_information_definition_of_tthe_term_low_information_voter.

20. American National Election Studies Pilot Study (ANES), 2016, http://www.electionstudies.org/studypages/anes_pilot_2016/anes_pilot_2016.htm.

21. John T. Cacioppo and Richard E. Petty, "The Need for Cognition," *Journal of Personality and Social Psychology* 42, 1 (1982): 116–31.

22. Cacioppo and Petty, "The Need for Cognition," p. 118.

23. Kevin Arceneaux and Ryan J. Vander Wielen, "The Effects of Need for Cognition and Need for Affect on Partisan Evaluations," *Political Psychology* 34, 1 (2013): 23–42.

24. The additional analyses are in the online Appendix.
25. William Van Til, "The American Democratic Experiment," *Educational Leadership*, October 1959, 6–10, http://www.ascd.org/ASCD/pdf/journals/ed_lead/el_195910_vantil.pdf.
26. Alexis de Tocqueville, *Democracy in America* (Chicago: University of Chicago Press, 2000).
27. William James, "On a Certain Blindness in Human Beings," in *Talks to Teachers on Psychology and to Students on Some of Life's Ideals* (New York: Henry Holt & Company, 1899), https://www.uky.edu/~eushe2/Pajares/jcertain.html.
28. Richard Hofstadter, "The Paranoid Style in American Politics," *Harper's Magazine*, November, 1964, http://harpers.org/archive/1964/11/the-paranoid-style-in-american-politics/.
29. Hofstadter, "The Paranoid Style in American Politics," p. 6.
30. Peter Baker and Michael D. Shear, "El Paso Shooting Suspect's Manifesto Echoes Trump's Language," *New York Times*, August 4, 2019, sec. U.S., https://www.nytimes.com/2019/08/04/us/politics/trump-mass-shootings.html.
31. Chris Sommerfeldt, "Donald Trump Supporter in Iowa Arrested for Voter Fraud," *Daily News*, October 29, 2016, http://www.nydailynews.com/news/politics/donald-trump-supporter-iowa-arrested-voter-fraud-article-1.2850101.
32. Josh Marshall, "Trump Rolls Out Anti-Semitic Closing Ad," Talking Points Memo, November 5, 2016, http://talkingpointsmemo.com/edblog/trump-rolls-out-anti-semitic-closing-ad.
33. Aaron Blake, "'The Poorly Educated' People of America Cut an Ad for Donald Trump," *Washington Post*, February 25, 2016, https://www.washingtonpost.com/news/the-fix/wp/2016/02/25/the-poorly-educated-people-of-america-cut-an-ad-for-donald-trump-video/.
34. Paul de Haye, "Microtargeting Low-Information Voters," Medium, December 30, 2016, https://medium.com/personaldata-io/microtargeting-of-low-information-voters-6eb2520cd473/; and Adam Henshall, "What Marketers Can Learn from Trump about the Science of Persuasion," process.st, March 31, 2017, https://www.process.st/science-of-persuasion/
35. Karoli Kuns, "Justice David Souter on Civic Ignorance: 'That Is How Democracy Dies,'" Crooks and Liars, October 22, 2016, http://crooksandliars.com/2016/10/justice-david-souter-civic- ignorance-how.
36. John Judis, *The Populist Explosion: How the Great Recession Transformed American and European Politics* (New York: Columbia Global Reports, 2016); and Jan-Werner Müller, *What Is Populism?* (Philadelphia: University of Pennsylvania Press 2016).

Chapter 8

1. See, for instance, Stephen L. Morgan and Jiwon Lee, "Economic Populism and Bandwagon Bigotry: Obama-to-Trump Voters and the Cross Pressures of the 2016 Election," *Socius: Sociological Research for a Dynamic World*, August 26, 2019, https://journals.sagepub.com/doi/10.1177/2378023119871119. For an alternative view,

see Ian Haney Lopez, *Dog Whistle Politics: Strategic Racism, Fake Populism, and the Dividing of America* (New York: Oxford University Press, 2013).

2. See John Sides, Michael Tesler, and Lynn Vavreck, *Identity Crisis: The 2016 Presidential Campaign and the Battle for the Meaning of America* (Princeton, NJ: Princeton University Press, 2018); and Ashley Jardina, *White Identity Politics* (New York: Cambridge University Press, 2019).

3. Douglas Kellner, "Brexit Plus, Whitelash, and the Ascendency of Donald J. Trump," *Cultural Politics* 13, 2 (2017): 135–49; Zack Beauchamp, "White Riot: How Racism and Immigration Gave Us Trump, Brexit, and a Whole New Kind of Politics," *Vox*, September 19, 2016, https://www.vox.com/2016/9/19/12933072/far-right-white-riot-trump-brexit; and Josiah Ryan, "'This Was a Whitelash': Van Jones' Take on the Election Results," *CNNPolitics*, November 9, 2016, https://www.cnn.com/2016/11/09/politics/van-jones-results-disappointment-cnntv/index.html.

4. Richard C. Fording and Sanford F. Schram, "The Cognitive and Emotional Sources of Trump Support: The Case of Low-Information Voters," *New Political Science* 39, 4 (2017): 670–86; Brian F. Schaffner, Matthew Macwilliams, and Tatishe Nteta, "Understanding White Polarization in the 2016 Vote for President: The Sobering Role of Racism and Sexism," *Political Science Quarterly* 133, 1 (2018): 9–34; and Sides, Tesler, and Vavreck, *Identity Crisis*.

5. Cara Wong and Grace E. Cho, "Two-Headed Coins or Kandinskys: White Racial Identification," *Political Psychology* 26, 5 (2005): 699–720.

6. Patricia Gurin, "Women's Gender Consciousness," *Public Opinion Quarterly* 49, 2 (1985): 143.

7. Gregory A. Petrow, John E. Transue, and Timothy Vercellotti, "Do White In-Group Processes Matter, Too? White Racial Identity and Support for Black Political Candidates," *Political Behavior* 40, 1 (2018): 197–222.

8. Eric D. Knowles and Linda R. Tropp, "The Racial and Economic Context of Trump Support: Evidence for Threat, Identity, and Contact Effects in the 2016 Presidential Election," *Social Psychological and Personality Science* 9, 3 (2019), https://journals.sagepub.com/doi/abs/10.1177/1948550618759326. Also see Sides, Tesler, and Vavreck, *Identity Crisis*; and Jardina, *White Identity Politics*.

9. Boris Bizumic and John Duckitt, "What Is and Is Not Ethnocentrism? A Conceptual Analysis and Political Implications," *Political Psychology* 33, 6 (2012): 887–909, https://doi.org/10.1111/j.1467-9221.2012.00907.x.

10. Jardina, *White Identity Politics*; Petrow, Transue, and Vercellotti, "Do White In-Group Processes Matter, Too?"; and Sides, Tesler, and Vavreck, *Identity Crisis*.

11. Maria Snegovaya, "The Economic Origins of Populist Support," *The American Interest*, February 22, 2018, https://www.the-american-interest.com/2018/02/22/economic-origins-populist-support/.; and Morgan and Lee "Economic Populism and Bandwagon Bigotry."

12. Details on all variables, including question wording and descriptive statistics, are included in our online Appendix.

13. Schaffner, Macwilliams, and Nteta, "Understanding White Polarization in the 2016 Vote for President"; and Nicholas A. Valentino, Carly Wayne, and Marzia Oceno,

"Mobilizing Sexism: The Interaction of Emotion and Gender Attitudes in the 2016 US Presidential Election," *Public Opinion Quarterly* 82, S1 (2018): 799–821.

14. Thomas B. Edsall, "The Great Democratic Inversion," *New York Times*, October 27, 2016, https://www.nytimes.com/2016/10/27/opinion/campaign-stops/the-great-democratic-inversion.html.

15. Sides, Tesler, and Vavreck, *Identity Crisis*.

16. Jardina, *White Identity Politics*.

17. Detailed results for these supplementary analyses of white racial identity are presented in our online Appendix.

18. Donald R. Kinder and Cindy D. Kam, *Us Against Them: Ethnocentric Foundations of American Opinion* (Chicago: University of Chicago Press, 2009).

19. Two additional differences between the two datasets are relevant to our analysis. First, the pilot survey did not include a feeling thermometer item for Christian fundamentalists. As the purpose of this indicator was to control for positions on morality-based policies such as LGBT rights and abortion, we therefore include a feeling thermometer for "feminists" as well as the average of the feeling theremometer scores for "gays" and "transgender" people. Second, the survey did not identify union households. Therefore, we are unable to control for this variable. The full results for this analyis are presented in our online Appendix.

20. Gordon W. Allport, *The Nature of Prejudice* (Oxford: Addison-Wesley, 1954).

21. Our preference for the feeling thermometer difference over a dichotomous vote choice variable is based on the fact that there is no consensus on how to compute indirect effects for path models with nonlinear outcome variables. Yet the use of the feeling thermometer scores does not alter our conclusions regarding the effects of the independent variables on support for Trump.

22. Marisa Abrajano and Zoltan L. Hajnal, *White Backlash: Immigration, Race, and American Politics* (Princeton, NJ: Princeton University Press, 2015); Zoltan Hajnal and Michael U. Rivera, "Immigration, Latinos, and White Partisan Politics: The New Democratic Defection," *American Journal of Political Science* 58, 4 (2014): 773–89; and Nicholas A. Valentino and David O. Sears, "Old Times There Are Not Forgotten: Race and Partisan Realignment in the Contemporary South," *American Journal of Political Science* 49, 3 (2005): 672–88.

23. John R. Alford, Carolyn L. Funk, and John R. Hibbing, "Are Political Orientations Genetically Transmitted?," *American Political Science Review* 99, 2 (2005): 153–67.

24. Ashley W. Doane Jr., "Dominant Group Ethnic Identity in the United States: The Role of 'Hidden' Ethnicity in Intergroup Relations," *The Sociological Quarterly* 38, 3 (1997): 375–97.

25. Although the path analysis using the VOTER data leads to the same substantive conclusions, we have a slight preference for the ANES analyses because we are able to control for authoritarianism in our models of outgroup hostility, modern sexism, and social issues. This is not possible for the VOTER analyses.

26. See for instance, Morgan and Lee, "Economic Populism and Bandwagon Bigotry: Obama-to-Trump Voters and the Cross Pressures of the 2016 Election."

27. Michael Tesler and David Sears, *Obama's Race: The 2008 Election and the Dream of a Post-Racial America* (Chicago: University of Chicago Press, 2010); and Michael Tesler, *Post-Racial or Most-Racial? Race and Politics in the Obama Era* (Chicago: University of Chicago Press, 2016).

28. Tali Mendelberg, *The Race Card: Campaign Strategy, Implicit Messages, and the Norm of Equality* (Princeton, NJ: Princeton University Press, 2001).

29. Jon Hurwitz and Mark Peffley, "Playing the Race Card in the Post–Willie Horton EraThe Impact of Racialized Code Words on Support for Punitive Crime Policy," *Public Opinion Quarterly* 69, 1 (2005): 99–112.

30. Peter M. Robinson, "Root-N-Consistent Semiparametric Regression," *Econometrica* 56, 4 (1988): 931–54.

31. Antoine J. Banks, *Anger and Racial Politics: The Emotional Foundation of Racial Attitudes in America* (New York: Cambridge University Press, 2014).

32. Charles S. Carver and Eddie Harmon-Jones, "Anger Is an Approach-Related Affect: Evidence and Implications," *Psychological Bulletin* 135, 2 (2009): 183–204.

33. Martijn van Zomeren et al., "Put Your Money Where Your Mouth Is! Explaining Collective Action Tendencies through Group-Based Anger and Group Efficacy," *Journal of Personality and Social Psychology* 87, 5 (2004): 649–64.

34. Eric W. Groenendyk and Antoine J. Banks, "Emotional Rescue: How Affect Helps Partisans Overcome Collective Action Problems," *Political Psychology* 35, 3 (2014): 359–78; Michael MacKuen, Jennifer Wolak, Luke Keele, and George E. Marcus, "Civic Engagements: Resolute Partisanship or Reflective Deliberation," *American Journal of Political Science* 54, 2 (2010): 440–58; George E. Marcus, "Emotions in Politics," *Annual Review of Political Science* 3, 1 (2000): 221–50; and Nicholas A. Valentino, Ted Brader, Eric W. Groenendyk, Krysha Gregorowicz, and Vincent L. Hutchings, "Election Night's Alright for Fighting: The Role of Emotions in Political Participation," *The Journal of Politics* 73, 1 (2011): 156–70.

35. Ted Brader, "Striking a Responsive Chord: How Political Ads Motivate and Persuade Voters by Appealing to Emotions," *American Journal of Political Science* 49, 2 (2005): 388–405; and Marcus, "Emotions in Politics."

36. Groenendyk and Banks, "Emotional Rescue"; David P. Redlawsk, Andrew J. W. Civettini, and Karen M. Emmerson, "The Affective Tipping Point: Do Motivated Reasoners Ever 'Get It'?," *Political Psychology* 31, 4 (2010): 563–93; and Valentino et al., "Election Night's Alright for Fighting."

37. Banks, "Anger and Racial Politics"; Groenendyk and Banks, "Emotional Rescue"; Redlawsk, Civettini, and Emmerson, "The Affective Tipping Point"; and Valentino et al., "Election Night's Alright for Fighting."

38. Abrajano and Hajnal, *White Backlash*; Kinder and Kam, *Us Against Them*; Tesler and Sears, *Obama's Race*; and Tesler, *Post-Racial or Most-Racial?*

39. The results for partisan-directed enthusiasm are nearly identical. We present these results in our online Appendix.

40. Hurwitz and Peffley, "Playing the Race Card in the Post–Willie Horton Era"; and Mendelberg, *The Race Card*.

Chapter 9

1. "The Frontline Interview: Brad Parscale," *Frontline*, August 18, 2018, https://www.pbs.org/wgbh/frontline/interview/brad-parscale/.
2. Ian Haney Lopez, *Dog Whistle Politics: Strategic Racism, Fake Populism, and the Dividing of America* (New York: Oxford University Press, 2013).
3. For background, see Tyler T. Reny, Loren Collingwood, and Ali A. Valenzuela, "Vote Switching in the 2016 Election: How Racial and Immigration Attitudes, Not Economics, Explain Shifts in White Voting," *Public Opinion Quarterly* 83, 1 (2019): 91–113.
4. John Sides, Michael Tesler, and Lynn Vavreck, *Identity Crisis: The 2016 Presidential Campaign and the Battle for the Meaning of America* (Princeton, NJ: Princeton University Press, 2018).
5. Nate Cohn, "The Obama-Trump Voters Are Real: Here's What They Think," *New York Times*, August 15, 2017, https://www.nytimes.com/2017/08/15/upshot/the-obama-trump-voters-are-real-heres-what-they-think.html.
6. Jens Manuel Krogstad and Mark Hugo Lopez, "Black Voter Turnout Fell in 2016 US Election," Pew Research Center, May 12, 2017, https://www.pewresearch.org/fact-tank/2017/05/12/black-voter-turnout-fell-in-2016-even-as-a-record-number-of-americans-cast-ballots/.
7. Rachelle Hampton, "The Most Underplayed Story of the 2016 Election Is Voter Suppression," *The New Republic*, October 19, 2017, https://newrepublic.com/minutes/145387/underplayed-story-2016-election-voter-suppression.
8. Julia Carrie Wong, "'It Might Work Too Well': The Dark Art of Political Advertising Online," *The Guardian*, March 19, 2018, https://www.theguardian.com/technology/2018/mar/19/facebook-political-ads-social-media-history-online-democracy.
9. David A. Graham, "Russian Trolls and the Trump Campaign Both Tried to Depress Black Turnout," *The Atlantic*, December 17, 2018, https://www.theatlantic.com/politics/archive/2018/12/shared-russia-trump-focus-depressing-black-votes/578302/.
10. David A. Graham, "Trump's 'Voter Suppression Operation' Targets Black Voters," *The Atlantic*, October 27, 2016, https://www.theatlantic.com/politics/archive/2016/10/trumps-black-voter-dilemma/505586/.
11. Philip Bump, "4.4 Million 2012 Obama Voters Stayed Home in 2016—More Than a Third of Them Black," *Washington Post*, March 12, 2018, https://www.washingtonpost.com/news/politics/wp/2018/03/12/4-4-million-2012-obama-voters-stayed-home-in-2016-more-than-a-third-of-them-black/.
12. Sides, Tesler, and Vavreck, *Identity Crisis*.
13. Josiah Ryan, "'This Was a Whitelash': Van Jones' Take on the Election Results," *CNN Politics*, November 9, 2016, https://www.cnn.com/2016/11/09/politics/van-jones-results-disappointment-cnntv/index.html.
14. Sabrina Tavernise and Robert Gebeloff, "They Voted for Obama, Then Went for Trump: Can Democrats Win Them Back?," *New York Times*, May 4, 2018, https://www.nytimes.com/2018/05/04/us/obama-trump-swing-voters.html.

15. Kevin Uhrmacher, Kevin Schaul, and Dan Keating, "These Former Obama Strongholds Sealed the Election for Trump," *Washington Post*, November 9, 2016, https://www.washingtonpost.com/graphics/politics/2016-election/obama-trump-counties/.

16. Shannon M. Monnat and David L.Brown, "More Than a Rural Revolt: Landscapes of Despair and the 2016 Presidential Election," *Journal of Rural Studies* 55 (2017): 227–36.

17. Sides, Tesler, and Vavreck, *Identity Crisis*, p. 172.

18. For one study that examines the validated vote for Obama-Trump switchers, see Stephen L. Morgan and Jiwon Lee, "Economic Populism and Bandwagon Bigotry: Obama-to-Trump Voters and the Cross Pressures of the 2016 Election, 2019," *Socius: Sociological Research for a Dynamic World*, August 26, 2019, https://doi.org/10.1177/2378023119871119.

19. These calculations are based on the validated vote from the 2016 Time Series Study from the American National Election Studies (ANES), http://www.electionstudies.org/studypages/anes_timeseries_2016/anes_timeseries_2016.htm.

20. J. M. Berger, "How White Nationalists Learned to Love Donald Trump," *Politico*, October 25, 2016, https://www.politico.com/magazine/story/2016/10/donald-trump-2016-white-nationalists-alt-right-214388.

21. Berger, "How White Nationalists Learned to Love Donald Trump."

22. Berger, "How White Nationalists Learned to Love Donald Trump."

23. WhiteGarden, "We Must Find Unity Now!!!," Stormfront, June 7, 2009, https://www.stormfront.org/forum/t605973/#post6949805.

24. Kampfgruppe88, "Re: 'We Must Find Unity Now!!!,'" Stormfront, June 9, 2009, https://www.stormfront.org/forum/t605973-2/.

25. Christina Wilkie, "White Supremacists Are Broadcasting from Inside Trump Rallies," *HuffPost*, March 2, 2016, https://www.huffpost.com/entry/white-supremacists-donald-trump-rallies_n_56d663cfe4b03260bf789a09.

26. J. M. Berger, *Nazis vs. ISIS on Twitter: A Comparative Study of White Nationalist and ISIS Online Social Media Networks* (Washington, DC: GW Program on Extremism, September 2016), p. 3, https://extremism.gwu.edu/sites/g/files/zaxdzs2191/f/downloads/Nazis%20v.%20ISIS.pdf

27. Jane Coaston, "Self-Described Nazis and White Supremacists Are Running as Republicans across the Country: The GOP Is Terrified," *Vox*, July 9, 2018, https://www.vox.com/2018/7/9/17525860/nazis-russell-walker-arthur-jones-republicans-illinois-north-carolina-virginia.

28. JaneCoaston,"HowWhiteSupremacistCandidatesFaredin2018,"*Vox*,November7,2018, https://www.vox.com/policy-and-politics/2018/11/7/18064670/white-supremacist-candidates-2018-midterm-elections.

29. Jessica Schulberg, "Spokane GOP Chair Cecily Wright Resigns After Defending White Nationalist Elected Official," *HuffPost*, August 2, 2018, https://www.huffpost.com/entry/james-allsup-cecily-wright-gop-label-lynching_n_5b60c7fae4b0fd5c73d4060b.

30. Danny Hakim and Stephanie Saul, "White Nationalists Love Corey Stewart: He Keeps Them Close," *New York Times*, August 5, 2018, https://www.nytimes.com/2018/08/05/us/politics/corey-stewart-virginia.html.

31. Maggie Astor, "How the Politically Unthinkable Can Become Mainstream," *New York Times*, February 26, 2019, https://www.nytimes.com/2019/02/26/us/politics/overton-window-democrats.html.

32. The difference between the effect of the county Trump vote in 2008 and 2016 is statistically significant. The full statistical results for this analysis can be found in our online Appendix.

33. *Richard von Busack*, "Forget Hillary's Deplorables. It's All About the Persuadables," *East Bay Express*, August 7, 2019, https://www.eastbayexpress.com/oakland/forget-hillarys-deplorables-its-all-about-the-persuadables/Content?oid=27250482.

Chapter 10

1. Sanford F. Schram, *The Return of Ordinary Capitalism: Neoliberalism, Precarity, Occupy* (New York: Oxford University Press, 2015), chapter 1. On the cyclical nature of racial politics specifically, see Michelle Alexander, "The Injustice of This Moment Is Not an 'Aberration,'" *New York Times*, January 17, 2020, https://www.nytimes.com/2020/01/17/opinion/sunday/michelle-alexander-new-jim-crow.html.

2. Doug McAdam, Sidney G. Tarrow, and Charles Tilly, *Dynamics of Contention* (New York: Cambridge University Press, 2001).

3. Ashley Jardina, *White Identity Politics* (New York: Cambridge University Press, 2019).

4. For background, see Nell Irvin Painter, *The History of White People* (New York: W. W. Norton & Company, 2011); and Carol Anderson, *White Rage: The Unspoken Truth of Our Racial Divide* (New York: Bloomsbury USA, 2016).

5. Michael Tesler, *Post-Racial or Most-Racial? Race and Politics in the Obama Era* (Chicago: University of Chicago Press, 2016).

6. Donald R. Kinder and Cindy D. Kam, *Us Against Them: Ethnocentric Foundations of American Opinion* (Chicago: University of Chicago Press, 2009).

7. George Packer, "A New Report Offers Insights into Tribalism in the Age of Trump," *The New Yorker*, October 13, 2018, https://www.newyorker.com/news/daily-comment/a-new-report-offers-insights-into-tribalism-in-the-age-of-trump.

8. For an alternative view, see Katherine Cramer, "Listening to Strengthen Democracy" (presentation at the Gerald R. Ford School of Public Policy, University of Michigan, October 23, 2019), http://fordschool.umich.edu/video/2019/katherine-cramer-listening-strengthen-democracy.

9. Ann M. Oberhauser, Daniel Krier, and Abdi M. Kusow, "Political Moderation and Polarization in the Heartland: Economics, Rurality, and Social Identity in the 2016 U.S. Presidential Election," *The Sociological Quarterly* 60, 2 (2019): 224–44. For an argument on behalf of a multiracial coalition that combats the intersections of racism and economic inequality, see Daniel Martinez HoSang and Joseph E. Lowndes,

Producers, Parasites, Patriots: Race and the New Right-Wing Politics of Precarity (Minneapolis: University of Minnesota Press, 2019). While wrong about Berne Sanders but right about the importance of a coalition that combines race and class considerations, see Keeanga-Yamahtta Taylor, "Don't Think Sanders Can Win? You Don't Understand His Campaign," *New York Times*, December 10, 2019, https://www.nytimes.com/2019/12/10/opinion/bernie-sanders-multiracial-workers.html.

10. Schram, *The Return of Ordinary Capitalism*, chapter 1.

11. McAdam, Tarrow, and Tilly, *Dynamics of Contention*.

12. Robert D. Benford and David A. Snow, "Framing Processes and Social Movements: An Overview and Assessment," *Annual Review of Sociology* 26 (2000): 611–39.

13. See Jeanne Theoharis, *A More Beautiful and Terrible History: The Uses and Misuses of Civil Rights History* (Boston: Beacon Press, 2018).

14. On the Civil Rights movement and the "socialization of conflict," see E. E. Schattschneider, *Semi-Sovereign People* (New York: Holt, Rinehart and Winston, 1960), p. 7.

15. Christopher S. Parker and Matt A. Barreto, *Change They Can't Believe In: The Tea Party and Reactionary Politics in America* (Princeton, NJ: Princeton University Press, 2014).

16. John D. McCarthy and Mayer N. Zald, "The Enduring Vitality of the Resource Mobilization Theory of Social Movements," in *Handbook of Sociological Theory*, Jonathan H. Turner, ed., *Handbook of Sociology and Social Research* (Boston: Springer US, 2001), 533–65.

17. Diana Mutz, "Status Threat, Not Economic Hardship, Explains the 2016 Presidential Vote," PNAS, May 8, 2018, https://www.pnas.org/content/115/19/E4330.

18. For an alternative view that suggests Obama-Trump switchers were critical to Trump's victory and that they switched on the basis of economic concerns, see Stephen L. Morgan and Jiwon Lee, "Economic Populism and Bandwagon Bigotry: Obama-to-Trump Voters and the Cross Pressures of the 2016 Election," *Socius: Sociological Research for a Dynamic World*, August 26, 2019, https://journals.sagepub.com/doi/10.1177/2378023119871119.

19. Joseph A. Wulfsohn, "Media Can't Recover Legitimacy Until It Stops Being Baited by Trump," *The Federalist*, May 15, 2018, https://thefederalist.com/2018/05/15/media-cant-recover-legitimacy-stops-baited-trumps-empty-threats/.

20. Aaron Rupar, "Why Trump Is Furiously Attacking Fox News," *Vox*, September 3, 2019, https://www.vox.com/2019/9/3/20836724/why-trump-is-attacking-fox-news-explained.

21. Yasha Mounk, *The People vs. Democracy Why Our Freedom Is in Danger and How to Save It* (Cambridge: Harvard University Press, 2018).

22. See Thomas B. Edsall, "The Deepening 'Racialization' of American Politics," *New York Times*, February 27, 2019, https://www.nytimes.com/2019/02/27/opinion/trump-obama-race.html.

23. Osita Nwanevu, "Conservative Nationalism Is Trumpism for Intellectuals," *The New Yorker*, July 21, 2019, https://www.newyorker.com/news/news-desk/conservative-nationalism-is-trumpism-for-intellectuals.

24. Zack Beauchamp, "White Riot: How Racism and Immigration Gave Us Trump, Brexit, and a Whole New Kind of Politics," *Vox*, September 19, 2016, https://www.vox.com/2016/9/19/12933072/far-right-white-riot-trump-brexit.

25. Lawrence M. Mead, *Burdens of Freedom: Cultural Difference and American Power* (New York: Encounter Books, 2019), pp. 2, 4, 18.

26. American exceptionalism is a much-abused appellation for U.S. alleged moral superiority that more often than not rationalized the Country's abuse of white privilege. Its return to justify the movement on behalf of conservative nationalism only reinforces that sad history. Colin Dueck, "Conservative American Nationalism: Our Oldest Foreign-Policy Tradition," *National Review*, October 21, 2019, https://www.nationalreview.com/2019/10/what-is-conservative-american-nationalism/.

27. Edsall, "The Deepening 'Racialization' of American Politics."

28. Ed Kilgore, "There Aren't Many True Independents, and They Aren't into Politics," Intelligencer, March 15, 2019, http://nymag.com/intelligencer/2019/03/true-independent-voters-are-few-in-number-often-apolitical.html.

29. Colby Itkowitz, "The Next Generation of Voters Is More Liberal, More Inclusive and Believes in Government," *Washington Post*, January 17, 2019, https://www.washingtonpost.com/politics/2019/01/17/next-generation-voters-are-more-liberal-more-inclusive-believe-government/.

30. Sarah Jaffe, "Why Did a Majority of White Women Vote for Trump?," *New Labor Forum* 27, 1 (2018): 18–26, https://doi.org/10.1177/1095796017744550.

31. Ronald Brownstein, "Will Trump's Racist Attacks Help Him? Ask Blue-Collar White Women," *The Atlantic*, July 25, 2019, https://www.theatlantic.com/politics/archive/2019/07/trumps-go-back-attacks-white-working-class-women/594805/.

32. Lara Putnam and Theda Skocpol, "Women Are Rebuilding the Democratic Party from the Ground Up," *The New Republic*, August 21, 2018, https://newrepublic.com/article/150462/women-rebuilding-democratic-party-ground.

33. For additional evidence for emphasizing resistance to racism, see Christopher S. Parker and Christopher Towler, "Why Bernie Sanders Isn't Winning Over Black Voters," *Politico*, March 7, 2020, https://www.politico.com/news/magazine/2020/03/07/why-bernie-sanders-economic-message-isnt-enough-to-win-over-black-voters-118197.

34. L. A. Kauffman, "First They Marched, Then They Mobilized: How the Resistance Swayed the Midterms," *The Guardian*, November 11, 2018, https://www.theguardian.com/commentisfree/2018/nov/11/how-the-resistance-trump-swayed-midterm-democrats.

35. Tim Hains, "Ann Coulter: 'The Only National Emergency Is That Our President Is an Idiot,'" Real Clear Politics, February 15, 2019, https://www.realclearpolitics.com/video/2019/02/15/ann_coulter_the_only_national_emergency_is_that_our_president_is_an_idiot.html.

36. Matthew Rosza, "White Supremacist Richard Spencer 'Deeply' Regrets Voting for Trump Amid Iran Crisis," *Salon*, January 9, 2020, https://www.salon.com/2020/01/08/white-supremacist-richard-spencer-deeply-regrets-voting-for-trump-amid-iran-crisis/.

37. Guy Molyneux, "Mapping the White Working Class," *The American Prospect*, December 20, 2016, https://prospect.org/economy/mapping-white-working-class/.

38. Cramer, "Listening to Strengthen Democracy." On how demographic change, not economic vulnerability, drives resurgent racism today, see David Neiwert, *Alt-America: The Rise of the Radical Right in the Age of Trump* (London: Verso Press, 2018); Eric Kaufmann, *Whiteshift: Populism, Immigration, and the Future of White Majorities*, 1st ed. (New York: Harry N. Abrams, 2019); and Ezra Klein, *Why We're Polarized* (New York: Simon & Schuster, 2020).

39. See HoSang and Lowndes, *Producers, Parasites, Patriots*, conclusion.

40. Pippa Norris and Ronald Inglehart, *Cultural Backlash and the Rise of Populism: Trump, Brexit, and Authoritarian Populism* (New York: Cambridge University Press, 2019).

41. See Marc Hetherington and Jonathan Weiler, *Prius or Pickup? How the Answers to Four Simple Questions Explain America's Great Divide* (New York: Houghton Mifflin Harcourt, 2018).

42. Thomas B. Edsall, "Is Politics a War of Ideas or of Us Against Them?," *New York Times*, November 6, 2019, https://www.nytimes.com/2019/11/06/opinion/is-politics-a-war-of-ideas-or-of-us-against-them.html.

43. Kinder and Kam, *Us Against Them* as discussed in Donald R. Kinder and Nathan P. Kalmoe, *Neither Liberal Nor Conservative: Ideological Innocence in the American Public* (Chicago: University of Chicago Press, 2017), pp. 136–39.

44. For the evidence that Trump is building on a broader movement of resurgent racial resentment, see Thomas B. Edsall, "Trump Has a Gift for Tearing Us Apart," *New York Times*, December 11, 2019, https://www.nytimes.com/2019/12/11/opinion/trump-immigration.html.

45. Steven Levitsky and Daniel Ziblatt, *How Democracies Die* (New York: Crown/Archetype, 2018).

46. Steven Miller and Nicholas Davis, "White Outgroup Intolerance and Declining Support for American Democracy," 2018, http://svmiller.com/research/white-outgroup-intolerance-democratic-support/.

47. Charlie Warzel, "Trump Chooses Disaster as His Re-Election Strategy: It's a Massive Bet that Political Polarization is a More Powerful Force than the Virus's Body Count," *New York Times*, March 27, 2020, https://www.nytimes.com/2020/03/27/opinion/trump-coronavirus-response.html?smid=fb-share.

48. Mike Magner, Bridget Bowman and Gopal Ratnam, "Democracy on the Ropes: The Pandemic's Threat to the 2020 Elections, *CQ Magazine,* March 30, 2020, https://plus.cq.com/shareExternal/doc/weeklyreport-5872116/-6ppqoxo8tUht CtW3KNKVwmGdWE?0&fbclid=IwAR3zdjCXtdzfPBOBttXnL6gKcTLS1PBBeejt 1ovd3VeW1YJWmERzdjwSwJM. Jeff Isaac. who originally drafted the petition, is quoted: "My biggest fear is that this president, and his supporters, will either explicitly call for the postponement or cancellation of the general election, or simply do nothing in the face of the logistical challenges presented by COVID, thereby making an election impossible."

Index

For the benefit of digital users, indexed terms that span two pages (e.g., 52–53) may, on occasion, appear on only one of those pages.

Tables and figures are indicated by *t* and *f* following the page number

National Policy Institute, 56
National Socialist White People's Party
    (NSWPP), 74
Nazism. *See* Neo-Nazism
Neo-Nazism, 12, 53–55, 58*f*, 74
New York Times, 136–37
Nix, Alexander, 127
Nixon, Richard, 3, 5, 40–41, 113–15
nonvoters
    Parscale on, 124, 141, 183, 190–91, 202
    Trump's mobilization of, 17–18, 125–26,
        140, 183, 189–93, 193*f*, 201–2, 212
Norris, Pippa, 144–45

Obama, Barack
    African American voters and,
        184–85, 207–8
    birther movement and, 4, 25–26, 99,
        128–29, 130–31, 206–7
    digital media campaign strategies of,
        125, 128
    increase in racialized attitudes among
        electorate since election of, 171–74
    low-information voters and,
        150*f*, 150–51
    misattribution of Muslim faith to, 79,
        142–43, 152*f*, 152–53
    Tea Party opposition to, 16, 25–26, 44,
        72, 76–77, 79, 97, 121
    voters' outgroup hostility and levels of
        anger toward, 180*t*, 181*f*, 182
    vote totals in states that switched from
        Obama to Trump for, 186–87, 186*t*
    white nationalist opposition to, 2, 4, 10–
        11, 33, 48, 63–71, 73, 74–75, 94–95,
        121, 196, 200–1, 202–3, 204–5, 206
Obama, Michelle, 130–31
Ocasio-Cortez, Alexandra, 6–9, 8*f*
Omar, Ilhan, 6–9, 8*f*
Orlando (Florida) mass shooting
    (2016), 111–12
outgroup hostility
    African Americans as target of, 9, 20–
        21, 24, 26–28, 27*t*, 34*f*, 79–81, 80*f*, 91,
        99, 101–2, 103–16*t*, 105*f*, 106, 109–
        10, 117–19, 130, 137–39, 139*f*, 141,
        152, 162*t*, 182, 183, 197, 204–5, 207,
        209, 220–21

age's correlation with, 30*t*
anger toward federal government and,
    66, 67*f*
Asians as target of, 27*t*, 162*t*
Congressional elections of 2018
    and, 214
democracy threatened by, 222–23
Democratic Party voters and, 174, 175*f*
economic pessimism and, 29–31,
    30*t*, 144
education levels' correlation with, 29
Fox News and, 136–39, 139*f*, 174
gender's correlation with, 30*t*
income levels' correlation with, 30*t*
independent voters and, 174, 175*f*
Latinx as target of, 20–21, 24–25, 26–28,
    27*t*, 34*f*, 61–62, 79–81, 80*f*, 91, 99,
    101–2, 103–16*t*, 105*f*, 106, 109–11,
    117–19, 130, 137–39, 139*f*, 141, 162*t*,
    182, 183, 204–5, 207, 209, 220–21
low-information voters and, 141, 144–
    45, 146, 152*f*, 152, 157, 158
Muslims as target of, 25–28, 27*t*, 34*f*,
    62, 79–81, 80*f*, 99, 102, 103–16*t*,
    105*f*, 106, 109, 111–12, 117–19, 130,
    137–39, 139*f*, 141, 152*f*, 152–53,
    160, 162*t*, 165, 182, 183, 204–5, 207,
    209, 220–21
older voters and, 144
partisan-directed anger and enthusiasm
    correlated with, 179–81, 180*t*, 181*f*
predicted participation levels'
    correlation with, 189, 190*f*,
    216–18, 218*f*
racial conservatives *versus* racial
    extremists and, 31–33, 32*t*, 34*f*
religiosity's correlation with, 30*t*
Republican Party voters and, 7–9, 79–
    81, 80*f*, 165–66, 167*t*, 169–75*f*, 174,
    188, 209
right-wing authoritarian scale
    correlated with, 27*t*, 28
social dominance orientation correlated
    with, 27*t*, 28–29
Tea Party and, 79–82, 80*f*, 97, 100–8,
    103–16*t*, 105–8*f*
traditional cultural values as factor
    in, 144–45